ACCOUNTING 1

FIFTH EDITION

Student Workbook

INCLUDING THE ACCOUNTING PAPER NEEDED FOR ALL EXERCISES

G. E. Syme

T. W. Ireland

Prentice Hall Canada Inc.
Scarborough, Ontario

Canadian Cataloguing in Publication Data

Syme, G. E.
Accounting 1, fifth edition. Student workbook

Supplement to: Syme, G. E. Accounting 1. 5th ed.
ISBN 0-13-334161-5

1. Accounting – Problems, exercises, etc.
I. Ireland, T. W. II. Title.

HF5635.S983 1993 657'.042 C93-094858-0

Also available:

Teacher's Key	0-13-334285-9
Student textbook	0-13-333825-8
Teacher's Guide and disk program	0-13-334179-8

PRENTICE-HALL INC., Englewood Cliffs, New Jersey
PRENTICE-HALL INTERNATIONAL, INC., London
PRENTICE-HALL OF AUSTRALIA, PTY., LTD., Sydney
PRENTICE-HALL OF INDIA, PVT., LTD., New Delhi
PRENTICE-HALL OF JAPAN INC., Tokyo
PRENTICE-HALL OF SOUTHEAST ASIA (PTE.) LTD., Singapore
EDITORA PRENTICE-HALL DO BRASIL, LTDA., Rio de Janeiro
PRENTICE-HALL HISPANOAMERICANA, S.A., Mexico

ISBN 0-13-334161-5

DEVELOPMENT AND PROJECT EDITOR: Denyse O'Leary
CREATIVE SERVICES: Deborah Starks
COMPOSITION: Jaytype Inc.

Printed and bound in Canada by WEBCOM Limited

12 WC 03

Contents

Preface

The *Accounting 1 Student Workbook* supplies all the business papers and accounting forms required to complete the exercises in the student text. The *Teacher's Key* is an exact replica of the *Workbook*, with the answers to all textbook and *Workbook* questions and exercises keyed in.

Many teachers find it useful to be able to show the correct answers to their students. For this reason, we are giving users of the *Accounting 1* text permission to reproduce any or all of the pages in the *Teacher's Key*. You may wish to make overheads, handouts, or displays for your bulletin board. However you wish to do it, we hope you will use this material to the full.

The *Teacher's Key* supplements the *Workbook*. This manual is designed to assist teachers by supplying worked-out solutions for all exercises, answers for all review questions, and comments on the case studies. Correct results of computer exercises are displayed in the *Teacher's Key*, but the templates are found in the Accounting 1 Computer Files with the *Teacher's Guide*. In the interests of saving paper, we have deleted pages from the *Workbook* where computer exercises have no manual applications. The corresponding pages in the *Key* show the correct results, as they should appear on the screen. A note in the *Workbook* at these points and the pagination continues to correspond exactly to the *Key*, for convenient reference.

Finally, a *Teacher's Guide* is available for the program. For the student text, this guide offers:

- an annotated teacher's edition. Teaching notes are placed in the margins of a one-colour edition of the textbook. This system makes all teaching notes conveniently available to you as you teach;
- black-line masters to illustrate the major concepts covered in each chapter;
- two tests, including comprehension questions as well as exercises. (There are no tests for Chapter 1.)
- an appendix on teaching about computers in accounting;
- disks containing the masters for the hands-on computer exercises.
- additional exercises, cases, etc.

G.E.S. T.W.I.

ANSWERS TO CHAPTER 1 REVIEW QUESTIONS (text p. 11)

1.

2.

3.

4.

5.

6.

7.

8.

9.

10.

11.

12.

13.

14.

15.

16.

17.

18.

19.

20.

21.

22.

Name ______________ Date ______________

ANSWERS TO CHAPTER 1 EXERCISES (text p. 11)

Exercise 1, p. 11 Using Your Knowledge

1. ____________________ 8. ____________________

2. ____________________ 9. ____________________

3. ____________________ 10. ____________________

4. ____________________ 11. ____________________

5. ____________________ 12. ____________________

6. ____________________ 13. ____________________

7. ____________________

Exercise 2, p. 12

1. The work of a(n)____________________is clerical in nature.
2. The work of a(n)____________________is concerned with routine matters.
3. The term__________is gradually being replaced with the term__________clerk.
4. A(n)____________________ensures that the supporting documents are present and correct for every transaction.
5. A(n)__________ensures that generally accepted accounting principles are followed.
6. A(n)____________________records the accounting entries in the books of account.
7. A(n)____________________makes the payroll calculations.
8. A(n)__________prepares reports based on the data produced by the accounting system.
9. A(n)____________________carries out all the necessary banking transactions.
10. A(n)__________participates in management meetings.
11. A qualified__________has a high-level position.
12. For centuries, all__________was handwritten.
13. Many small businesses still do their__________by hand.

Name____________________ Date__________

ANSWERS TO CHAPTER 1 EXERCISES (cont.)

Underline the correct answer.

Exercise 3, p. 13

1. Which of the following statements does not fit the job title?
   - **a.** An accounting clerk verifies source documents.
   - **b.** An accounting clerk ensures that the ledger balances.
   - **c.** An accounting clerk works neatly to guard against errors.
   - **d.** An accounting clerk studies tax bulletins to keep up to date.
2. Which of the following statements does not fit the job title?
   - **a.** An accounting clerk works out accounting entries.
   - **b.** An accounting clerk, together with the owner, compares this year's and last year's income statements.
   - **c.** An accounting clerk records accounting entries in the books.
   - **d.** An accounting clerk inquires about a suspected error made by the bank.
3. Which of the following statements does not fit the job title?
   - **a.** An accountant is a professional person.
   - **b.** An accountant has a broad knowledge of accounting.
   - **c.** An accountant ensures the accuracy of the payroll deductions.
   - **d.** An accountant discusses the business's "cash flow" with the owners.
4. Which of the following statements does not fit the job title?
   - **a.** An accountant talks about revising a spreadsheet model.
   - **b.** An accountant investigates the credit rating of a new customer.
   - **c.** An accountant is promoted to vice-president.
   - **d.** An accountant is ill; a meeting with the bank manager has to be cancelled.
5. Which of the following statements does not fit the facts about computers?
   - **a.** The computer is an ideal machine for use in an accounting environment.
   - **b.** The computer can handle large quantities of data.
   - **c.** The computer produces better profit figures.
   - **d.** The computer can provide information for management very quickly.

CAREER Melissa Porchuk/Student

ANSWERS TO DISCUSSION QUESTIONS (text p. 15)

1. ______________________________

2. ______________________________

3. ______________________________

____

____

4. ______________________________

____

5. ______________________________

____

Name______________________ Date______________________

ANSWERS TO SECTION 2.1 REVIEW QUESTIONS (text p. 19) Financial Position

1.

2.

3.

4.

5.

6.

7.

8.

ANSWERS TO SECTION 2.1 EXERCISES (text p. 19)

Exercise 1, p. 19

Exercise 2, p. 19

Exercise 3, p. 19

Exercise 4, p. 19

Name Date

ANSWERS TO SECTION 2.1 EXERCISES (cont.)

Exercise 5, p. 19

Exercise 6, p. 19

Exercise 7, p. 19

Exercise 8, p. 19

Exercise 9, p. 20

1. ASSETS

2. LIABILITIES

3. EQUITY

ANSWERS TO SECTION 2.2 REVIEW QUESTIONS (text p. 27) The Balance Sheet

1.

2.

Name Date

ANSWERS TO SECTION 2.2 REVIEW QUESTIONS (cont.)

3. ______

4. ______

5. ______

6. ______

7. ______

8. ______

9. ______

10. ______

11. ______

12. ______

13. ______

14. ______

15. ______

16. ______

17. ______

ANSWERS TO SECTION 2.2 EXERCISES (text p. 28)

Exercise 1, p. 28

Name______ Date______

ANSWERS TO SECTION 2.2 EXERCISES (cont.)

Exercise 2, p. 28

Exercise 3, p. 28

Name________________ Date____________

ANSWERS TO SECTION 2.3 REVIEW QUESTIONS (text p. 30) Claims against the Assets

1. ____________________

2. ____________________

3. ____________________

4. ____________________

5. ____________________

ANSWERS TO SECTION 2.3 EXERCISES (text p. 30)

Exercise 1, p. 30

1. ____________________

2. ____________________

Name____________________ Date____________________

ANSWERS TO SECTION 2.3 EXERCISES (cont.)

Exercise 2, p. 31

1. ______________________

____

____

2. ______________________

____

ANSWERS TO SECTION 2.4 REVIEW QUESTIONS (text p. 33) Generally Accepted Accounting Principles

1. ______________________

____

2. ______________________
3. ______________________
4. ______________________

____

5. ______________________

____

6. ______________________

____

Name______________________ Date______________________

ANSWERS TO SECTION 2.4 EXERCISES (text p. 33)

Exercise 1, p. 33

	AMOUNT	BUSINESS	PERSONAL
ASSETS			
Accounts Receivable	$ 27 460		
Boat and Motor	16 520		
Business Bank Balance	1 852		
Business Automobiles	48 054		
Furniture and Appliances	6 528		
Government Bonds of Owner	20 000		
House and Lot	99 600		
Office Furniture and Equipment	18 324		
Office Supplies	3 545		
Owner's Automobiles	18 657		
Paving Materials	55 326		
Personal Bank Balance	1 258		
Plant Property and Buildings	125 358		
Summer Cottage	65 874		
Trucks and Equipment	285 657		
Total Assets			
LIABILITIES			
Accounts Payable	3 500		
Business Bank Loan	56 000		
Mortgage on Plant Property	75 000		
Mortgage on House and Lot	60 000		
Mortgage on Summer Cottage	22 300		
Owed to Finance Co.— Business Equipment	136 522		
Total Liabilities			
OWNER'S EQUITY			

Exercise 2, p. 34 **Cases for Further Thought**

1. a. ____________________
   b. ____________________

2. a. ____________________
   b. ____________________

3. a. ____________________
   b. ____________________

Name________________ Date____________

ANSWERS TO SECTION 2.4 EXERCISES (cont.)

4. a. ______
   b. ______
   ______

5. a. ______
   b. ______
   ______

6. a. ______
   b. ______
   ______

ANSWERS TO SECTION 2.5 COMPUTER REVIEW QUESTIONS (text p. 39)
A Spreadsheet for Personal Balance Sheets

1. ______
   ______
2. ______
   ______
3. ______
   ______
4. ______
   ______
5. ______
   ______
6. ______
   ______
7. ______
   ______
   ______
8. ______
   ______
9. ______
   ______
10. ______
   ______

Name______ Date______

ANSWERS TO SECTION 2.5 COMPUTER EXERCISES (text p. 39)

1.

	A	B	C	D	E	F
1						
2						
3						
4						
5						
6						
7						
8						
9						
10						
11						
12						
13						
14						
15						

1., 5. ______________________________

Communicate It (text p. 40)

____

ANSWERS TO CHAPTER 2 EXERCISES (text p. 41)

Exercise 1, p. 41 Using Your Knowledge

For each of the following questions, write the letter that represents the best possible answer.

1. The financial position of a business is ___
   a. the difference between total assets and total liabilities.
   b. represented by the assets, liabilities, and the capital.
   c. the same as the net worth of the business.

2. If the total assets increase by $10 000 and the total liabilities decrease by $10 000, the capital will ___
   a. increase by $20 000.
   b. be unchanged.
   c. decrease by $20 000.

Name______________________ Date______________

ANSWERS TO CHAPTER 2 EXERCISES (cont.)

Exercise 1 (cont.)

3. Which one of the following is not true? ___

a. A – C = L
b. A – L = E
c. A + L = E
d. A = L + E

4. A balance sheet shows ___

a. all of the owner's assets and liabilities.
b. a financial picture of the business on a certain date.
c. the progress of the business over a period of time.

5. Which one of the following is not true? ___

a. The heading of a balance sheet shows the date as of which it was prepared.
b. Assets are listed in the order of their liquidity.
c. Accounts receivable are considered to be a liquid asset.
d. Personal assets have no place on the business balance sheet.
e. A truck which cost $10 000 and for which $6 000 is owed is listed on the balance sheet at $4 000.

6. Abbreviations may be used on financial statements ___

a. when it is necessary to crowd things to conserve space.
b. to save time in preparing the statements.
c. in a company name if the abbreviation is a formal part of the name.

7. Which one of the following is least true? ___
Columnar paper helps the accountant to:

a. add columns more accurately.
b. make records easier to read.
c. make the records more appealing.
d. make recordkeeping go more quickly.

8. Which one of the following is not true? ___
Ruled lines are:

a. used to underline headings.
b. used to indicate that columns of numbers are to be totaled.
c. necessary to separate sections of the balance sheet.
d. doubled to indicate a final total.

9. Before a business is closed down, the equation for it is:
Assets ($125 000) = Liabilities ($37 000) + Equity ($88 000).
If assets of $70 000 are sold for $20 000, assets of $50 000 are sold for $90 000, and the remaining assets stay the same, the equation will become ___

a. $ 55 000 = $ 37 000 + $ 18 000.
b. $ 115 000 = $ 37 000 + $ 78 000.
c. $ 75 000 = $ 37 000 + $ 38 000.
d. $ 135 000 = $ 47 000 + $ 88 000.
e. $ 115 000 = $ 27 000 + $ 88 000.

Name________________ Date________________

ANSWERS TO CHAPTER 2 EXERCISES (cont.)

10. Which of the following is not true? ___
    a. In the liability section on a balance sheet, accounts payable may be listed first.
    b. On a balance sheet there are three main totals.
    c. On a balance sheet the owner's name appears only in the heading.
    d. On a balance sheet the final totals are always on the same line.

Exercise 2, p. 42 *(Use more paper if necessary.)*

Exercise 3, p. 43 *(Use more paper if necessary.)*

Exercise 4, p. 43 **For Further Thought** *(Use more paper if necessary.)*

1. ______
2. ______
3. ______
4. ______
5. ______
6. ______
7. ______
8. ______
9. ______

Name______ Date______

CASE STUDIES (text p. 44)

Case 1 *Is Money Better?*, p. 44 *(Use more paper if necessary.)*

Case 2 *Can You Spend the Equity?*, p. 46 *(Use more paper if necessary.)*

Challenge Case 3 *Are the Assets Worth What the Balance Sheet Says?*, p. 46 *(Use more paper if necessary.)*

1.

2.

3.

4.

5.

6.

Name Date

CASE STUDIES (cont.)

Co-Operative Learning Case 4 *Should Your Friends Purchase This Business?*, p. 47

Here are some good questions to ask:

1. ______
2. ______
3. ______
4. ______
5. ______
6. ______
7. ______
8. ______
9. ______
10. ______
11. ______

CAREER Julia Stavreff/Founder of Accounting Firm Gory & Stavreff Chartered Accountants

ANSWERS TO DISCUSSION QUESTIONS (text p. 49)

1. ______
2. ______
3. ______
4. ______

Name ______ Date ______

ANSWERS TO SECTION 3.1 REVIEW QUESTIONS (text p. 51)

Business Transactions

1. ______
2. ______
3. ______

ANSWERS TO SECTION 3.1 EXERCISES (text p. 52)

Exercise 1, p. 52

1. ______ 4. ______ 7. ______
2. ______ 5. ______ 8. ______
3. ______ 6. ______

Exercise 2, p. 52

1. ______ 4. ______ 7. ______
2. ______ 5. ______ 8. ______
3. ______ 6. ______

ANSWERS TO SECTION 3.2 REVIEW QUESTIONS (text p. 60)

Equation Analysis Sheet

1. ______
2. ______
3. ______
4. ______
5. ______

Name______ Date______

ANSWERS TO SECTION 3.2 EXERCISES (text p. 60)

Exercise 1, p. 60

	ASSETS					LIABILITIES		OWNER'S EQUITY
	Cash	Accounts Receivable	Supplies	Office Furniture	Truck	Accounts Payable		S. Kostiuk, Capital
		D. Murray				Ace Supply	Pine Motors	
Opening balances	1 000	50						1 050

Name________________________ Date________________

ANSWERS TO SECTION 3.2 EXERCISES (cont.)

Exercise 2, p. 61, 1, 2.

		ASSETS					LIABILITIES	OWNER'S EQUITY

3.

Name ________________ Date ________________

ANSWERS TO SECTION 3.2 EXERCISES (cont.)

Exercise 3, p. 62, 1., 2.

		ASSETS						LIABILITIES		OWNER'S EQUITY

3.

____

____

____

Name______________________ Date______________

ANSWERS TO SECTION 3.3. REVIEW QUESTIONS (text p. 63)

Summary of Steps in Analyzing a Transaction

1. ______________________________

2. ______________________________

3. ______________________________

4. ______________________________

5. ______________________________

ANSWERS TO SECTION 3.4 REVIEW QUESTIONS (text p. 65)

Introduction to Source Documents

1. ______________________________

2. ______________________________

3. ______________________________

4. ______________________________

5. ______________________________

6. ______________________________

7. ______________________________

Name ______________________ Date ______________________

ANSWERS TO SECTION 3.4 EXERCISES (text p. 65)

Exercise 1, p. 65

1.
2.
3.
4.
5.
6.
7.

Exercise 2, p. 66

1.
2.
3.
4.
5.
6.
7.
8.
9.

Exercise 3, p. 67

1.
2.
3.
4.
5.

Exercise 4, p. 67

1.
2.

Name __________ Date __________

ANSWERS TO SECTION 3.5 COMPUTER REVIEW QUESTIONS (text p. 71)

A Spreadsheet for Transaction Analysis

1. ______
2. ______
3. ______
4. ______
5. ______
6. ______
7. ______
8. ______
9. ______
10. ______

ANSWERS TO SECTION 3.5 COMPUTER EXERCISES (text p. 71)

1.

	A	B	C	D	E	F	G	H
1								
2								
3								
4								
5								
6								
7								
8								
9								
10								
11								
12								
13								
14								
15								
16								
17								
18								
19								

Name______ Date______

ANSWERS TO SECTION 3.5 COMPUTER EXERCISES (cont.)

Extending Your Computer Skills (text p. 72)

1. Cell Display

	I	J	K	L
25				
26				
27				
28				
29				
30				
31				
32				
33				
34				
35				
36				

Cell Contents

	I	J	K	L
25				
26				
27				
28				
29				
30				
31				
32				
33				
34				
35				
36				

2. See p. 26 if you are doing this exercise manually.

Communicate It (text p. 72) *(Use more paper if necessary.)*

Name____________________ Date__________

ANSWERS TO CHAPTER 3 EXERCISES (text p. 73)

Exercise 1, p. 73 **Using Your Knowledge**

1. ____________________
2. ____________________
3. ____________________
4. ____________________
5. ____________________

Exercise 2, p. 74

1. ____________________
2. ____________________
3. ____________________
4. ____________________
5. ____________________

Exercise 3, p. 74

Year	Assets	Liabilities	Equity
19-1	$ 85 000	Step 1.	$60 000
19-2	$115 000	Step 2.	Step 3.

Make the calculations in the order shown: Step 1, Step 2, then Step 3.

Exercise 4, p. 74

Exercise 5, p. 74

Name____________________ Date____________________

ANSWERS TO CHAPTER 3 EXERCISES (cont.)

Exercise 6, p. 74, 1., 2. **Challenge Exercise**

	ASSETS						LIABILITIES				OWNER'S EQUITY

Name____________________ Date______________

ANSWERS TO CHAPTER 3 EXERCISES (cont.)

3.

Exercise 7, p. 75 For Further Thought *(Use more paper if necessary.)*

1.

2.

3.

4.

5. a.

b.

c.

d.

e.

f.

Name________________ Date________________

ANSWERS TO CHAPTER 3 EXERCISES (cont.)

Exercise 7 (cont.) *(Use more paper if necessary.)*

6. **a.** ______
b. ______
c. ______
______
d. ______
e. ______
f. ______
______

7. ______
______

8. ______

Exercise 8, p. 77 **Cases for Further Thought** *(Use more paper if necessary.)*

1. ______
2. ______
3. ______
______

CASE STUDIES (text p. 77)

Case 1 *An Objective Balance Sheet?*, p. 77 *(Use more paper if necessary.)*

1. ______
______
2. ______
______
3. ______
4. ______

Case 2 *Checking Out a New Customer*, p. 78 *(Use more paper if necessary.)*

1. ______
2. ______
______
______
______
______
______
______
3. ______

Name______ Date______

CASE STUDIES (cont.)

Challenge Case 3 *The Balance Sheet Shuffle*, p. 78 *(Use more paper if necessary.)*

1. The revised amounts are: Total Assets ____________

Total Liabilities ____________

Cash	Truck	Accounts Payable	Loan Payable (Brother)

2. ____________________

3. ____________________

____

4. ____________________

a. ____________________

b. ____________________

c. ____________________

CAREER Larry Lancefield/Forensic Accountant

ANSWERS TO DISCUSSION QUESTIONS (text p. 80)

1. ____________________

____

2. ____________________

____

3. ____________________

____

4. ____________________

____

____

____

____

____

5. ____________________

Research and Writing Question *(Use additional paper as necessary.)*

6. ____________________

____

____

____

Name____________________ Date____________________

ANSWERS TO SECTION 4.1 REVIEW QUESTIONS (text p. 85)

Ledger Accounts

1. ______

2. ______

3. ______

4. ______

5. ______

6. ______

7. ______

8. ______

ANSWERS TO SECTION 4.1 EXERCISES (text p. 85)

Cash

A/R – A. Marks

A/R – C. Prentice

Land

Building

Equipment

Truck

Bank Loan

A/P – Gem Lumber

Mortgage Payable

T. Stevens, Capital

Name______ Date______

ANSWERS TO SECTION 4.1 EXERCISES (cont.)

Exercise 2, p. 86

Cash	A/R – P. Auul	A/R – S. Wouke
Supplies	Furniture and Equipment	Automobile
A/P – A.B. Associates	A/P – Medico Supply	Pauline Inaba, Capital

Exercise 3, p. 86

Assets: ______

Liabilities: ______

ANSWERS TO SECTION 4.2 REVIEW QUESTIONS (text p. 94)
Debit and Credit Theory

1. ______
2. ______
3. ______
4. ______
5. ______
6. ______
7. ______
8. ______
9. ______
10. ______
11. ______
12. ______

Name______ Date______

ANSWERS TO SECTION 4.2 EXERCISES (text p. 94)

Exercise 1, p. 94

ASSETS		=	LIABILITIES		+	OWNER'S EQUITY	
Debit	Credit		Debit	Credit		Debit	Credit

Exercise 2, p. 94

Transaction No.	Account Names	Account Classification: Asset, Liability or Owner's Equity	Increase (+) or Decrease (–)	Debit or Credit	Amount	
1	Cash	Asset	+	DR	300	–
	A/R – J. Parker	Asset	–	CR	300	–

Name____________________________ Date____________________

ANSWERS TO SECTION 4.2 EXERCISES (cont.)

Exercise 3, p. 95

Transaction No.	Account Names	Account Classification: Asset, Liability or Owner's Equity	Increase (+) or Decrease (–)	Debit or Credit	Amount	

Name________________________ Date________________

Chapter 4 The Simple Ledger

ANSWERS TO SECTION 4.3 REVIEW QUESTIONS (text p. 99) Account Balances

1.

2. The two steps are:

3.

4.

5.

6.

7. Two examples of situations that result in an exceptional balance are:
   1.
   2.

8. a. c.
   b. d.

ANSWERS TO SECTION 4.3 EXERCISES (text p. 99)

Exercise 1, p. 99

Bank		A/R — H. Devrie		A/P — P. Helka		R. Smart, Capital	
250	190	25	175	30	75	150	3 140
1 210	48	150		45	40		
360	512	70			175		
29		35					

1.

2.

Name Date

ANSWERS TO SECTION 4.3 EXERCISES (cont.)

Exercise 2, p. 100

1. ______________________________

2. Possible causes for exceptional balances:
____

Exercise 3, p. 100

		Debit	Credit
1.	The left side of an account.		
2.	The balance of an account receivable.		
3.	The balance of a supplier's account.		
4.	A decrease in a liability.		
5.	An exceptional balance in the Bank account.		
6.	The balance in the Equipment account.		
7.	The right side of an account.		
8.	The balance in the Bank Loan account.		
9.	An exceptional balance in an account payable.		
10.	The larger side of a liability account.		
11.	A creditor's account.		
12.	A customer's account.		
13.	An increase in an asset.		
14.	A debtor's account.		

ANSWERS TO SECTION 4.4 REVIEW QUESTIONS (text p. 104) Trial Balance

1. ______________________________

2. To balance a ledger:
   1. ______________________________
   2. ______________________________
   3. ______________________________

Name______________________ Date______________________

ANSWERS TO SECTION 4.4 REVIEW QUESTIONS (cont.)

3. ______________________________

4. ______________________________

5. ______________________________

6. ______________________________

7. ______________________________

8. ______________________________

9. a. ______________________________
   b. ______________________________
   c. ______________________________
   d. ______________________________

ANSWERS TO SECTION 4.4 EXERCISES (text p. 105)

Exercise 1, p. 105

ACCOUNTS	DEBIT	CREDIT

Name____________ Date____________

ANSWERS TO SECTION 4.4 EXERCISES (cont.)

Exercise 2, p. 105 ______________________

____

____

ACCOUNTS	DEBIT	CREDIT

Exercise 3, p. 106 ______________________

____

____

ACCOUNTS	DEBIT	CREDIT

Name______________________ Date______________________

ANSWERS TO SECTION 4.5 REVIEW QUESTIONS (text p. 107)

Analyzing Financial Data: Comparing Balance Sheets

1. ______

2. a. ______
   b. ______

Exercise 1, p.107 *Analytical Observations* *(Use more paper if necessary.)*

1. ______
2. ______
3. ______
4. ______

Exercise 2, p. 107 *(Use more paper if necessary.)*

1. *Observations*
   1. ______
   2. ______
   3. ______
   4. ______
   5. ______
   6. ______
2. ______
3. ______

ANSWERS TO SECTION 4.6 COMPUTER REVIEW QUESTIONS (text p. 113)

Using a Computer: A Spreadsheet for Trial Balances

1. ______
2. ______
3. ______
4. ______
5. ______
6. ______

Name______ Date______

ANSWERS TO SECTION 4.6 COMPUTER EXERCISES (text p. 113)

1., 2

4.

	A	B	C	D	E
1					
2					
3					
4					
5					
6					
7					
8					
9					
10					
11					
12					
13					
14					
15					
16					
17					

3. ______________________________

Communicate It (text p. 114)

The sentences that would not apply are:

Name__________________ Date____________

ANSWERS TO CHAPTER 4 EXERCISES (text p. 114)

Exercise 1, p. 114 Using Your Knowledge

Indicate whether each of the following statements is true or false by entering a "T" or an "F" in the box indicated. Explain the reason for each "F" response in the space provided.

1. A number of individual balance sheet items may appear on one account page, as long as they are shown separately. ☐
2. Many accountants use the equation analysis sheet instead of the ledger. ☐
3. There is a page in the ledger for the total assets figure. ☐
4. T-accounts are ideal for small businesses. ☐
5. The first dollar amount recorded in an account is placed on the same side as it appears on a simple balance sheet. ☐
6. There is no account for capital because it can always be found by subtracting the total assets from the total liabilities. ☐
7. A transaction analysis sheet is a permanent accounting record. ☐
8. For every transaction, there is always one debit amount and one credit amount, which are equal. ☐
9. A balanced accounting entry is a correct accounting entry. ☐
10. The balance of an account that is not zero must be either a debit or a credit. ☐
11. The J.R. Dahl account in the ledger of C. Jacob is either an account payable or an account receivable. ☐
12. Eric Lai's account has a credit balance. This means that he purchased our services on credit. ☐
13. An exceptional balance is opposite to what would be normal. ☐
14. A customer is given a refund because of unsatisfactory service. The account of this customer will now have an exceptional balance. ☐
15. A ledger contains an exceptional balance. A trial balance cannot be taken until the exceptional item is transferred to another part of the ledger. ☐
16. A trial balance that is in balance proves that there are no errors in the accounts. ☐
17. A trial balance is taken using a printing calculator. When the "total" key is pressed, the figure 89.00 comes up. This is the amount of the error. ☐
18. The business buys supplies and pays cash. The accounting entry made in the accounts is Dr Bank and Cr Supplies. This causes the ledger to be out of balance. ☐
19. A correct trial balance needs to be kept only until the next one is taken. ☐

Name________________________ Date______________

ANSWERS TO CHAPTER 4 EXERCISES (cont.)

Exercise 1 (cont.) **Explanations for "F" Responses**

Exercise 2, p. 115

1.

2.

3.

Exercise 3, p. 115

The debit balance could still exist because

Exercise 4, p. 116

1.

2.

3.

4.

Name ______________________ Date ____________________

ANSWERS TO CHAPTER 4 EXERCISES (cont.)

Exercise 5, p. 116

1., 2.

Name____________________________ Date____________________

ANSWERS TO CHAPTER 4 EXERCISES (cont.)

Exercise 5 (cont.)

3.

____

____

____

ACCOUNTS	DEBIT	CREDIT

Exercise 6, p. 117

Bank	
1 056	

A/R – V. Morris	

A/R – D. Murray	
1 351	

A/R – A. Niemi	
2 516	

Name______________________ Date______________

ANSWERS TO CHAPTER 4 EXERCISES (cont.)

Exercise 6 (cont.)

Office Supplies	
1 115	

Furniture and Equipment	
11 916	

Properties Owned	
18 042	

Automobile	
27 965	

Bank Loan	
	19 000

A/P – Pioneer Furniture	

A/P – Tuck Corporation	
	1 520

Cathy Rogers, Capital	

ACCOUNTS	DEBIT	CREDIT

Name________________ Date________________

ANSWERS TO CHAPTER 4 EXERCISES (cont.)

Exercise 7, p. 117 **For Further Thought** *(Use more paper if necessary.)*

1. ______________________________

2. ______________________________

3. ______________________________
____
____

4. ______________________________

5. ______________________________
____

6. a. ______________________________
b. ______________________________
c. ______________________________
d. ______________________________
e. ______________________________

7. ______________________________

8. ______________________________
____
____
____

9. ______________________________
____

10. ______________________________
____

11. ______________________________

12. ______________________________

13. ______________________________
____
____

14. ______________________________
____

15. ______________________________
____

Name______________________ Date______________

Chapter 4 The Simple Ledger

CASE STUDIES (text p. 118)

Case 1 *Are Debits and Credits Confusing?*, p. 118 *(Use more paper if necessary.)*

1.

Case 2 *Property Value: A Matter of Opinion?*, p.119 *(Use more paper if necessary.)*

1.

2.

3.

Challenge Case 3 *Choosing between Two Companies*, p.120 *(Use more paper if necessary.)*

1.

2.

3.

Name ______________________ Date ______________

CAREER Tony Constantino / Co-operative Education Student

ANSWERS TO DISCUSSION QUESTIONS (text p. 122)

1. ______

2. ______

3. a. ______

   b. ______

   c. ______

4. ______

5. ______

6. ______

Name______ Date______

ANSWERS TO SECTION 5.1 REVIEW QUESTIONS (text p. 131)

Expanding the Ledger

1.

2.

3.

4.

5.

6.

7.

8.

9.

10.

Name Date

ANSWERS TO SECTION 5.1 EXERCISES (text p. 131)

Exercise 1, p. 131

A business has the beginning financial position recorded in the schedule below. Ten simple transactions are listed in the left-hand column. **Work out the revised totals for assets, liabilities, and owner's equity after each transaction. Enter these totals below. Complete the last two columns of the chart by recording: a) the amount of change in equity (if any), and b) whether the change in equity represents revenue, expense, or drawings.**

Transactions	*Total Assets*	*Total Liabs.*	*Owner's Equity*	*Change in Equity*	*Revenue? Expense? Drawings?*
Beginning financial position	10 000	6 000	4 000	–	–
1. Purchased $400 of supplies for future use and paid cash.					
2. Reduced bank loan by $1 000.					
3. Received $800 cash from a debtor.					
4. Sold services for $900 cash.					
5. Sold services on credit, $1 500.					
6. Paid hydro for month just ended, $125.					
7. Owner withdrew $750 cash for personal use.					
8. Paid employee's wages, $600.					
9. Purchased truck on credit, $20 000.					
10. Owner took supplies for personal use, $250.					

Name____________________ Date________________

ANSWERS TO SECTION 5.1 EXERCISES (cont.)

Exercise 2, p. 131

DATE	DEBITS		CREDITS	
	ACCOUNT(S)	AMOUNT	ACCOUNT(S)	AMOUNT

Exercise 3, p. 133

1. The Bank account normally has a ________ balance.
2. A revenue account normally has a ________ balance.
3. An expense account normally has a ________ balance.
4. Paying a creditor involves a ________entry to the creditor's account.
5. The Drawings account receives a ________ entry when the owner withdraws money for personal use.
6. A lawyer gives a refund to a customer. The Bank account will receive a ________ entry and the Revenue account will receive a ________ entry.
7. Supplies are bought on credit. The Supplies account will receive a ________ entry and the supplier's account payable will receive a ________ entry.
8. The Drawings account will not normally receive ________entries.
9. An increase in equity can be thought of as a ________ to the Capital account.
10. Net profit can be thought of as a ________ to the Capital account.
11. Net loss can be thought of as a________ to the Capital account.
12. The owner takes a computer from the business for his personal (permanent) use. The Drawings account will receive a________entry.

Name________________________ Date________________

ANSWERS TO SECTION 5.1 EXERCISES (cont.)

Exercise 4, p. 133 **Ace Repair Answer Key**

No.	Asset Increase	Asset Decrease	Liability Decrease	Liability Increase	Revenue (Equity) (Increase)	Expense (Equity) (Decrease)	Drawings (Equity) (Decrease)
1.	✓				✓		
2.							
3.							
4.							
5.							
6.							
7.							
8.							
9.							
10.							

ANSWERS TO SECTION 5.2 REVIEW QUESTIONS (text p. 140)

Completing Ledger Theory

1. ______________________________

2. ______________________________

3. ______________________________

4. ______________________________

Name______________________ Date______________________

ANSWERS TO SECTION 5.2 REVIEW QUESTIONS (cont.)

5. The types of accounts and their normal balances are:

6. The equity equation is:

7.

8. The term "on account" is used as follows:
   1. ______ 3. ______
   2. ______ 4. ______

9.

10.

11.

12.

13.

ANSWERS TO SECTION 5.2 EXERCISES (text p. 140)

Exercise 1, p. 140 **Using the table at right, complete the exercise that follows.**

1.	Asset debit	7.	Drawings debit
2.	Asset credit	8.	Drawings credit
3.	Liability debit	9.	Revenue debit
4.	Liability credit	10.	Revenue credit
5.	Capital debit	11.	Expense debit
6.	Capital credit	12.	Expense credit

A series of transactions is given below. **Show the effect of the accounting entry for each transaction.** The first transaction is done for you.

	Transaction	DR	CR
1.	Purchase a new car on account.	1	4
2.	Receive payment on account from a customer.		
3.	Owner withdraws cash for personal use.		
4.	Owner starts a new business by investing cash.		
5.	The car is repaired and paid for in cash immediately.		
6.	Perform a service for a customer for cash.		
7.	Perform a service for a customer on account.		
8.	Purchase supplies for cash.		
9.	Receive a bill for gas and oil for the car.		
10.	Pay a creditor on account.		
11.	Throw out some ruined supplies.		

Name______________ Date______________

ANSWERS TO SECTION 5.2 EXERCISES (cont.)

Exercise 2, p. 141

1.

ACCOUNTS	DEBIT	CREDIT

Name ____________ Date ____________

ANSWERS TO SECTION 5.2 EXERCISES (cont.)

Exercise 2 (cont.)

2.

E. Stokaluk
Chart of Accounts

Assets	No.	Equity	No.

Liabilities	No.

Name_______________ Date_______________

ANSWERS TO SECTION 5.2 EXERCISES (cont.)

Exercise 2 (cont.)

3. ______________________________

ANSWERS TO SECTION 5.2 EXERCISES (cont.)

Exercise 3, p. 142

1.

Karen's Air Service
Chart of Accounts

Assets	*No.*	*Equity*	*No.*

Liabilities	*No.*

Exercise 4, p. 142

A = L + OE

Assets

DEBIT	CREDIT

Liabilities

DEBIT	CREDIT

Capital

DEBIT	CREDIT

Revenue

DEBIT	CREDIT

Drawings

DEBIT	CREDIT

Expense

DEBIT	CREDIT

Name________________ Date________________

ANSWERS TO SECTION 5.2 EXERCISES (cont.)

Exercise 5, p. 143

ANSWERS TO SECTION 5.2 EXERCISES (cont.)

Exercise 6, p. 143

Complete the following schedule for each of the five separate equity section relationships.

Financial Information	*Company 1*	*Company 2*	*Company 3*	*Company 4*	*Company 5*
Beginning capital	6 000	6 000	15 000		62 000
Total revenues	10 000		29 000		
Total expenses	8 000	11 000		30 000	35 000
Net income or loss (–)		14 000	11 000	20 000	–5 000
Drawings	3 000	12 000		15 000	
Increase or decrease (–) in equity			–6 000		–10 000
Ending capital				10 000	

ANSWERS TO SECTION 5.3 REVIEW QUESTIONS (text p. 144)

Analyzing Financial Data: Comparing Income Statements

1. ______________________________

2. ______________________________

3. ______________________________

4. ______________________________

____

Name______________________ Date______________

ANSWERS TO SECTION 5.3 EXERCISES (text p. 144)

Exercise 1, p. 144 1., 2.

Professional Engineering and Consulting
Income Statement
Years Ended June 30, 19–7 and 19–6

Items	19–7			19–6			Dollar Increase or Decrease	Percentage Increase or Decrease
Revenues								
Consulting	62	250	–	60	402	–		
Construction	202	365	–	290	201	–		
Designing	35	250	–	36	603	–		
Total Revenue	299	865	–	387	206	–		
Operating Expenses								
Advertising Expense	3	520	–	3	400	–		
Automobiles Expense	25	025	–	16	350	–		
Bank Charges Expense	15	850	–	11	200	–		
Building Expense	4	200	–	3	700	–		
Equipment Maintenance Expense	1	525	–	1	750	–		
Insurance Expense	5	014	–	3	000	–		
Light, Heat, and Water Expense	3	124	–	3	107	–		
Miscellaneous Expense		312	–		250	–		
Property Taxes Expense	1	215	–		950	–		
Telephone Expense	1	507	–		904	–		
Wages Expense	102	301	–	78	201	–		
Total Expenses	163	593	–	122	812	–		
Net Income	136	272	–	264	394	–		

Name____________________ Date______________

ANSWERS TO SECTION 5.3 EXERCISES (cont.)

Exercise 1 (cont.)

3.

4.

Name____________________ Date________________

ANSWERS TO SECTION 5.3 EXERCISES (cont.)

Exercise 2, p. 145

1.

Fiesta Restaurant
Income Statement
Years Ended March 31, 19–3 and 19–4

Items	19–3			19–4			Dollar Increase or Decrease			Percentage Increase or Decrease
Revenues										
Food and Dining	150	290	–	163	595	–				
Liquor and Bar	181	410	–	197	492	–				
Total Revenues	331	700	–	361	087	–				
Operating Expenses										
Bank Charges Expense	1	520	–		920	–				
Car Expense	3	725	–	3	516	–				
Insurance Expense	1	800	–	1	800	–				
Light and Heat Expense	1	570	–	1	610	–				
Food and Liquor Expense	140	290	–	157	315	–				
Miscellaneous Expense		950	–		920	–				
Rent Expense	24	000	–	24	000	–				
Telephone Expense	1	290	–	1	350	–				
Wages Expense	51	374	–	49	316	–				
Total Expenses	226	519	–	240	747	–				
Net Income	105	181	–	120	340	–				

2.

Name__________ Date__________

ANSWERS TO SECTION 5.4 COMPUTER REVIEW QUESTIONS (text p. 153)

How Accountants Use Computers: Identifying Problems in Company Performance

1. __________
2. __________
3. __________
4. __________
5. __________
6. __________
7. __________
8. __________
9. __________
10. __________

ANSWERS TO CHAPTER 5 EXERCISES (text p. 154)

Exercise 1, p. 154 **Using Your Knowledge**

ACCOUNT	NORMAL BALANCE
Supplies	____
Advertising Expense	____
A. Bryce, Drawings	____
G. Wright, a creditor	____
Rent Expense	____
Fees Earned	____
Bank Loan	____
W. Magill, a debtor	____
A. Bryce, Capital	____
Mortgage Payable	____
Automobile	____

Exercise 2, p. 155

1. __________
2. __________

Name__________ Date__________

ANSWERS TO CHAPTER 5 EXERCISES (cont.)

Exercise 3, p. 155

Exercise 4, p. 155

1.

Bank	
1 745	

A/R – P. Alder	
50	

A/R – A. Jackson	
70	

Equipment	
5 000	

Supplies	
610	

Automobiles	
7 900	

A/P – B & B Stone	
	110

A/P – Century Finance	
	5 500

P. Garside, Capital	
	5 625

P. Garside, Drawings	
200	

Revenue	
	11 920

Car Expense	
500	

Light, Heat, Water Expense	
280	

Rent Expense	
300	

Wages Expense	
6 500	

Name____________________ Date____________________

ANSWERS TO CHAPTER 5 EXERCISES (cont.)

Exercise 4 (cont.)

1. (cont.)

No.	DEBITS ACCOUNT(S)	DEBITS AMOUNT	CREDITS ACCOUNT(S)	CREDITS AMOUNT

2. The corrected net income will be ______

Exercise 5, p. 156

	Assets	=	Liabilities	+	Beginning Capital	+	Revenue	−	Expenses	−	Drawings
End of Year 1	100	=	20	+	70	+	60	−	45	−	5
Year 2	120	=	30	+		+	90	−	60	−	
Year 3	130	=		+		+	105	−	80	−	20
Year 4		=	30	+		+	110	−	95	−	10

Exercise 6, p. 156

	Assets	*Liabilities*	*Equity*
End of 19–1		$27 400	
End of 19–2			$19 300

Name________________________ Date____________________

ANSWERS TO CHAPTER 5 EXERCISES (cont.)

Exercise 7, p. 157 **Comprehensive Exercise**

	DEBITS		CREDITS	
	ACCOUNT	AMOUNT	ACCOUNT	AMOUNT
1.				
2.				
3.				
4.				
5.				
6.				
7.				
8.				
9.				
10.				
11.				
12.				
13.				
14.				
15.				
16.				

Name____________________ Date________________

ANSWERS TO CHAPTER 5 EXERCISES (cont.)

Exercise 7 (cont.)

Bank

A/R – Jenkins and Co.

Office Supplies

Office Equipment

Automobile

A/P – Office Supply Company

N.A. James, Capital

N.A. James, Drawings

Fees Earned

Advertising Expense

Car Expense

Donations Expense

Miscellaneous Expense

Rent Expense

Name____________________ Date____________

ANSWERS TO CHAPTER 5 EXERCISES (cont.)

Exercise 7 (cont.)

____

____

____

ACCOUNTS	DEBIT	CREDIT

Name______________________ Date______________

ANSWERS TO CHAPTER 5 EXERCISES (cont.)

Exercise 7 (cont.)

Exercise 8, p. 158 **For Further Thought** *(Use more paper if necessary)*

1.

2.

3.

4.

5.

6.

Name __________ Date __________

ANSWERS TO CHAPTER 5 EXERCISES (cont.)

Exercise 8 (cont.)

7. ______
   a. ______
   b ______
   c. ______
   d. ______
   e. ______
   f. ______

8. ______

9. ______

10. ______

11. ______

12. ______

13. ______

Exercise 9, p. 159 Cases for Further Thought *(Use more paper if necessary.)*

1. 1. ______
   2. ______
   3. ______

2. a. ______
   b. ______

Name ______ Date ______

ANSWERS TO CHAPTER 5 EXERCISES (cont.)

Exercise 9 (cont.)

CASE STUDIES (text p. 160)

Case 1 *"Timing Is Everything"*, p. 160 *(Use more paper if necessary.)*

1.

2.

3.

4.

Case 2 *Pumping Profits*, p. 161 *(Use more paper if necessary.)*

1.

2.

3.

Name____________________ Date__________

CASE STUDIES (cont.)

Challenge Case 3 *Revenue Roulette*, p. 162

1. ______________________________

2. ______________________________

   a. ______________________________

   b. ______________________________

3. ______________________________

Group Discussion Case 4 *Perspective on Financial Statements*, p. 163

1. ______________________________

2. ______________________________

3. ______________________________

4. ______________________________

5. ______________________________

6. ______________________________

7. ______________________________

8. ______________________________

CAREER Brian Van Der Lugt/Self-Employed (semi-retired) Accountant

ANSWERS TO DISCUSSION QUESTIONS (text p. 165)

1. ______________________________

2. ______________________________

3. ______________________________

4. ______________________________

Name______________________ Date______________________

CAREER (cont.)

ANSWERS TO DISCUSSION QUESTIONS (cont.)

Exercise 5 (cont.)

5a.

Professional Engineering and Consulting
Percentage Increase or Decrease
Expenses: 19–6 to 19–7

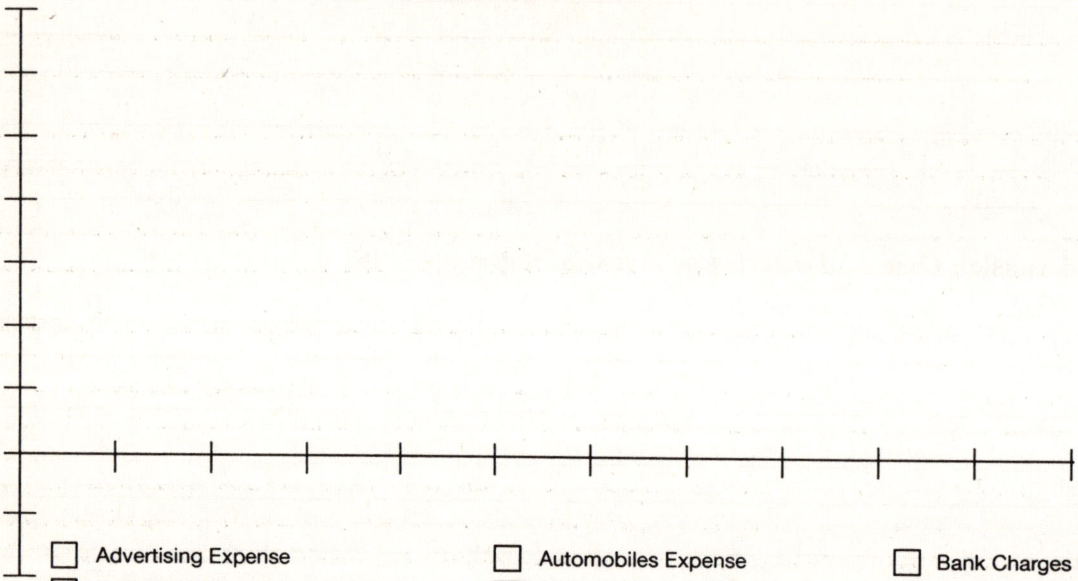

☐ Advertising Expense
☐ Automobiles Expense
☐ Bank Charges Expense
☐ Building Expense
☐ Equipment Maintenance Expense
☐ Insurance Expense
☐ Light, Heat and Water Expense
☐ Miscellaneous Expense
☐ Property Taxes Expense
☐ Telephone Expense
☐ Wages Expense

5b.

Fiesta Restaurant
Total Expenses
Year Ending March 31, 19–4

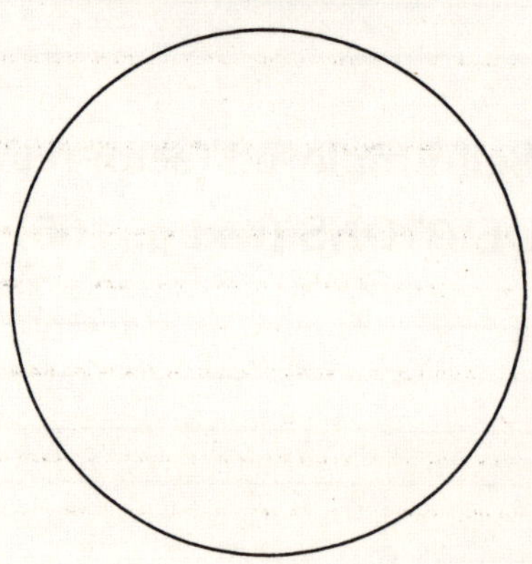

☐ Bank Charges Expense
☐ Car Expense
☐ Insurance Expense
☐ Light and Heat Expense
☐ Food and Liquor Expense
☐ Miscellaneous Expense
☐ Rent Expense
☐ Telephone Expense
☐ Wages Expense

Name____________________ Date________________

ANSWERS TO SECTION 6.1 REVIEW QUESTIONS (text p. 171)

The Journal

1. ______

2. ______

3. ______

4. ______

5. ______

6. ______

7. ______

8. ______

9. ______

10. a. ______
 b. ______
 c. ______
 d. ______
 e. ______

11. ______

12. ______

13. ______

14. ______

15. ______

Name______ Date______

ANSWERS TO SECTION 6.1 EXERCISES (text p. 171)

Exercise 1, p. 171

GENERAL JOURNAL

PAGE ______

DATE		PARTICULARS	P.R.	DEBIT	CREDIT

Name______________________ Date______________

ANSWERS TO SECTION 6.1 EXERCISES (cont.)

Exercise 1 (cont.)

GENERAL JOURNAL PAGE ______

DATE		PARTICULARS	P.R.	DEBIT	CREDIT

Exercise 2, p. 172

1.

ANSWERS TO SECTION 6.1 EXERCISES (cont.)

Exercise 2 (cont.)

2. GENERAL JOURNAL PAGE ____

DATE		PARTICULARS	P.R.	DEBIT	CREDIT

Name________________ Date________

ANSWERS TO SECTION 6.1 EXERCISES (cont.)

Exercise 2 (cont.)

3. GENERAL JOURNAL PAGE ______

DATE		PARTICULARS	P.R.	DEBIT	CREDIT

Name____________________ Date____________________

ANSWERS TO SECTION 6.1 EXERCISES (cont.)

Exercise 3, p. 173

1. ____________________
2. ____________________
3. ____________________
4. ____________________
5. ____________________
6. ____________________
7. ____________________
8. ____________________
9. ____________________

Exercise 4, p.174

Transaction 1 ____________________

Transaction 2 ____________________

Transaction 3 ____________________

Transaction 4 ____________________

Transaction 5 ____________________

Exercise 5, p. 174

GENERAL JOURNAL

PAGE 1

DATE		PARTICULARS	P.R.	DEBIT	CREDIT

Name____________________ Date____________________

ANSWERS TO SECTION 6.1 EXERCISES (cont.)

Exercise 6, p. 174

GENERAL JOURNAL

PAGE ____

DATE		PARTICULARS	P.R.	DEBIT	CREDIT

Name ____________ Date ____________

ANSWERS TO SECTION 6.2 REVIEW QUESTIONS (text p. 185) Source Documents

1. ______________________________

2. ______________________________

3. ______________________________

4. ______________________________

5. ______________________________

6. ______________________________

7. ______________________________

8. ______________________________

9. ______________________________

10. ______________________________

11. ______________________________

12. ______________________________

13. ______________________________

14. ______________________________

15. ______________________________

16. ______________________________

17. ______________________________

18. ______________________________

19. ______________________________

Name______________________ Date______________

ANSWERS TO SECTION 6.2 REVIEW QUESTIONS (cont.)

20. ____________________

21. ____________________

22. ____________________

23. ____________________

24. ____________________

ANSWERS TO SECTION 6.2 EXERCISES (text p. 186)

Exercise 1, p. 186

1. ____________________
2. ____________________
3. ____________________
4. ____________________
5. ____________________
6. ____________________
7. ____________________

Exercise 2, p. 187

1. ____________________
2. ____________________
3. ____________________
4. ____________________

Name____________________ Date____________________

ANSWERS TO SECTION 6.2 EXERCISES (cont.)

Exercise 2 (cont.)

5. ______________________________

Exercise 3, p. 188

1. ______________________________
2. ______________________________
3. ______________________________
4. ______________________________
5. ______________________________

Exercise 4, p. 189

1. ______________________________
2. ______________________________
3. ______________________________
4. ______________________________
5. ______________________________
6. ______________________________
7. ______________________________

Exercise 5, p. 190

1. ______________________________
2. ______________________________
3. ______________________________

Name______________________ Date______________

ANSWERS TO SECTION 6.3 REVIEW QUESTIONS (text p. 193)

Provincial Sales Tax

1. ______
2. ______
3. ______
4. ______
   1. ______
   2. ______
   3. ______
   4. ______
5. ______
6. ______
7. ______
8. ______

ANSWERS TO SECTION 6.3 EXERCISES (text p. 194)

Exercise 1, p. 194

1.

Amount before PST	PST at 8 per cent	Total amount
1. $75.00		
2. $120.00		
3. $58.60		
4. $98.00		
5. $130.75		

Name______ Date______

ANSWERS TO SECTION 6.3 EXERCISES (cont.)

Exercise 1 (cont.)

2. **GENERAL JOURNAL** PAGE ______

DATE		PARTICULARS	P.R.	DEBIT	CREDIT
	1.				
	2.				
	3.				
	4.				
	5.				

Name______________________ Date______________

ANSWERS TO SECTION 6.3 EXERCISES (cont.)

Exercise 2, p.194

GENERAL JOURNAL PAGE ______

DATE		PARTICULARS	P.R.	DEBIT	CREDIT
1.					

GENERAL JOURNAL PAGE ______

DATE		PARTICULARS	P.R.	DEBIT	CREDIT
2.					

Exercise 3, p. 195

1. ______

2. ______

3. ______

Exercise 4, p. 195

1. ______
2. ______
3. ______
4. ______
5. ______
6. ______

ANSWERS TO SECTION 6.3 EXERCISES (cont.)

Exercise 5, p. 195

1.

MOORE'S MARINA

16 HARBOURFRONT RD.
VANCOUVER, B.C.
V7C 8T8
Phone 888-6666
Fax 888-6645

Date *Feb. 28* 19—

Name *Valerie Miniaci*

Address *Bear Island, Alberta*

Qty	Description	Price	Amount

RECEIVED ABOVE IN GOOD ORDER

PST	
Total	

Cash	Charge

SALES SLIP 9124

2. Journal entry:

GENERAL JOURNAL

DATE		PARTICULARS	P.R.	DEBIT	CREDIT

Name__________ Date__________

ANSWERS TO SECTION 6.4 REVIEW QUESTIONS (text p. 203)

The Goods and Services Tax

1. ____________________
2. ____________________
3. ____________________
4. ____________________
5. ____________________
6. ____________________
7. ____________________
8. ____________________
9. ____________________
10. ____________________
11. ____________________
12. ____________________
13. ____________________
14. ____________________
15. ____________________
16. ____________________
17. ____________________

ANSWERS TO SECTION 6.4 EXERCISES (text p. 203)

Exercise 1, p. 203 **Complete the following schedule.**

End of Period	GST Recoverable	GST Payable	Amount of Remittance	Refund Claimed	Due Date
March 31	$904.72	$1 507.20			
Sept. 30	$1 565.20	$2 074.21			
Dec. 31	$700.40	$608.32			
Aug. 31	$2 764.35	$1 964.32			
Jan. 31	$3 750.00	$4 209.64			

Name________________ Date____________

ANSWERS TO SECTION 6.4 EXERCISES (cont.)

Exercise 2, p. 204

GENERAL JOURNAL

DATE		PARTICULARS	P.R.	DEBIT	CREDIT

Name____________________ Date________________

ANSWERS TO SECTION 6.4 EXERCISES (cont.)

Exercise 3, p. 204

1.

CUSTODIAL SERVICES
900 LANSDOWNE AVENUE
TORONTO, ONTARIO
M6K 2V7

INVOICE NUMBER 953

Phone 767-8569 Fax 767-8533

GST No. 102620110	Terms Net 30	Date April 26, 19—	
TO Oakridge Ski Club Box 500 Medonte, Ontario L4M 4Y8			
FOR 2 #152 Floor Mops @ $12			$24.00
6 gals. Floor Cleaner @ $15			$90.00
		GST 7%	
		PST 8%	
		TOTAL	

2.

DATE		PARTICULARS	P.R.	DEBIT	CREDIT

3.

DATE		PARTICULARS	P.R.	DEBIT	CREDIT

Name____________________ Date________________

ANSWERS TO SECTION 6.4 EXERCISES (cont.)

Exercise 4, p. 205

2. GENERAL JOURNAL PAGE 6

DATE		PARTICULARS	P.R.	DEBIT	CREDIT

Name______________________ Date______________

ANSWERS TO SECTION 6.4 EXERCISES (cont.)

Exercise 4 (cont.)

GENERAL JOURNAL PAGE 7

DATE		PARTICULARS	P.R.	DEBIT	CREDIT

ANSWERS TO SECTION 6.5 EXERCISES (text p. 207)

Analyzing Financial Data: Trend Analysis

Exercise 1, p. 207

1.

SALES DATA

19-1	*19-2*	*19-3*	*19-4*	*19-5*
$20 700	$22 356	$23 184	$23 805	$24 219
100.0 %				
Increase in Percentage				

2. ____________________

____

____

____

____

Name____________________ Date____________________

ANSWERS TO SECTION 6.5 EXERCISES (cont.)

Exercise 2, p. 207

1. **Sales, Expenses, and Net Income Data**

		19–5	*19–6*	*19–7*	*19–8*	*19–9*
Sales	$	$57 000	$58 254	$58 767	$59 223	$59 451
	%					
Expenses	$	$35 000	$36 050	$36 575	$36 785	$37 520
	%					
Net Income	$	$22 000	$22 204	$22 192	$22 438	$21 931
	%					

2. ______________________________

Exercise 3, p. 207

1. **Soul Foods**
Selected Sales Data

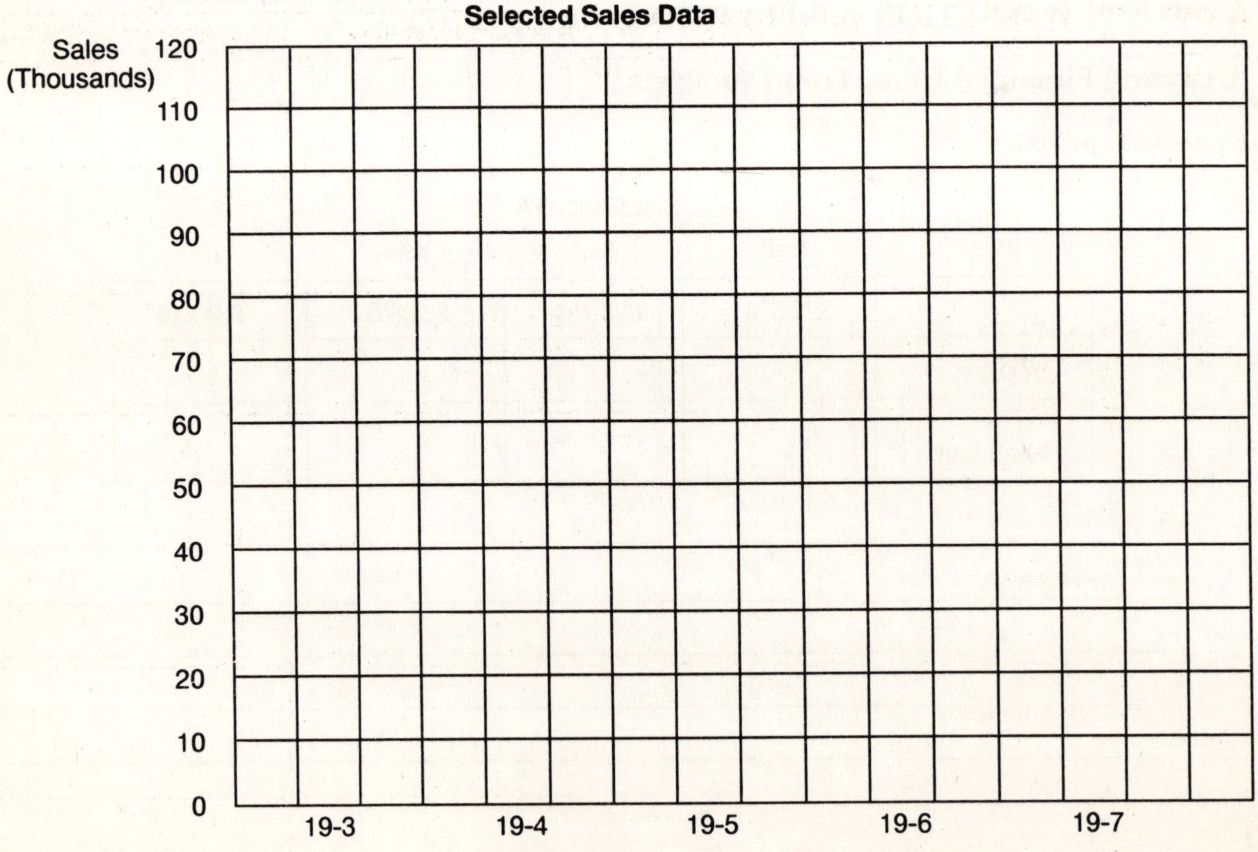

2. ______________________________

Name______________________ Date______________

ANSWERS TO CHAPTER 6 EXERCISES (text p. 208)

Exercise 1, p. 208 **Using Your Knowledge**

1. ______
2. ______
3. ______
4. ______
5. ______
6. ______
7. ______
8. ______
9. ______
10. ______
11. ______
12. ______

Exercise 2, p. 209

Complete the following summary.

Nature of Transaction	Source Document(s)	Required Journal Entry	
		Accounts Debited	Accounts Credited
Payment on account			
Sale on account			
Bank service charge (GST – exempt item)			
Cash payment of phone bill			
Cash received on account			
Purchase of equipment on account			
Cash sale			

Name______________ Date______________

ANSWERS TO CHAPTER 6 EXERCISES (cont.)

Exercise 3, p. 209

Source Document	Document Number	Transactions	Document Number
Bank credit memo	1	1. Owner withdraws money.	
Bank debit memo	2	2. Purchase of equipment on account.	
Cheque copy	3	3. Payment on account.	
Cash sales slip	4	4. Cash sale.	
Sales invoice	5	5. Sale on account.	
Purchase invoice	6	6. Cheques received from customers on account.	
Cash receipts list	7	7. Increase bank loan.	
Owner's written memo	8	8. Owner invests additional money in the business.	
Bank statement	9	9. Bank service charge.	

Exercise 4, p. 210

Indicate whether each of the following statements is true or false by placing a "T" or an "F" in the box provided. Explain the reason for each "F" response in the space provided.

1. Anyone in the business can initiate a business transaction. ☐
2. Every journal entry is based on a source document. ☐
3. The only purpose of source documents is to provide the basis for a journal entry. ☐
4. A business that sells to its customers on a cash basis does not normally use a sales invoice. ☐
5. Journal entries for all cash sales slips are essentially the same. ☐
6. Sales invoices are used by businesses that make most of their sales on account. ☐
7. For every sales invoice, there is a debit to an account receivable. ☐
8. Dual purpose sales slips are the choice of businesses that sell for cash and also on account. ☐
9. Every sales invoice is also a purchase invoice. ☐
10. The debit entry for every purchase invoice is always the same. ☐
11. The supporting document for a payment on account is the tear-off portion of a cheque. ☐
12. The credit entry for every cheque copy payment is always the same. ☐
13. Cheques received are considered to be cash received. ☐
14. The bank has no right to make deductions from the accounts of its customers. ☐
15. We debit Bank when we receive a bank debit memo. ☐

Name________________________ Date________________

ANSWERS TO CHAPTER 6 EXERCISES (cont.)

Exercise 4 (cont.)

16. The cost principle states that every asset acquired is to be recorded at its cost price. ☐

17. The best objective evidence of a purchase is a purchase invoice received from an independent supplier. ☐

18. Only provincial governments are allowed to levy retail sales taxes. ☐

19. The purchaser of goods or services is required to make accounting entries for sales tax. ☐

20. The PST account is an expense account. ☐

Explanations for "F" Responses:

Name______________________ Date______________

ANSWERS TO CHAPTER 6 EXERCISES (cont.)

Exercise 5, p. 211 **Comprehensive Exercise**

GENERAL JOURNAL PAGE 7

DATE		PARTICULARS	P.R.	DEBIT	CREDIT

Name________________ Date________________

ANSWERS TO CHAPTER 6 EXERCISES (cont.)

Exercise 5 (cont.)

GENERAL JOURNAL PAGE ____

DATE		PARTICULARS	P.R.	DEBIT	CREDIT

Name______________________ Date______________________

ANSWERS TO CHAPTER 6 EXERCISES (cont.)

Exercise 6, p. 212 **Comprehensive Exercise**

GENERAL JOURNAL PAGE 12

DATE		PARTICULARS	P.R.	DEBIT	CREDIT

Name________________ Date__________

ANSWERS TO CHAPTER 6 EXERCISES (cont.)

Exercise 6 (cont.) GENERAL JOURNAL PAGE ______

DATE		PARTICULARS	P.R.	DEBIT	CREDIT
19—					

Name ______________________ Date ______________

ANSWERS TO CHAPTER 6 EXERCISES (cont.)

Exercise 7, p. 213 **Comprehensive Exercise**

GENERAL JOURNAL PAGE 36

DATE		PARTICULARS	P.R.	DEBIT	CREDIT

Name________________ Date__________

ANSWERS TO CHAPTER 6 EXERCISES (cont.)

Exercise 7 (cont.) GENERAL JOURNAL PAGE ____

DATE		PARTICULARS	P.R.	DEBIT	CREDIT

Name________________ Date____________

ANSWERS TO CHAPTER 6 EXERCISES (cont.)

Exercise 7 (cont.) GENERAL JOURNAL PAGE ____

DATE		PARTICULARS	P.R.	DEBIT	CREDIT

2. GST Recoverable: ________

Exercise 8, p. 215 **For Further Thought** *(Use more paper if necessary.)*

1. ____________________

2. ____________________

3. ____________________

4. ____________________

5. ____________________

6. ____________________

7. ____________________

Name________________ Date________________

ANSWERS TO CHAPTER 6 EXERCISES (cont.)

Exercise 8 (cont.)

8. ______________________________

9. ______________________________

10. ______________________________

11. ______________________________

12. ______________________________

Exercise 9, p. 215 **Cases for Further Thought** *(Use more paper if necessary.)*

1. ______________________________

2. ______________________________

3. ______________________________

4. ______________________________

5. ______________________________

6. ______________________________

Name______________________ Date______________

CASE STUDIES (text p. 216)

Case 1 *Can Net Income Be Increased?*, p. 216 *(Use more paper if necessary.)*

1.

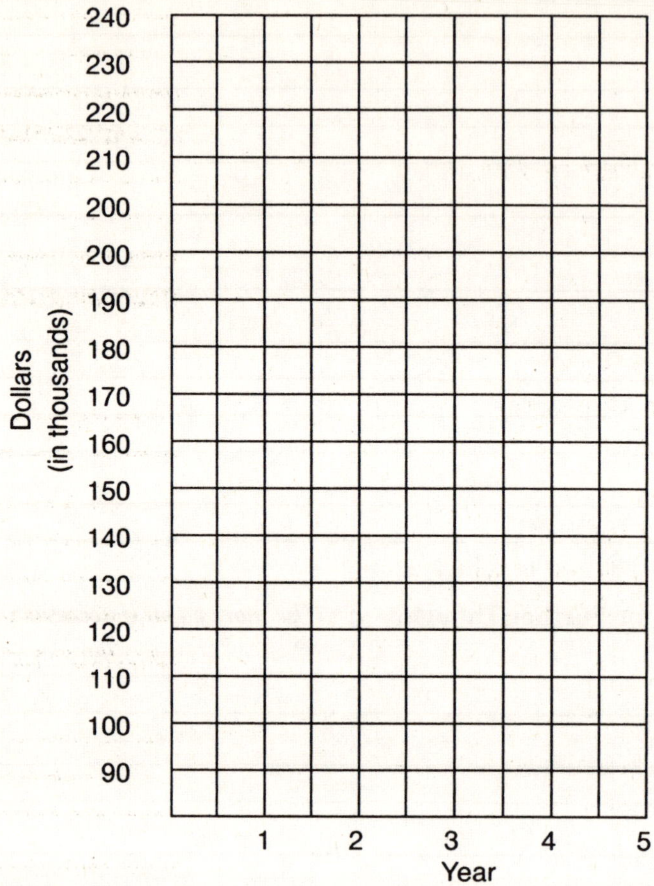

2. ____________________

3. ____________________

4. ____________________

5. ____________________

Name____________________ Date____________________

CASE STUDIES (cont.)

Case 2 *Analyzing Business Data*, p. 217 *(Use more paper if necessary.)*

1. **a.** Increase in total assets ____________

b. Increase in A/P ____________
New mortgage ____________
Increase in equity ____________

c. The funds came from: trade creditors ____________
the mortgage ____________
retained profits ____________

d. Owner's drawings
Net income for year $35 000
Less amount retained in business ____________
Amount taken out by owner ____________

2. **a.** Increase in total assets ____________
b. To make the mortgage payment ____________
c. The funds came from: increase in bank loan ____________
retained profits ____________

d. Owner's drawings
Net income for the year ____________
Less amount retained in business ____________
Amount taken out by owner ____________

3. **a.** Increase in total assets ____________
b. To make the mortgage payment ____________
To pay off the bank loan ____________

c. The funds came from: trade creditors ____________
retained profits ____________

d. Calculation of profit for 19—6
Amount taken out by owner ____________
Amount retained in business ____________

Name____________________ Date____________

CASE STUDIES (cont.)

Challenge Case 3 *Accounting for a Package Deal*, p. 218 *(Use more paper if necessary.)*

1.

2.

3.

4.

Item	Appraised Values in Dollars per Item	Appraised Values in Fractions of Total	Times	Total Cost Price	Cost Price per Item
			×		
			×		
			×		
			×		
			×		
			×		
			×		
			×		
			×		

5.

6.

Name______________________ Date______________

CASE STUDIES (cont.)

Group Discussion Case 4 *Is a Profit Always a Profit?*, p. 219 *(Use more paper if necessary.)*

1.
2.
3.
4.
5.
6.
7.

CAREER Phil Quackenbush/President, Q.W. Page Associates

ANSWERS TO DISCUSSION QUESTIONS (text p. 221)

1.
2.
3.
4.

Name ____________ Date ____________

ANSWERS TO SECTION 7.1 REVIEW QUESTIONS (text p. 233)

Posting

1. ______
2. ______
3. ______
4. ______
5. ______
6. ______
7. ______
8. ______
9. ______
    1. ______
    2. ______
    3. ______
    4. ______
    5. ______
10. ______
11. ______
12. 1. ______
    2. ______
    3. ______
13. ______
14. ______
15. ______
16. ______
    1. ______
    2. ______
    3. ______
    4. ______

Name______ Date______

ANSWERS TO SECTION 7.1 EXERCISES (text p. 233)

Exercise 1, p. 233

A. Asset

						Balance			
Debit			Credit			DR/CR	Amount		
1	000	00							
	250	00							
	310	00							
			1	250	00				
	200	00							
	350	00							
				860	00				
	850	00							
			1	000	00				
1	500	00							
	200	00							

B. Liability

						Balance			
Debit			Credit			DR/CR	Amount		
			3	500	00				
			1	600	00				
3	500	00							
1	000	00							
			2	000	00				
	600	00							
2	000	00							
				450	00				
	500	00							
				50	00				
				375	00				

Name____________________ Date________________

ANSWERS TO SECTION 7.1 EXERCISES (cont.)

Exeercise 2, p. 234 (Workbook Exercise)

The journal and ledger of C. Fries appear below and on the following pages. **Post the journal entries to the ledger accounts.** When this is completed, **take off a trial balance to ensure that your work is accurate.**

GENERAL JOURNAL PAGE 40

DATE		PARTICULARS	P.R.	DEBIT	CREDIT
19— Jan.	4	Bank		805 –	
		Revenue			700 –
		GST Payable			49 –
		PST Payable			56 –
		Cash sale			
	7	Wages Expense		1500 –	
		Bank			1500 –
		Wages for week			
	10	Bank		370 –	
		A/R – P. Berry			370 –
		Received on account			
	15	Supplies		1100 –	
		GST Recoverable		77 –	
		A/P – General Supply Co.			1177 –
		Paper products			
	21	A/R – P. Berry		575 –	
		Revenue			500 –
		GST Payable			35 –
		PST Payable			40 –
		Sale on account			
	25	C. Fries, Drawings		800 –	
		Bank			800 –
		For personal use			
	30	General Expense		240 –	
		GST Recoverable		16 80	
		Bank			256 80
		Materials used			

Name________________ Date________________

ANSWERS TO SECTION 7.1 EXERCISES (cont.)

Exercise 2 (cont.)

ACCOUNT Bank **No.** 105

Date		Particulars	P.R.	Debit	Credit	DR/CR	Balance
19— Dec	31	Forwarded	–			DR	1 900 –

ACCOUNT A/R – P. Berry **No.** 110

Date		Particulars	P.R.	Debit	Credit	DR/CR	Balance
19— Dec	31	Forwarded	–			DR	370 –

ACCOUNT Supplies **No.** 115

Date		Particulars	P.R.	Debit	Credit	DR/CR	Balance
19— Dec	31	Forwarded	–			DR	1 420 –

ACCOUNT Equipment **No.** 120

Date		Particulars	P.R.	Debit	Credit	DR/CR	Balance
19— Dec.	31	Forwarded	–			DR	9 075 –

ACCOUNT A/P – General Supply Company **No.** 205

Date		Particulars	P.R.	Debit	Credit	DR/CR	Balance
19— Dec	31	Forwarded	–			CR	2 030 –

Name____________________ Date________________

ANSWERS TO SECTION 7.1 EXERCISES (cont.)

Exercise 2 (cont.)

ACCOUNT GST Payable **No.** 210

Date		Particulars	P.R.	Debit	Credit	DR/CR	Balance
19— Dec.	31	Forwarded	–			CR	105 –

ACCOUNT GST Recoverable **No.** 215

Date		Particulars	P.R.	Debit	Credit	DR/CR	Balance
19— Dec.	31	Forwarded	–			DR	75 –

ACCOUNT PST Payable **No.** 220

Date		Particulars	P.R.	Debit	Credit	DR/CR	Balance
19— Dec	31	Forwarded	–			CR	120 –

ACCOUNT C. Fries, Capital **No.** 305

Date		Particulars	P.R.	Debit	Credit	DR/CR	Balance
19— Dec.	31	Forwarded	–			CR	10 585 –

ACCOUNT C. Fries, Drawings **No.** 310

Date		Particulars	P.R.	Debit	Credit	DR/CR	Balance

ACCOUNT Revenue **No.** 400

Date		Particulars	P.R.	Debit	Credit	DR/CR	Balance

Name____________________ Date______________

ANSWERS TO SECTION 7.1 EXERCISES (cont.)

Exercise 2 (cont.)

ACCOUNT General Expense **No.** 500

Date		Particulars	P.R.	Debit	Credit	DR/CR	Balance

ACCOUNT Wages Expense **No.** 505

Date		Particulars	P.R.	Debit	Credit	DR/CR	Balance

____

____

____

ACCOUNTS	DEBIT	CREDIT

Name______________________ Date________________

ANSWERS TO SECTION 7.1 EXERCISES (cont.)

Exercise 3, p. 233 (Workbook Exercise)

The Bank account page shown below is filled. **Forward the balance to a new account page.**

ACCOUNT Bank **No.** 1

Date		Particulars	P.R.	Debit	Credit	DR/CR	Balance
19— July	1		J1	1900 –		DR	1900 –
	7		J1	1900 –		DR	3800 –
	13		J1		500 –	DR	3300 –
	19		J2		275 –	DR	3025 –
	21		J2		50 –	DR	2975 –
	25		J2		75 –	DR	2900 –
	27		J3	1000 –		DR	3900 –
	29		J3		100 –	DR	3800 –

ACCOUNT **No.**

Date		Particulars	P.R.	Debit	Credit	DR/CR	Balance

Name____________________ Date____________________

ANSWERS TO SECTION 7.2 REVIEW QUESTIONS (text p. 236)

Trial Balance Out of Balance

1. ______________________________

2. ______________________________
   1. ______________________________
   2. ______________________________
   3. ______________________________
   4. ______________________________
   5. ______________________________

3. ______________________________

4. ______________________________

5. ______________________________

6. ______________________________

7. ______________________________

8. ______________________________

9. ______________________________

10. ______________________________

11. ______________________________

Name______________________ Date______________________

ANSWERS TO SECTION 7.2 EXERCISES (text p. 237)

Exercise 1, p. 237 (Workbook Exercise)

The exercise below, involving a journal, ledger, and trial balance, has errors in it. **Locate and correct the errors and balance the trial balance.**

GENERAL JOURNAL **PAGE 12**

DATE		PARTICULARS	P.R.	DEBIT	CREDIT
19– Nov.	4	Automobile	125	13 500 –	
		GST Recoverable	215	1 015 –	
		Bank	105		4 000 –
		A/P – Ace Finance	205		11 515 –
		Purchase of new car for $15 515 incl. tax			
	6	Furniture	120	900 –	
		GST Recoverable	215	36 –	
		Bank	105		936 –
		Purchase of new desk for $936 incl. tax			
	7	A/R – A. Boyd	110	460 –	
		Revenue	400		400 –
		GST Payable	210		28 –
		PST Payable	220		32 –
		Sale on account			
	10	Bank	105	345 –	
		Revenue	400		300 –
		GST Payable	210		21 –
		PST Payable	220		24 –
		Cash sale			
	12	Rent Expense	410	700 –	
		GST Recoverable	215	49 –	
		Bank	105		749 –
		Rent for the month			
	15	Car Expense	405	200 –	
		GST Recoverable	215	14 –	
		Bank	105		214 –
		Car repairs paid by cash			

Assume that $36 is Correct GST

Name____________________ Date____________

ANSWERS TO SECTION 7.2 EXERCISES (cont.)

Exercise 1 (cont.) THE LEDGER

ACCOUNT Bank **No.** 105

Date		Particulars	P.R.	Debit	Credit	DR/CR	Balance
19— Oct.	31	Forwarded	–			DR	12 048 88
Nov.	4		J12		4 000 –	DR	8 048 88
	6		J12		936 –	DR	7 112 88
	10		J12	245 –		DR	7 357 88
	12		J12		749 –	DR	6 608 88
	15		J12		214 –	DR	6 394 88

ACCOUNT A/R – A. Boyd **No.** 110

Date		Particulars	P.R.	Debit	Credit	DR/CR	Balance
19— Nov.	7		J12	460 –		DR	460 –

ACCOUNT Supplies **No.** 115

Date		Particulars	P.R.	Debit	Credit	DR/CR	Balance
19— Oct.	31	Forwarded	–			DR	570 –

ACCOUNT Furniture **No.** 120

Date		Particulars	P.R.	Debit	Credit	DR/CR	Balance
19— Oct.	31	Forwarded	–			DR	1 971 50
Nov.	6		J12	900 –		DR	2 871 50

ACCOUNT Automobile **No.** 125

Date		Particulars	P.R.	Debit	Credit	DR/CR	Balance
19— Nov.	4		J12	13 500 –		DR	13 500 –

Name________________________ Date__________________

ANSWERS TO SECTION 7.2 EXERCISES (cont.)

Exercise 1 (cont.)

ACCOUNT A/P – Ace Finance **No.** 205

Date		Particulars	P.R.	Debit	Credit	DR/CR	Balance
19— Nov.	4		J12		11 515 –	CR	11 515 –

ACCOUNT GST Payable **No.** 210

Date		Particulars	P.R.	Debit	Credit	DR/CR	Balance
19— Oct.	31	Forwarded	–			CR	251 90
Nov.	7		J12		28 –	CR	279 90

ACCOUNT GST Recoverable **No.** 215

Date		Particulars	P.R.	Debit	Credit	DR/CR	Balance
19— Oct.	31	Forwarded	–			DR	193 50
Nov.	4		J12	1 015 –		DR	1 208 50
	6		J12	36 –		DR	1 244 50
	10		J12	21 –		DR	1 265 50
	12		J12	49 –		DR	1 314 50
	15		J12	14 –		DR	1 328 50

ACCOUNT PST Payable **No.** 220

Date		Particulars	P.R.	Debit	Credit	DR/CR	Balance
19— Oct.	31	Forwarded	–			CR	365 –
Nov.	7		J12		23 –	CR	388 –

ANSWERS TO SECTION 7.2 EXERCISES (cont.)

Exercise 1 (cont.)

ACCOUNT A. Holmes, Capital **No.** 305

Date		Particulars	P.R.	Debit	Credit	DR/CR	Balance
19— Oct.	31	Forwarded	–			CR	9 024 44

ACCOUNT Revenue **No.** 400

Date		Particulars	P.R.	Debit	Credit	DR/CR	Balance
19— Oct.	31	Forwarded	–			CR	19 409 –
Nov.	7		J12		400 –	CR	19 709 –
	10		J12		300 –	CR	20 009 –

ACCOUNT Car Expense **No.** 405

Date		Particulars	P.R.	Debit	Credit	DR/CR	Balance
19— Oct.	31	Forwarded	–			DR	2 964 30
Nov.	15		J12		200 –	DR	3 164 30

ACCOUNT Rent Expense **No.** 410

Date		Particulars	P.R.	Debit	Credit	DR/CR	Balance
19— Oct.	31	Forwarded	–			DR	7 000 –
Nov.	12		J12	700 –		DR	7 700 –

ACCOUNT Wages Expense **No.** 415

Date		Particulars	P.R.	Debit	Credit	DR/CR	Balance
19— Oct.	31	Forwarded	–			DR	4 302 16

Name____________________ Date____________

ANSWERS TO SECTION 7.2 EXERCISES (cont.)

Exercise 1 (cont.)

A. Holmes

Trial Balance

November 15, 19 —

ACCOUNTS	DEBIT		CREDIT	
Bank	6 394	88		
A/R – A. Boyd	460	–		
Supplies	570	–		
Furniture	2 871	50		
Automobile	13 500	–		
A/P – Ace Finance			11 515	–
GST Payable			279	90
GST Recoverable			1 328	50
PST Payable			388	–
A. Holmes, Capital			9 024	44
Revenue			20 009	–
Car Expense	3 164	30		
Rent Expense	7 700	–		
Wages Expense	4 302	16		
	38 962	84	42 544	84

Name________________ Date________________

ANSWERS TO SECTION 7.2 EXERCISES (cont.)

Exercise 2, p. 237

1. Why does it not balance?

JOURNAL

DATE	PARTICULARS	DR	CR
19— Jan. 1	Bank	4 500	
	Equipment	3 600	
	Capital		8 100
3	Supplies	73	
	Accounts Payable		73
6	Expense	47	
	Bank		47
10	Bank	195	
	Revenue		195
15	Drawings	100	
	Bank		100
19	Accounts Receivable	63	
	Revenue		63
24	Supplies	38	
	Bank		38

LEDGER

Bank

DR	CR
4 500	47
195	100
	38
(4 510) 4 695	185

Accounts Receivable

DR	CR
63	

Supplies

DR	CR
73	
38	
111	

Equipment

DR	CR
3 600	

Accounts Payable

DR	CR
	73

Capital

DR	CR
	8 100

Drawings

DR	CR
100	

Revenue

DR	CR
	159
	63
	222

Expense

DR	CR
47	

TRIAL BALANCE

DR	CR
4 510	73
63	8 100
111	222
3 600	
100	
47	
8 431	8 395

Name____________________ Date____________________

ANSWERS TO SECTION 7.2 EXERCISES (cont.)

Exercise 2 (cont.)

2. Why does it not balance?

JOURNAL

DATE	PARTICULARS	DR	CR
19— Feb. 3	Bank	3 000	
	Equipment	2 000	
	Capital		5 000
5	Supplies	490	
	Bank		490
9	Accounts Receivable	155	
	Revenue		155
15	Expense	56	
	Bank		56
25	Expense	72	
	Accounts Payable		72
28	Bank	312	
	Revenue		312
29	Drawings	97	
	Bank		97

LEDGER

Bank

	Debit	Credit
	3 000	490
	312	56
		97
(2 669)	3 312	643

Accounts Receivable

Debit	Credit
155	

Supplies

Debit	Credit
490	

Equipment

Debit	Credit
2 000	

Accounts Payable

Debit	Credit
	72

Capital

Debit	Credit
	5 000

Drawings

Debit	Credit
97	

Revenue

Debit	Credit
	155
	312
	467

Expense

Debit	Credit
56	

TRIAL BALANCE

DR	CR
2 669	72
155	5 000
490	467
2 000	
97	
56	
5 467	5 539

Name____________________ Date________________

ANSWERS TO SECTION 7.2 EXERCISES (cont.)

Exercise 2 (cont.)

3. Why does it not balance?

JOURNAL

DATE	PARTICULARS	DR	CR
19— Apr. 3	Bank	2 500	
	Equipment	7 000	
	Capital		9 500
4	Accounts Receivable	371	
	Revenue		371
8	Bank	269	
	Revenue		269
10	Supplies	53	
	Accounts Payable		53
11	Drawings	127	
	Bank		127
13	Expense	86	
	Bank		86
17	Expense	49	
	Accounts Payable		49

LEDGER

Bank

2 500	127
269	86
(2 556) 2 769	213

Accounts Receivable

371	

Supplies

53	

Equipment

7 000	

Accounts Payable

	53
	49
	102

Capital

	9 500

Drawings

127	

Revenue

	371
	269
	540

Expense

86	
49	
135	

TRIAL BALANCE

DR	CR
2 556	102
371	9 500
53	540
7 000	
127	
135	
10 242	10 142

Name________________ Date________________

ANSWERS TO SECTION 7.2 EXERCISES (cont.)

Exercise 2 (cont.)

4. Why does it not balance?

JOURNAL

DATE	PARTICULARS	DR	CR
19— Jul. 4	Bank	4 000	
	Equipment	3 000	
	Capital		7 000
5	Supplies	216	
	Accounts Payable		216
10	Accounts Receivable	321	
	Revenue		321
15	Expense	73	
	Bank		73
20	Expense	34	
	Accounts Payable		34
25	Drawings	41	
	Bank		41
30	Bank	150	
	Accounts Receivable		150

LEDGER

Bank

DR	CR
4 000	73
150	41
(4 036) 4 150	114

Accounts Receivable

DR	CR
321	150
(171)	

Supplies

DR	CR
216	

Equipment

DR	CR
3 000	

Accounts Payable

DR	CR
	216
	34
	250

Capital

DR	CR
	7 000

Drawings

DR	CR
41	

Revenue

DR	CR
	321

Expense

DR	CR
73	
34	
107	

TRIAL BALANCE

DR	CR
4 036	250
171	7 000
216	41
3 000	321
107	
7 530	7 612

Name__________ Date__________

ANSWERS TO SECTION 7.3 EXERCISES

Analyzing Financial Data: Common-Size Income Statement (text p. 243)

Exercise 1, p. 243

1.

INCOME STATEMENTS
YEAR ENDED DECEMBER 31, 19–5

Items	*Company A*		*Company B*	
	$	*%*	*$*	*%*
Revenue				
Sales	$197 000		$421 000	
Expenses				
Automotive Expense	$40 200		$80 270	
Bank Interest Expense	3 500		27 050	
Rent Expense	12 000		30 000	
Wages Expense	86 750		214 860	
Other Expenses	1 800		10 900	
Total Expenses	$144 250		$363 080	
Net Income	$52 750		$57 920	

2. Observations:

1. ____________________
2. ____________________
3. ____________________
4. ____________________

Conclusion:

____

____

Additional Information Required:

____

____

Name____________________ Date____________________

ANSWERS TO SECTION 7.3 EXERCISES (cont.)

Exercise 2, p. 243

1.

INCOME STATEMENTS
YEAR ENDED DECEMBER 31, 19–6

Items	Ace Cleaning		Tip Top Cleaners	
Revenues	$294 325		$147 821	
Operating Expenses				
Bank Charges Expense	$6 700		$7 100	
Car Expense	28 070		11 190	
Cleaning Supplies Expense	52 950		36 960	
Insurance Expense	2 800		500	
Light and Heat Expense	6 500		2 100	
Miscellaneous Expense	1 800		750	
Rent Expense	18 000		12 000	
Telephone Expense	3 721		1 570	
Wages Expense	100 971		75 360	
Total Expenses	$221 512		$147 530	
Net Income	$72 813		$291	

2. ______________________________

3. ______________________________

Name________________ Date________________

ANSWERS TO SECTION 7.4 COMPUTER REVIEW QUESTIONS (text p. 248)

Using a Computer: A Spreadsheet To Find Trial Balance Errors

1. ______________________________
2. ______________________________
3. ______________________________
4. ______________________________
____
5. ______________________________
____
____
6. ______________________________
7. ______________________________
8. ______________________________

ANSWERS TO SECTION 7.4 COMPUTER EXERCISES (text p. 249)

Exercise 1, p. 249

1.

	A	B	C	D	E	F	G
1							
2							
3							
4							
5							
6							
7							
8							
9							
10							
11							
12							
13							
14							
15							
16							
17							
18							
19							
20							
21							
22							
23							
24							
25							
26							
27							
28							
29							
30							
31							
32							
33							
34							
35							

Name______________________ Date______________________

ANSWERS TO SECTION 7.4 COMPUTER EXERCISES (cont.)

Extending Your Computer Skills (text p. 249) *(These Exercises have no manual applications.)*

1. ______________________________

2. ______________________________

ANSWERS TO CHAPTER 7 EXERCISES (text p. 250)

Exercise 1, p. 250 Using Your Knowledge

Indicate whether each of the following statements is true or false by placing a "T" or an "F" in the space indicated. Explain the reason for each "F" response in the space provided.

1. The chief advantage of the three column account is that there is room for the account balance. ☐
2. Both sides of an account page (front and back) are used for the same item, (for example, Bank). ☐
3. Entering the journal page number in the account is the sixth step in the posting process. ☐
4. The step described in 3 above is performed in the journal. ☐
5. The process of setting up an account is known as "forwarding." ☐
6. The fourth step in the accounting cycle, as we know it, is the taking off of a trial balance. ☐
7. It is not possible for the ledger to be out of balance and also to be correct. ☐
8. If the trial balance difference is an even amount, the error could not be a transposition error. ☐
9. If the trial balance difference is zero, the ledger is in balance. ☐
10. Posting a debit item incorrectly as a credit produces a trial balance credit total that is smaller than the debit total by twice the amount of the error. ☐
11. Very rarely does a transaction affect only one account. ☐
12. Ledger accounts are arranged alphabetically to make them easier to find. ☐
13. The presence of the account number in the journal indicates that the posting of an item has been completed. ☐

Explanations for "F" Responses:

Name______________ Date______________

ANSWERS TO CHAPTER 7 EXERCISES (cont.)

Exercise 1 (cont.)

Exercise 2, p. 251

Error Situations	*Trial Balance will not balance*		*Trial Balance will balance but will not be correct*
	Debits greater than Credits by ($$)	*Credits greater than Debits by ($$)*	
1. An entire journal entry is posted as $400 instead of $100.			
2. A debit of $200 is posted twice.			
3. A debit of $150 is posted as a credit.			
4. The Bank account is over-added by $80.			
5. The Drawings account balance of $5 500 is missed when preparing the trial balance.			
6. The Revenue account balance of $72 000 is listed on the trial balance as a debit.			
7. An entire general journal entry for $325 is not posted.			
8. An entire general journal entry for $50 is posted in reverse.			
9. A $40 debit is not posted.			
10. A $500 credit is posted as $50.			
11. A debit of $60 to Bank was also posted to a customer's account.			
12. A $40 debit is posted as $400.			

Name____________________ Date_______________

ANSWERS TO CHAPTER 7 EXERCISES (cont.)

Exercise 3, p. 252

Exercise 4, p. 252

Exercise 5, p. 252

Exercise 6, p. 252

Name________________________ Date________________

ANSWERS TO CHAPTER 7 EXERCISES (cont.)

Exercise 7, p. 252 **Comprehensive Exercise**

1., 2. **GENERAL JOURNAL** **PAGE** *1*

DATE		PARTICULARS	P.R.	DEBIT	CREDIT

Name ________________ Date ____________

ANSWERS TO CHAPTER 7 EXERCISES (cont.)

Exercise 7 (cont.)

GENERAL JOURNAL PAGE ____

DATE		PARTICULARS	P.R.	DEBIT	CREDIT

Name________________ Date________________

ANSWERS TO CHAPTER 7 EXERCISES (cont.)

Exercise 7 (cont.)

GENERAL JOURNAL

PAGE____

DATE		PARTICULARS	P.R.	DEBIT	CREDIT

Name________________ Date____________

ANSWERS TO CHAPTER 7 EXERCISES (cont.)

Exercise 7 (cont.)

GENERAL JOURNAL PAGE ____

DATE		PARTICULARS	P.R.	DEBIT	CREDIT

Name________________ Date________

ANSWERS TO CHAPTER 7 EXERCISES (cont.)

Exercise 7 (cont.)

ACCOUNT Bank — No. 101

Date		Particulars	P.R.	Debit	Credit	DR/CR	Balance

ACCOUNT A/R – L. Pero — No. 111

Date		Particulars	P.R.	Debit	Credit	DR/CR	Balance

ACCOUNT A/R – K. Puna — No. 113

Date		Particulars	P.R.	Debit	Credit	DR/CR	Balance

ACCOUNT A/R – Spectrum Co. — No. 115

Date		Particulars	P.R.	Debit	Credit	DR/CR	Balance

Name____________________ Date____________________

ANSWERS TO CHAPTER 7 EXERCISES (cont.)

Exercise 7 (cont.)

ACCOUNT A/R – W.J. Thomson **No.** 117

Date		Particulars	P.R.	Debit	Credit	DR/CR	Balance

ACCOUNT Supplies **No.** 120

Date		Particulars	P.R.	Debit	Credit	DR/CR	Balance

ACCOUNT Equipment **No.** 125

Date		Particulars	P.R.	Debit	Credit	DR/CR	Balance

ACCOUNT Automobiles **No.** 130

Date		Particulars	P.R.	Debit	Credit	DR/CR	Balance

ACCOUNT Bank Loan **No.** 201

Date		Particulars	P.R.	Debit	Credit	DR/CR	Balance

Name______________________________ Date____________________

ANSWERS TO CHAPTER 7 EXERCISES (cont.)

Exercise 7 (cont.)

ACCOUNT A/P – Imperial Garage **No.** 211

Date		Particulars	P.R.	Debit	Credit	DR/CR	Balance

ACCOUNT A/P – Home Hardware **No.** 213

Date		Particulars	P.R.	Debit	Credit	DR/CR	Balance

ACCOUNT GST Payable **No.** 220

Date		Particulars	P.R.	Debit	Credit	DR/CR	Balance

ACCOUNT GST Recoverable **No.** 225

Date		Particulars	P.R.	Debit	Credit	DR/CR	Balance

Name________________________ Date____________________

ANSWERS TO CHAPTER 7 EXERCISES (cont.)

Exercise 7 (cont.)

ACCOUNT PST Payable **No.** 230

Date		Particulars	P.R.	Debit	Credit	DR/CR	Balance

ACCOUNT Pat Schelling, Capital **No.** 301

Date		Particulars	P.R.	Debit	Credit	DR/CR	Balance

ACCOUNT Pat Schelling, Drawings **No.** 302

Date		Particulars	P.R.	Debit	Credit	DR/CR	Balance

ACCOUNT Service Revenue **No.** 401

Date		Particulars	P.R.	Debit	Credit	DR/CR	Balance

ACCOUNT Automobile Expense **No.** 505

Date		Particulars	P.R.	Debit	Credit	DR/CR	Balance

Name____________________ Date____________

ANSWERS TO CHAPTER 7 EXERCISES (cont.)

Exercise 7 (cont.)

ACCOUNT Bank Charges Expense **No.** 510

Date	Particulars	P.R.	Debit	Credit	DR/CR	Balance

ACCOUNT General Expense **No.** 515

Date	Particulars	P.R.	Debit	Credit	DR/CR	Balance

ACCOUNT Rent Expense **No.** 520

Date	Particulars	P.R.	Debit	Credit	DR/CR	Balance

ACCOUNT Telephone Expense **No.** 525

Date	Particulars	P.R.	Debit	Credit	DR/CR	Balance

ACCOUNT Wages Expense **No.** 530

Date	Particulars	P.R.	Debit	Credit	DR/CR	Balance

ACCOUNT Loss on Sale of Equipment **No.** 535

Date	Particulars	P.R.	Debit	Credit	DR/CR	Balance

Name____________________ Date________________

ANSWERS TO CHAPTER 7 EXERCISES (cont.)

Exercise 7 (cont.)

3.

ACCOUNTS	DEBIT	CREDIT

Name____________________ Date________________

ANSWERS TO CHAPTER 7 EXERCISES (cont.)

Exercise 7 (cont.)

4.

Name________________________ Date__________________

ANSWERS TO CHAPTER 7 EXERCISES (cont.)

Exercise 7 (cont.)

5.

Name____________________ Date____________

ANSWERS TO CHAPTER 7 EXERCISES (cont.)

Exercise 8, p. 255

1. GENERAL JOURNAL PAGE 28

DATE		PARTICULARS	P.R.	DEBIT	CREDIT

Name________________ Date____________

ANSWERS TO CHAPTER 7 EXERCISES (cont.)

Exercise 8 (cont.)

1. (cont.)

GENERAL JOURNAL

PAGE ____

DATE		PARTICULARS	P.R.	DEBIT	CREDIT

Name ____________________ Date ____________________

ANSWERS TO CHAPTER 7 EXERCISES (cont.)

Exercise 8 (cont.)

1. (cont.) GENERAL JOURNAL PAGE ____

DATE		PARTICULARS	P.R.	DEBIT	CREDIT

Name________________ Date________________

ANSWERS TO CHAPTER 7 EXERCISES (cont.)

Exercise 8 (cont.)

1. (cont.) **GENERAL JOURNAL** **PAGE ______**

DATE		PARTICULARS	P.R.	DEBIT	CREDIT

Name______________________ Date________

ANSWERS TO CHAPTER 7 EXERCISES (cont.)

Exercise 8 (cont.)

ACCOUNT Bank **No.** 100

Date		Particulars	P.R.	Debit	Credit	DR/CR	Balance
19— Sep.	30	Forwarded	–			DR	3 7 5 0 20

ACCOUNT Supplies – Golf Course **No.** 105

Date		Particulars	P.R.	Debit	Credit	DR/CR	Balance
19— Sep.	30	Forwarded	–			DR	10 2 3 6 –

Name________________ Date________________

ANSWERS TO CHAPTER 7 EXERCISES (cont.)

Exercise 8 (cont.)

ACCOUNT Supplies – Office **No. 110**

Date		Particulars	P.R.	Debit	Credit	DR/CR	Balance
19– Sep.	30	Forwarded	–			DR	3 265 25

ACCOUNT Property **No. 115**

Date		Particulars	P.R.	Debit	Credit	DR/CR	Balance
19– Sep.	30	Forwarded	–			DR	95 000 –

ACCOUNT Buildings **No. 120**

Date		Particulars	P.R.	Debit	Credit	DR/CR	Balance
19– Sep.	30	Forwarded	–			DR	85 360 –

ACCOUNT Automotive Equipment **No. 125**

Date		Particulars	P.R.	Debit	Credit	DR/CR	Balance
19– Sep.	30	Forwarded	–			DR	40 956 –

ACCOUNT Maintenance Equipment **No. 130**

Date		Particulars	P.R.	Debit	Credit	DR/CR	Balance
19– Sep.	30	Forwarded	–			DR	22 650 60

ACCOUNT Bank Loan **No. 201**

Date		Particulars	P.R.	Debit	Credit	DR/CR	Balance
19– Sep.	30	Forwarded	–			CR	120 000 –

ACCOUNT A/P – Blair's Automotive **No. 205**

Date		Particulars	P.R.	Debit	Credit	DR/CR	Balance

Name______________________ Date______________

ANSWERS TO CHAPTER 7 EXERCISES (cont.)

Exercise 8 (cont.)

ACCOUNT A/P – Main Supply **No.** 210

Date		Particulars	P.R.	Debit	Credit	DR/CR	Balance
19— Sep.	30	Forwarded	–			CR	1 8 9 0 65

ACCOUNT A/P – Pro Equipment **No.** 215

Date		Particulars	P.R.	Debit	Credit	DR/CR	Balance
19— Sep.	30	Forwarded	–			CR	3 5 8 2 10

ACCOUNT GST Payable **No.** 220

Date		Particulars	P.R.	Debit	Credit	DR/CR	Balance
19— Sep.	30	Forwarded	–			CR	7 1 0 –

ACCOUNT GST Recoverable **No.** 225

Date		Particulars	P.R.	Debit	Credit	DR/CR	Balance
19— Sep.	30	Forwarded	–			DR	1 8 5 –

Name____________________ Date________________

ANSWERS TO CHAPTER 7 EXERCISES (cont.)

Exercise 8 (cont.)

ACCOUNT GST Recoverable **No.** 225

Date		Particulars	P.R.	Debit	Credit	DR/CR	Balance

ACCOUNT PST Payable **No.** 230

Date		Particulars	P.R.	Debit	Credit	DR/CR	Balance
19— Sep.	30	Forwarded	–			CR	2 5 0 50

ACCOUNT Mortgage Payable **No.** 240

Date		Particulars	P.R.	Debit	Credit	DR/CR	Balance
19— Sep.	30	Forwarded	–			CR	100 0 0 0 –

Name________________ Date____________

ANSWERS TO CHAPTER 7 EXERCISES (cont.)

Exercise 8 (cont.)

ACCOUNT Shirley Iris, Capital **No.** 301

Date		Particulars	P.R.	Debit	Credit	DR/CR	Balance
19— Sep.	30	Forwarded	–			CR	37 027 46

ACCOUNT Shirley Iris, Drawings **No.** 305

Date		Particulars	P.R.	Debit	Credit	DR/CR	Balance
19— Sep.	30	Forwarded	–			DR	18 000 –

ACCOUNT Revenue – Golf **No.** 401

Date		Particulars	P.R.	Debit	Credit	DR/CR	Balance
19— Sep.	30	Forwarded	–			CR	52 655 –

ACCOUNT Revenue – Food **No.** 405

Date		Particulars	P.R.	Debit	Credit	DR/CR	Balance
19— Sep.	30	Forwarded	–			CR	9 250 50

Name____________________ Date________________

ANSWERS TO CHAPTER 7 EXERCISES (cont.)

Exercise 8 (cont.)

ACCOUNT Automotive Expense **No.** 500

Date		Particulars	P.R.	Debit	Credit	DR/CR	Balance
19— Sep.	30	Forwarded	–			DR	5 9 6 3 01

ACCOUNT Bank Charges Expense **No.** 505

Date		Particulars	P.R.	Debit	Credit	DR/CR	Balance
19— Sep.	30	Forwarded	–			DR	6 8 4 2 25

ACCOUNT Light and Heat Expense **No.** 510

Date		Particulars	P.R.	Debit	Credit	DR/CR	Balance
19— Sep.	30	Forwarded	–			DR	2 8 5 0 45

ACCOUNT Maintenance Expense **No.** 515

Date		Particulars	P.R.	Debit	Credit	DR/CR	Balance
19— Sep.	30	Forwarded	–			DR	7 2 3 0 85

ACCOUNT Miscellaneous Expense **No.** 520

Date		Particulars	P.R.	Debit	Credit	DR/CR	Balance
19— Sep.	30	Forwarded	–			DR	1 5 2 5 75

Name__________ Date__________

ANSWERS TO CHAPTER 7 EXERCISES (cont.)

Exercise 8 (cont.)

ACCOUNT Mortgage Interest Expense **No.** 525

Date		Particulars	P.R.	Debit	Credit	DR/CR	Balance
19— Sep.	30	Forwarded	–			DR	4 5 0 0 –

ACCOUNT Telephone Expense **No.** 530

Date		Particulars	P.R.	Debit	Credit	DR/CR	Balance
19— Sep.	30	Forwarded	–			DR	6 8 5 55

ACCOUNT Wages Expense **No.** 535

Date		Particulars	P.R.	Debit	Credit	DR/CR	Balance
19— Sep.	30	Forwarded	–			DR	16 3 6 5 30

Name________________ Date____________

ANSWERS TO CHAPTER 7 EXERCISES (cont.)

Exercise 8 (cont.)

2.

ACCOUNTS	DEBIT	CREDIT

Name____________________ Date________________

ANSWERS TO CHAPTER 7 EXERCISES (cont.)

Exercise 8 (cont.)

3.

ANSWERS TO CHAPTER 7 EXERCISES (cont.)

Exercise 9, p. 257 For Further Thought *(Use more paper if necessary.)*

1.

2.

3.

4.

5.

6.
   1.
   2.
   3.

Exercise 10, p. 258 Cases for Further Thought *(Use more paper if necessary.)*

1.

2.

3.

4.

Name____________________ Date________________

CASE STUDIES (text p. 258)

Case 1 *A Stitch in Time,* p. 258 *(Use more paper if necessary.)*

1.

2.

Case 2 *Does the Order of Accounts Matter?* p. 258 *(Use more paper if necessary.)*

1.

2.

Name____________________ Date__________

CASE STUDIES (cont.)

Challenge Case 3 *Frustration for the Auditor*, p. 260 *(Use more paper if necessary.)*

1. GENERAL JOURNAL PAGE ______

DATE		PARTICULARS	P.R.	DEBIT	CREDIT

Name______________________ Date______________

CASE STUDIES (cont.)

Challenge Case 3 (cont.)

1. **GENERAL JOURNAL** PAGE ____

DATE		PARTICULARS	P.R.	DEBIT	CREDIT

2. ______________________________

Name ____________________ Date ____________

CASE STUDIES (cont.)

Group Discussion Case 4 *"To Fire or Not To Fire"*, p. 260 *(Use more paper if necessary.)*

1.

2.

3.

4.

5.

6.

CAREER Fred Branch/Corporate Controller, Nestle Enterprises Ltd.

ANSWERS TO DISCUSSIONS QUESTIONS (text p. 262)

1.

2.

3.

4.

5.

Name __________ Date __________

ANSWERS TO SECTION 8.1 REVIEW QUESTIONS (text p. 273)

The Six-Column Work Sheet

1. ______

2. ______

3. ______

4. ______

5. ______

6. ______

7. ______

8. ______

9. ______

10. ______

11. ______

12. ______

13. ______

14. ______

15. ______

16. ______

17. 1. ______
    2. ______
    3. ______
    4. ______
    5. ______
    6. ______

Name______ Date______

ANSWERS TO SECTION 8.1 EXERCISES (text p. 273)

Exercise 1, p. 273

Indicate to which column in the work sheet each account should be extended by placing a check mark in the appropriate column.

Account	Income Statement Debit	Income Statement Credit	Balance Sheet Debit	Balance Sheet Credit
Accounts Payable				
Miscellaneous Expense				
Revenue				
Advertising Expense				
Wages Expense				
Mortgage Payable				
Light and Heat Expense				
Equipment				
G. Rojek, Capital				
Delivery Expense				
GST Payable				
GST Recoverable				
Bank Loan				
Accounts Receivable				
Automobile				
Bank				
G. Rojek, Drawings				
Sales				
Bank Charges Expense				
Rent Expense				
Supplies				
Trucks				

Name____________________ Date________________

ANSWERS TO SECTION 8.1 EXERCISES (cont.)

Exercise 2, p. 273 **N. Foreman and Company**

N. Foreman and Company
Work Sheet
Month Ended April 30, 19__

ACCOUNTS	TRIAL BALANCE DR	TRIAL BALANCE CR	INCOME STATEMENT DR	INCOME STATEMENT CR	BALANCE SHEET DR	BALANCE SHEET CR
Bank	750 20					
Accounts Receivable	15 375 10					
Supplies	1 250 –					
Equipment	18 500 –					
Automobiles	29 300 88					
Bank Loan		30 000 –				
Accounts Payable		5 331 –				
GST Payable		106 17				
GST Recoverable	74 12					
PST Payable		121 33				
N. Foreman, Capital		24 772 50				
N. Foreman, Drawings	3 000 –					
Fees Revenue		18 200 –				
Bank Charges	250 –					
Car Expense	1 750 –					
Miscellaneous Expense	512 20					
Light and Heat Expense	746 –					
Rent Expense	1 100 –					
Telephone Expense	276 50					
Wages Expense	5 646 –					
	78 531 –	78 531 –				

Name______________________ Date______________________

ANSWERS TO SECTION 8.1 EXERCISES (cont.)

Exercise 3, p. 274

Boa Bodyworks and Repairs

Work Sheet

Year Ended December 31, 19–8

ACCOUNTS	TRIAL BALANCE		INCOME STATEMENT		BALANCE SHEET	
	DR	CR	DR	CR	DR	CR

Name________________ Date________________

ANSWERS TO SECTION 8.1 EXERCISES (cont.)

Exercise 4, p. 275

1.

Work Sheet — The Arthur Company — Month Ended Oct. 31, 19—

ACCOUNTS	TRIAL BALANCE DR	TRIAL BALANCE CR	INCOME STATEMENT DR	INCOME STATEMENT CR	BALANCE SHEET DR	BALANCE SHEET CR
Bank	1 722.16				1 722.16	
A/R – J. Young	323.–				332.–	
A/R – M. Watson	72.–				72.–	
A/R – H. Chan	116.–				116.–	
Supplies	1 255.–				1 255.–	
Office Equipment	5 863.–				5 863.–	
Automobiles	13 200.–				1 320.–	
A/P – City Hydro		1 116.42				1 116.42
A/P – O.K. Supply		4 21.72				4 21.72
A/P – Slick Oil Co.		331.19				331.19
Bank Loan		10 000.–				10 000.–
P. Arthur, Capital		10 504.82				10 504.82
P. Arthur, Drawings	1 000.–			1 000.–		
Revenue		4 903.17		4 903.17		
Advertising Expense	465.12		465.12			
Automobile Expense	270.–		270.–		270.–	
Bank Charges	56.40		56.40			
Miscellaneous Expense	113.74		113.74			
Rent Expense	400.–		400.–			
Salaries Expense	1 280.–		1 280.–		1 280.–	
Telephone Expense	25.60		25.60			
Utilities Expense	115.30					
	26 277.32	26 277.32	2 340.86	5 903.17	12 230.16	21 074.15
Net Income			3 562.31			8 843.99
			5 903.17	5 903.17	12 230.16	29 918.14

Name______________________ Date______________________

ANSWERS TO SECTION 8.1 EXERCISES (cont.)

Exercise 4 (cont.)

2. Accounts Receivable Control ____________
Accounts Payable Control ____________

Exercise 5, p. 275 Workbook Exercise

Show where each step in the accounting cycle should appear in the chart below by entering the number of its location in the circle provided.

STEPS IN THE ACCOUNTING CYCLE

WORK SHEET PREPARED

LEDGER BALANCED BY MEANS OF A TRIAL BALANCE

TRANSACTIONS OCCUR SOURCE DOCUMENTS

PERFORMED BY SENIOR PERSONNEL

ACCOUNTING ENTRIES RECORDED IN THE JOURNAL

BALANCE SHEET AND INCOME STATEMENT PREPARED

PERFORMED BY JUNIOR PERSONNEL

JOURNAL ENTRIES POSTED TO THE LEDGER ACCOUNTS

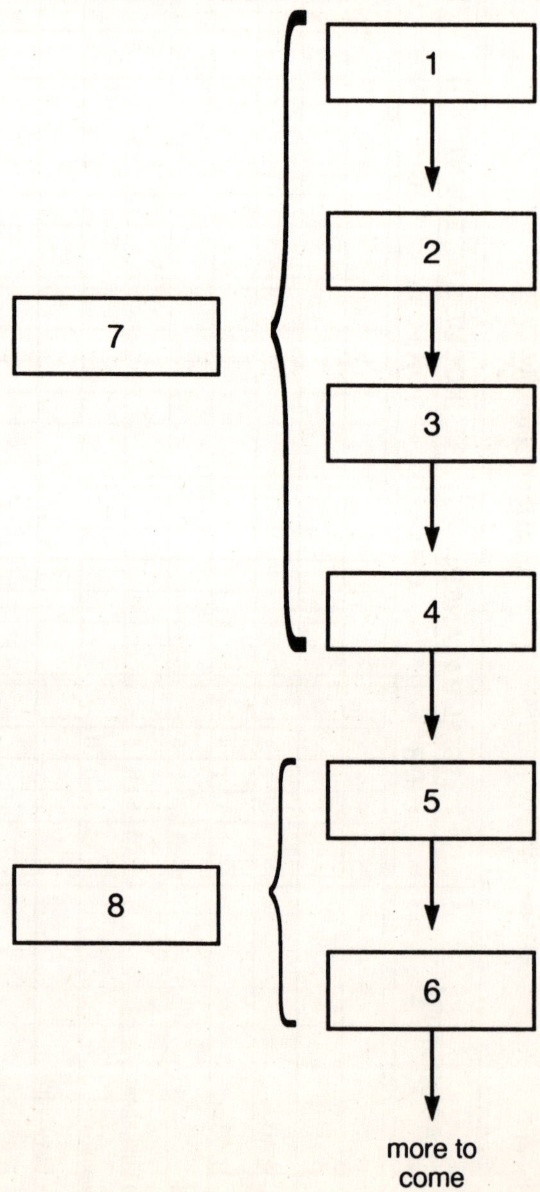

Name____________________ Date____________________

ANSWERS TO SECTION 8.2 REVIEW QUESTIONS (text p. 278) Formal Financial Statements: Income Statement

1. ______

2. ______

3.
   1. ______
   2. ______
   3. ______

4. ______

5. ______

6. ______

ANSWERS TO SECTION 8.2 EXERCISES (text p. 278)

Exercise 1, p. 278

1. ______
   1. ______
   2. ______
   3. ______

2. ______

3. ______

4. ______

5. ______

Name______ Date______

ANSWERS TO SECTION 8.2 EXERCISES (cont.)

Exercise 2, p. 278

Exercise 3, p. 279

1. a.
   b.
   c.
   d.
   e.
   f.
2.

Name Date

ANSWERS TO SECTION 8.3 REVIEW QUESTIONS (text p. 286)

Formal Financial Statements: Balance Sheet

1. ______
2. ______
3. ______
4. ______
5. ______
6. ______
7. ______
8. ______
______
9. ______
10. ______
11. ______
12. 1. ______
    2. ______
13. ______

ANSWERS TO SECTION 8.3 EXERCISES (text p. 286)

Exercise 1, p. 286

ACCOUNTS	CLASSIFICATION
Accounts Payable	______
Accounts Receivable	______
Advertising Expense	______
Automobiles	______
Bank Charges Expense	______
Bank Loan	______
Bank	______
Buildings	______
GST Payable	______
Commissions Earned	______
Delivery Expense	______
F. Ryback, Capital	______
F. Ryback, Drawings	______
General Expense	______
Insurance Expense	______
Mortgage Payable (current instalment)	______
Mortgage Payable (non-current portion)	______
Postage Expense	______
Rent Expense	______
Supplies	______
Telephone Expense	______
Wages Expense	______

Name______ Date______

ANSWERS TO SECTION 8.3 EXERCISES (cont.)

Exercise 2, p. 287

1. Current assets: ____________
2. Fixed assets: ____________
3. Current liabilities: ____________
4. Long-term liabilities: ____________
5. ______________________________
6. ______________________________
7. Mortgage payable: ____________

Exercise 3, p. 288

Complete the following schedule by filling in the blanks.

Items	*Opening Capital*	*Net Income or Net Loss (–)*	*Drawings*	*Ending Capital*
a.	$ 30 000	$15 000	$ 10 000	$
b.	50 000	–2 000	7 000	
c.	70 000	32 000		75 500
d.		16 000	19 500	33 200
e.	56 000		30 000	40 000
f.	45 000		25 000	15 000
g.	22 000		10 000	28 000
h.		25 000	18 000	42 000
i.	120 000	42 000		112 000

Exercise 4, p. 288

Name______________________ Date______________

ANSWERS TO SECTION 8.3 EXERCISES (cont.)

Exercise 4 (cont.)

ANSWERS TO SECTION 8.3 EXERCISES (cont.)

Exercise 5, p. 289

Name____________________ Date____________

ANSWERS TO SECTION 8.3 EXERCISES (cont.)

Exercise 6, p. 289

ANSWERS TO SECTION 8.4 EXERCISES (text p. 290)

Analyzing Financial Data: Common-Size Balance Sheet

Exercise 1, p. 290

1.

BALANCE SHEETS
DECEMBER 31, 19–6

Items	Neon Company		Radon Company	
	$	%	$	%
Assets				
Bank	$3 000		$14 500	
Accounts Receivable	10 000		5 500	
Plant and Equipment	132 000		53 000	
Automobiles	38 000		26 000	
Total Assets	$183 000		$99 000	
Liabilities and Equity				
Accounts Payable	$19 000		$2 200	
Mortgage Payable	92 500		18 000	
Owner's Equity	71 500		78 800	
Total Liabilities and Equity	$183 000		$99 000	

2.

3.

Name__________ Date__________

ANSWERS TO SECTION 8.4 EXERCISES (cont.)

Exercise 2, p. 291

BALANCE SHEETS
DECEMBER 31, 19–4

Items	Leo Company		Capricorn Company	
	$	%	$	%
Assets				
Bank	$1 000		$31 000	
Accounts Receivable	25 000		–	
Plant and Equipment	150 000		160 000	
Automobiles	50 000		29 000	
Total Assets	$226 000		$220 000	
Liabilities and Equity				
Accounts Payable	$25 000		$11 000	
Debt Payable (Automobile)	20 000		20 000	
Mortgage Payable	–		150 000	
Owner's Equity	181 000		39 000	
Total Liabilities and Equity	$226 000		$220 000	

Observations about each company's position:

Name____________________ Date____________________

ANSWERS TO SECTION 8.5 COMPUTER REVIEW QUESTIONS (text p. 297)

Using a Computer: A Spreadsheet For Work Sheets and Financial Statements

1. ______________________________
2. ______________________________
3. ______________________________
4. ______________________________
5. ______________________________
6. ______________________________

ANSWERS TO SECTION 8.5 COMPUTER EXERCISES (text p. 297)

Work Sheet

	A	B	C	D	E	F	G	H	I
1									
2									
3									
4									
5									
6									
7									
8									
9									
10									
11									
12									
13									
14									
15									
16									
17									
18									
19									
20									
21									
22									
23									
24									
25									
26									
27									
28									
29									

Name______________________ Date______________

ANSWERS TO SECTION 8.5 COMPUTER EXERCISES (cont.)

Income Statement

	J	K	L	M
38				
39				
40				
41				
42				
43				
44				
45				
46				
47				
48				
49				
50				
51				
52				
53				
54				
55				
56				

Balance Sheet

	O	P	Q	R	S
56					
57					
58					
59					
60					
61					
62					
63					
64					
65					
66					
67					
68					
69					
70					
71					
72					
73					
74					
75					
76					
77					
78					
79					
80					
81					
82					

Name______________________ Date________________

ANSWERS TO SECTION 8.5 COMPUTER EXERCISES (cont.)

Extending Your Computer Skills (text p. 298)

	A	B	C	D	E	F
1						
2						
3						
4						
5						
6						
7						
8						
9						
10						
11						
12						
13						
14						
15						
16						
17						
18						
19						
20						
21						

Communicate It (text p. 298)

ANSWERS TO CHAPTER 8 EXERCISES (text p. 299)

Exercise 1, p. 299 Using Your Knowledge

1.

2.

Name ____________________ Date ____________

ANSWERS TO CHAPTER 8 EXERCISES (cont.)

Exercise 2, p. 300

Ying Lo — Work Sheet — Six Months Ended June 30, 19–5

ACCOUNTS	TRIAL BALANCE DR	TRIAL BALANCE CR	INCOME STATEMENT DR	INCOME STATEMENT CR	BALANCE SHEET DR	BALANCE SHEET CR
Bank	516.20					
Accounts Receivable	9 255.50					
Office Supplies	1 525.–					
Office Equipment	10 356.–					
Automobile	19 255.65					
Professional Library	5 363.25					
Accounts Payable		2 618.25				
GST Payable		650.–				
GST Recoverable	410.–					
Ying Lo, Capital		34 024.81				
Ying Lo, Drawings	20 000.–					
Fees Earned		55 285.–				
Car Expense	4 592.36					
Light and Heat Expense	589.25					
Miscellaneous Expense	1 254.85					
Rent Expense	7 200.–					
Salaries Expense	9 235.–					
Telephone Expense	3 025.–					
	92 578.06	92 578.06				

Name__________ Date__________

ANSWERS TO CHAPTER 8 EXERCISES (cont.)

Exercise 2 (cont.) Balance Sheet

Name______________________ Date______________

ANSWERS TO CHAPTER 8 EXERCISES (cont.)

Exercise 2 (cont.) Income Statement

ANSWERS TO CHAPTER 8 EXERCISES (cont.)

Exercise 3, p. 301

Star Delivery — Work Sheet — Year Ended December 31, 19–4

ACCOUNTS	TRIAL BALANCE DR	TRIAL BALANCE CR	INCOME STATEMENT DR	INCOME STATEMENT CR	BALANCE SHEET DR	BALANCE SHEET CR
Bank	1 852 25					
Accounts Receivable	15 325 –					
Office Supplies	1 863 –					
Furniture and Equipment	7 258 36					
Land	45 500 –					
Buildings	52 365 50					
Automobile	9 255 65					
Trucks	36 252 95					
Accounts Payable		3 579 25				
GST Payable		730 –				
GST Recoverable	450 –					
Bank Loan		25 000 –				
Mortgage Payable		75 000 –				
Danielle Nowak, Capital		58 099 98				
Danielle Nowak, Drawings	32 000 –					
Revenue		125 254 –				
Gas and Oil Expense	26 215 24					
Insurance Expense	2 657 25					
Miscellaneous Expense	1 526 85					
Telephone Expense	965 32					
Truck Repairs Expense	4 240 65					
Utilities Expense	1 575 65					
Wages Expense	48 359 56					
	287 663 23	287 663 23				

Name________________ Date________________

ANSWERS TO CHAPTER 8 EXERCISES (cont.)

Exercise 3 (cont.)

Name________________ Date________________

ANSWERS TO CHAPTER 8 EXERCISES (cont.)

Ex. 3 (cont.)

Name____________ Date____________

ANSWERS TO CHAPTER 8 EXERCISES (cont.)

Exercise 4, p. 301

For each of the following, check off the most appropriate response in the space provided.

1. Financial statements are prepared:

- **a.** once a year. ☐
- **b.** at the end of the fiscal period. ☐
- **c.** whenever management requires them. ☐
- **d.** all of the above. ☐
- **e.** none of the above. ☐

2. A work sheet is:

- **a.** one of the books of account. ☐
- **b.** one of the financial statements. ☐
- **c.** used instead of the financial statements. ☐
- **d.** all of the above. ☐
- **e.** none of the above. ☐

3. Extending amounts on a work sheet means:

- **a.** adding to the amounts because of additional transactions. ☐
- **b.** placing debit amounts in debit columns and credit amounts in credit columns. ☐
- **c.** transferring amounts into the Balance Sheet section or the Income Statement section. ☐
- **d.** all of the above. ☐
- **e.** none of the above. ☐

4. The process of balancing the work sheet involves:

- **a.** totaling the four right-hand money columns. ☐
- **b.** calculating the difference between the two money columns in each of the last two sections. ☐
- **c.** ensuring that the differences in **b)** above are equal to each other. ☐

Name________________________________ Date______________________

ANSWERS TO CHAPTER 8 EXERCISES (cont.)

Exercise 4 (cont.)

d. all of the above. ☐

e. none of the above. ☐

5. A work sheet will not balance if:

a. the Telephone Expense amount is extended to the Balance Sheet section Debit Column. ☐

b. the Drawings amount is extended to the Income Statement section Debit column. ☐

c. the Capital amount is extended to the Balance Sheet section Debit column. ☐

d. all of the above. ☐

e. none of the above. ☐

6. You can tell what the net income or net loss figure is by:

a. looking at the balancing figure in the Balance Sheet section of the work sheet. ☐

b. looking at the balancing figure in the Income Statement section of the work sheet. ☐

c. looking at the equity section of the completed balance sheet. ☐

d. all of the above. ☐

e. none of the above. ☐

7. All of the following statements, except one, are false. Indicate which statement is true.

a. The report form of balance sheet is the only style used in the real business world. ☐

b. The report form of balance sheet is common because it uses standard-sized paper. ☐

c. The report form of balance sheet is horizontal in form. ☐

d. The style of the report form of balance sheet eliminates the need for "balancing" totals. ☐

e. The report form of balance sheet is more difficult to understand. ☐

Name_______________________________ Date_______________________

ANSWERS TO CHAPTER 8 EXERCISES (cont.)

Exercise 4 (cont.)

8. All of the following statements, except one, are false. Indicate the one that is true.

On a classified balance sheet:

- **a.** automobiles are not included in the Fixed Assets section because their value decreases over time. ☐
- **b.** a mortgage payable is deducted from the asset, Building. ☐
- **c.** supplies are not included as a current asset because they are normally converted into cash. ☐
- **d.** a bank loan is included in long-term liabilities. ☐
- **e.** the values shown for the fixed assets are not necessarily their true market value. ☐

9. All of the following statements, except one, are true. Indicate which statement is false.

- **a.** The data in the books of account are considered to be "raw" data. ☐
- **b.** Accountants are judged on the basis of the accounting statements and reports that they prepare. Therefore, their work should be first-class in form and content. ☐
- **c.** All of the data necessary for the financial statements can be found on the work sheet. ☐
- **d.** An overall decrease in capital can occur in two ways. An overall increase in capital can occur in only one way. Therefore, decreases in capital are more common. ☐
- **e.** The beginning balance in the equity section of the balance sheet is not always that of January 1. ☐

10. During a fiscal period, a business suffered a loss of $12 000, began the period with a capital balance of $20 000, and ended the period with a minus capital balance of $2 000. The drawings for the fiscal period were:

- **a.** $ 6 000 ☐
- **b.** $10 000 ☐
- **c.** $30 000 ☐
- **d.** $18 000 ☐
- **e.** $14 000 ☐

Name________________________ Date________________

ANSWERS TO CHAPTER 8 EXERCISES (cont.)

Exercise 5, p. 303 **For Further Thought** *(Use more paper if necessary.)*

1. __________

2. __________

3. __________
   1. __________
   2. __________
   3. __________
   4. __________
   5. __________

4. __________

5. __________

6. __________

7. __________

8. __________
   1. __________
   2. __________
   3. __________
   4. __________
   5. __________

9. __________

10. __________

Name__________ Date__________

CASE STUDIES (text p. 304)

Case 1 *Why Doesn't Net Income Equal Cash?*, p. 304 *(Use more paper if necessary.)*

1.

2.

3.

Case 2 *Interpreting Condensed Balance Sheets*, p. 305 *(Use more paper if necessary.)*

1.

2.

3.

4.

Challenge Case 3 *Could You Get Student Council out of the Hole?*, p. 306 *(Use more paper if necessary.)*

1.

Name____________________ Date________________

CASE STUDIES (cont.)

Challenge Case 3 (cont.)

2.

3.

4.

CAREER LILIAN GOH / MANAGER, AUDIT OPERATIONS BRANCH, DEPARTMENT OF INDIAN AFFAIRS AND NORTHERN DEVELOPMENT

ANSWERS TO DISCUSSION QUESTIONS (text p. 308)

Name____________________ Date________________

ANSWERS TO SECTION 9.1 REVIEW QUESTIONS (text p. 311)

Accountability

1. ______
2. ______
3. ______
4. ______
5. ______
6. ______
7. ______
8. ______
9. ______
10. ______
11. ______
12. ______
13. ______
14. ______

ANSWERS TO SECTION 9.1 EXERCISE (text p. 312)

Exercise 1, p. 312

1. ______
2. ______
3. a. ______
   b. ______
   c. ______
4. ______
5. ______
6. ______
7. ______

Name______ Date______

ANSWERS TO SECTION 9.1 EXERCISE (cont.)

8. __________
9. __________
10. __________
11. __________
12. __________

ANSWERS TO SECTION 9.2 REVIEW QUESTIONS (text p. 323)

Simple Adjustments and Expanded Work Sheets

1. __________
2. __________
3. __________
4. __________
5. __________
6. __________
7. __________
8. __________
9. __________
10. __________
11. __________
12. __________
13. __________
14. __________
15. __________
16. __________
17. __________
18. __________
19. __________

Name__________ Date__________

ANSWERS TO SECTION 9.2 EXERCISES (text p. 325)

Exercise 1, p. 325

Complete the following schedule.

Supplies	*Trial Balance Figure*	*Supplies Closing Inventory Figure*	*Supplies Expense Figure*
1.	$300.00	$100.00	
2.		$175.00	$250.00
3.	$950.00		$740.00
Prepaid Insurance	***Trial Balance Figure***	***Prepaid Insurance Final Calculation***	***Insurance Expense Figure***
1.	$875.00	$325.00	
2.	$925.00		$315.00
3.		$410.00	$375.00

Exercise 2, p. 325

Using the following information, complete the inventory sheet and make the adjusting entry in the T-accounts.

Inventory Item	*Quantity*	*Unit Price*	*Value*
Rubber bands	3 boxes	*$ 1.50 per box*	
Envelopes #8	10 boxes	*32.00 per box*	
Envelopes #10	4 1/2 boxes	*36.00 per box*	
Envelopes, manila	2 boxes	*28.00 per box*	
Typing paper	4M sheets	*15.60 per M*	
Letterhead	10M sheets	*22.50 per M*	
Copy paper	4M sheets	*10.00 per M*	
Carbon paper	2 boxes	*6.00 per box*	
Paper clips	12 boxes	*1.50 per box*	
Staples	15 boxes	*4.10 per box*	
Pencils, regular	4 doz	*5.50 per doz*	
Pencils, red	2 doz	*6.10 per doz*	
		Total	

Supplies	
2 018–	

Supplies Used	

ANSWERS TO SECTION 9.2 EXERCISES (cont.)

Exercise 3, p. 326

Year	Insurance Expense	Prepaid Insurance (Dec. 31)
19–1		
19–2		
	Total Expense $216	

Exercise 4, p. 326

	Total number of months of insurance used as of the designated year-end	Total number of months of insurance unused as of the designated year-end	Value of the prepaid insurance at the designated year-end
a.			
b.			
c.			
d.			
e.			
f.			

Exercise 5, p. 326

1. Prepaid Licences ______________
   Bank ______________
2. Prepaid licences = ______________
3. Truck licences expense = ______________
4. Truck Licence Expense ______________
   Prepaid Licences ______________
5. ______________
6. ______________
7. ______________

Name______________ Date______________

ANSWERS TO SECTION 9.2 EXERCISES (cont.)

Exercise 6, p. 327

Work Sheet | P. Pahl and Company | Year Ended December 31, 19—8

ACCOUNTS	TRIAL BALANCE DEBIT	TRIAL BALANCE CREDIT	ADJUSTMENTS DEBIT	ADJUSTMENTS CREDIT	INCOME STATEMENT DEBIT	INCOME STATEMENT CREDIT	BALANCE SHEET DEBIT	BALANCE SHEET CREDIT
Bank	1 800							
Accounts Receivable	19 500							
Supplies	1 000							
Prepaid Insurance	1 750							
Equipment	22 000							
Automobile	21 000							
Accounts Payable		4 360						
P. Pahl, Capital		54 040						
P. Pahl, Drawings	15 000							
Fees Earned		60 300						
Car Expense	3 800							
General Expense	2 950							
Miscellaneous Expense	700							
Rent Expense	7 200							
Wages Expense	22 000							
	118 700	118 700						

Name________________ Date________________

ANSWERS TO SECTION 9.2 EXERCISES (cont.)

Exercise 6 (cont.)

2. GENERAL JOURNAL PAGE ____

DATE 19—8		PARTICULARS	P.R.	DEBIT	CREDIT

3.

Bank	
1 800	

Accounts Receivable	
19 500	

Supplies	
1 000	

Prepaid Insurance	
1 750	

Equipment	
22 000	

Automobile	
21 000	

Accounts Payable	
	4 360

P. Pahl, Capital	
	54 040

P. Pahl, Drawings	
15 000	

Name____________________ Date____________

ANSWERS TO SECTION 9.2 EXERCISES (cont.)

Exercise 6 (cont.)

3. (cont.)

Fees Earned

	60 300

Car Expense

3 800	

General Expense

2 950	

Miscellaneous Expense

700	

Rent Expense

7 200	

Wages Expense

22 000	

Supplies Expense

Insurance Expense

P. Pahl and Company

Adjusted Trial Balance

December 31, 19–8

Name________________ Date__________

ANSWERS TO SECTION 9.2 EXERCISES (cont.)

Exercise 6 (cont.)

Optional

4.

P. Pahl and Company
Income Statement
Year Ended December 31, 19–8

Name________________ Date________________

ANSWERS TO SECTION 9.2 EXERCISES (cont.)

Exercise 6 (cont.)

4. (cont.)

P. Pahl and Company

Balance Sheet

December 31, 19 – 8

Name__________ Date__________

ANSWERS TO SECTION 9.2 EXERCISES (cont.)

Exercise 7, p. 328

1.

Work Sheet | Mission Marketing | Year Ended December 31, 19-5

ACCOUNTS	TRIAL BALANCE		ADJUSTMENTS		INCOME STATEMENT		BALANCE SHEET	
	DEBIT	CREDIT	DEBIT	CREDIT	DEBIT	CREDIT	DEBIT	CREDIT
Bank	2 490							
Accounts Receivable	21 600							
Supplies	4 250							
Prepaid Insurance	1 254							
Equipment	19 200							
Automobile	44 200							
Accounts Payable		6 565						
GST Payable		780						
GST Recoverable	510							
C. Ans, Capital		71 275						
C. Ans, Drawings	40 000							
Fees Earned		135 700						
Car Expense	13 214							
Light and Power Exp.	2 800							
Miscellaneous Exp.	1 563							
Rent Expense	18 000							
Wages Expense	45 239							
	214 320	214 320						

Name________________ Date________________

ANSWERS TO SECTION 9.2 EXERCISES (cont.)

Exercise 7 (cont.)

2. **GENERAL JOURNAL** **PAGE** ____

DATE 19—5		PARTICULARS	P.R.	DEBIT	CREDIT

3.

Bank	
2 490	

Accounts Receivable	
21 600	

Supplies	
4 250	

Prepaid Insurance	
1 254	

Equipment	
19 200	

Automobile	
44 200	

Accounts Payable	
	6 565

GST Payable	
	780

GST Recoverable	
510	

C. Ans, Capital	
	71 275

C. Ans, Drawings	
40 000	

Fees Earned	
	135 700

Name________________ Date________________

ANSWERS TO SECTION 9.2 EXERCISES (cont.)

Exercise 7 (cont.)

3. (cont.)

Car Expense

13 214	

Light & Power Expense

2 800	

Miscellaneous Expense

1 563	

Rent Expense

18 000	

Wages Expense

45 239	

Supplies Expense

Insurance Expense

Mission Marketing
Adjusted Trial Balance
December 31, 19—5

Name____________________ Date________________

ANSWERS TO SECTION 9.2 EXERCISES (cont.)

Exercise 7 (cont.)

Optional

4. Mission Marketing

Income Statement

Year Ended December 31, 19 – 5

ANSWERS TO SECTION 9.2 EXERCISES (cont.)

Exercise 7 (cont.)

Optional

4. (cont.)

Mission Marketing

Balance Sheet

December 31, 19–5

Name ______________ Date ______________

ANSWERS TO SECTION 9.2 EXERCISES (cont.)

Exercise 8, p. 328

Work Sheet — J. Soo and Associates — Year Ended December 31, 19 – 5

ACCOUNTS	TRIAL BALANCE		ADJUSTMENTS		INCOME STATEMENT		BALANCE SHEET	
	DEBIT	CREDIT	DEBIT	CREDIT	DEBIT	CREDIT	DEBIT	CREDIT
Bank	2 160 –							
Accounts Receivable	11 500 –							
Supplies	1 950 –							
Prepaid Insurance	624 –							
Equipment	9 200 –							
Automobile	18 350 –							
Accounts Payable		5 920 –						
GST Payable		310 –						
GST Recoverable	340 –							
J. Soo, Capital		36 662 –						
J. Soo, Drawings	7 500 –							
Commissions		35 650 –						
Car Expense	3 214 –							
Light and Power Expense	1 563 –							
Miscellaneous Expense	902 –							
Rent Expense	6 000 –							
Wages Expense	15 239 –							
	78 542 –	78 542 –						

Name__________ Date__________

ANSWERS TO SECTION 9.2 EXERCISES (cont.)

Exercise 8 (cont.)

2. GENERAL JOURNAL PAGE ____

DATE		PARTICULARS	P.R.	DEBIT	CREDIT

3.

Bank	
2160	

Accounts Receivable	
11 500	

Supplies	
1 950	

Prepaid Insurance	
624	

Equipment	
9 200	

Automobiles	
18 350	

Accounts Payable	
	5 920

GST Payable	
	310

GST Recoverable	
340	

J. Soo, Capital	
	36 662

J. Soo, Drawings	
7 500	

Commissions	
	35 650

Car Expense	
3 214	

Light and Power Expense	
1 563	

Miscellaneous Expense	
902	

Name__________________________ Date__________________

ANSWERS TO SECTION 9.2 EXERCISES (cont.)

Exercise 8 (cont.)

3. (cont.)

Rent Expense	
6 000	

Wages Expense	
15 239	

Supplies Expense	

Insurance Expense	

J. Soo & Associates

Adjusted Trial Balance

Year Ended December 31, 19–5

Name________________ Date________________

ANSWERS TO SECTION 9.2 EXERCISES (cont.)

Exercise 8 (cont.)

Optional

4.

J. Soo and Associates

Income Statement

Year Ended December 31, 19 – 5

Name________________ Date____________

ANSWERS TO SECTION 9.2 EXERCISES (cont.)

Exercise 8 (cont.)

Optional

4. (cont.)

J. Soo and Associates

Balance Sheet

December 31, 19 – 5

ANSWERS TO SECTION 9.3 REVIEW QUESTIONS (text p. 332)

Closing Entries Concepts

1. ____________________

2. ____________________

3. ____________________
4. ____________________

5. ____________________
6. ____________________
7. ____________________

8. ____________________
9. ____________________
   1. ____________________
   2. ____________________
   3. ____________________
10. ____________________
    1. ____________________
    2. ____________________
    3. ____________________

ANSWERS TO SECTION 9.3 EXERCISES (text p. 332)

Exercise 1, p. 332

Name____________________ Date____________________

ANSWERS TO SECTION 9.3 EXERCISES (cont.)

Exercise 2, p. 332 1., 2.

Bank	
100	

Bank Loan	
	300

S. Mosar, Capital	
	740

S. Mosar, Drawings	
750	

Accounts Receivable	
200	

Accounts Payable	
	150

Advertising Revenue	
	1 750

Sales Revenue	
	450

Supplies	
50	

Bank Charges	
20	

Light and Heat Expense	
40	

Equipment	
1 050	

Miscellaneous Expense	
5	

Printing Expense	
500	

Rent	
250	

Telephone Expense	
25	

Wages Expense	
400	

1.

2.

Name____________________ Date________________

ANSWERS TO SECTION 9.3 EXERCISES (cont.)

Exercise 3, p. 332 (Workbook Exercise)

In the chart below, the steps in the accounting cycle are given in incorrect order.

Required: 1. In the column headed Step No., enter the correct step number according to the sequence of steps given in the text on page 331.

2. In two of the remaining five columns, place check marks to indicate when the step is performed and by whom.

STEPS IN THE ACCOUNTING CYCLE	STEP NO.	DONE DAILY	DONE MONTHLY	DONE AT THE END OF THE FISCAL PERIOD	DONE BY JUNIOR PERSONNEL	DONE BY SENIOR PERSONNEL
Journal entries posted to the ledger accounts.						
Adjusting and closing entries journalized and posted.						
Post-closing trial balance.						
Financial statements prepared.						
Ledger balanced by means of a trial balance.						
Accounting entries recorded in the journal.						
Work sheet prepared.						
Transactions occur.						

Exercise 4, p. 332

1. Accounting is________________in nature.
2. The ____________________________ states that financial reporting is done in equal periods of time.
3. Asset and liability accounts are considered to be_________________accounts.
4. _________________are ones that have their balances continue on into the succeeding fiscal period.
5. Revenue, expense, and drawings accounts are considered to be_________________accounts.
6. The balances in__________________________do not continue into the_________________fiscal period.

Name______________________________ Date____________________

ANSWERS TO SECTION 9.3 EXERCISES (cont.)

Exercise 4 (cont.)

7. Another name for a nominal account is a ______________________.
8. Nominal accounts begin each fiscal period with ______________________.
9. The process of removing the "old" balances from the nominal accounts is known as ______________________.
10. ______________________ means to cause it to have no balance.
11. During a fiscal period, the Capital account shows ______________________.
12. Changes in equity during a fiscal period (except for additional investments by the owner) are contained in ______________________ accounts.
13. At the end of the fiscal period the ledger is brought up to date by ______________________ ______________________.
14. One of the final steps in the accounting cycle is to bring the Capital account ______________________ and to ______________________ the nominal accounts.
15. The final step in the accounting cycle is ______________________.

ANSWERS TO SECTION 9.4 REVIEW QUESTIONS (text p. 341)

Journalizing and Posting the Closing Entries

1. ______________________
2. ______________________
3. ______________________
4. ______________________
5. ______________________
6. ______________________
7. ______________________
8. ______________________
   1. ______________________
   2. ______________________
   3. ______________________
   4. ______________________

Name ______________________ Date ______________________

ANSWERS TO SECTION 9.4 EXERCISES (text p. 341)

Note: *Do* **not** *separate journal entries with a blank line when doing this exercise.*

Exercise 1, p. 341

GENERAL JOURNAL PAGE ____

DATE		PARTICULARS	P.R.	DEBIT	CREDIT

Name________________ Date________________

ANSWERS TO SECTION 9.4 EXERCISES (cont.)

Exercise 2, p. 342

1. GENERAL JOURNAL PAGE _____

DATE		PARTICULARS	P.R.	DEBIT	CREDIT

ANSWERS TO SECTION 9.4 EXERCISES (cont.)

Exercise 2 (cont.)

2. **General Ledger for Golden Tresses Hair Stylists**

Account	Debit	Credit
Bank	790	
Supplies & Materials	2 755	
Prepaid Insurance	2 450	
Equipment	17 005	
Accounts Payable		1 075
GST Payable		580
GST Recoverable	365	
R. Tompko, Capital		9 342
R. Tompko, Drawings	42 000	
Revenue		98 370
Advertising Expense	1 200	
Bank Charges Expense	96	
Light & Heat Expense	2 104	
Materials Used Expense	6 950	
Miscellaneous Expense	1 902	
Rent Expense	6 000	
Wages Expense	25 750	
Income Summary		
Insurance Expense		

Name________________________ Date________________

ANSWERS TO SECTION 9.4 EXERCISES (cont.)

Exercise 2 (cont.)

3. Golden Tresses Hair Stylists

Post-Closing Trial Balance

December 31, 19—

ACCOUNTS	DEBIT	CREDIT

Exercise 3, p. 342

1. Journalizing and posting the adjusting and closing entries is a routine task that can be done by any knowledgeable accounting clerk. ☐

2. All of the data required to journalize the adjusting and closing entries can be found on the work sheet. ☐

3. It can be assumed that all adjustments have been thought of once the work sheet is completed. ☐

4. The adjusting entries must be journalized and posted to bring the ledger into agreement with the figures on the financial statements. ☐

5. An explanation is needed for each individual adjusting entry being journalized. ☐

Name____________________ Date______________

ANSWERS TO SECTION 9.4 EXERCISES (cont.)

Exercise 3 (cont.)

6. The adjusting and closing entries in the journal are dated as of the end of the fiscal period. ☐

7. The closing entries can only be processed using the four-step method. ☐

8. The figures for the first closing entry (as described in the textbook) are taken from the Income Statement section, Debit column, of the work sheet. ☐

9. Since revenue accounts have debit balances, credit entries are needed to close them out. ☐

10. The second closing entry (as described in the textbook) transfers the balances in the expense accounts to the Income Summary account. ☐

11. When the adjusting entries and the first two closing entries are journalized and posted, all of the accounts in the equity section of the ledger except three will have nil balances. ☐

12. A loss has been suffered if the Income Summary account has a credit balance before it is closed out. ☐

13. The first two entries in the Income Summary account are the same as the subtotals of the Income Statement section of the work sheet ☐

14. The Income Summary account is not closed out if a loss occurs. ☐

15. A work sheet is not necessary in a computer accounting system because the mathematical accuracy of the figures is assured. ☐

Explanations for "F" Responses

___

___

___

___

___

___

___

___

___

___

___

___

Name_______________ Date_______________

ANSWERS TO SECTION 9.5 REVIEW QUESTIONS (text p. 351)

Adjusting for Depreciation

1. ______________________________

2. ______________________________

3. ______________________________

4. ______________________________

5. ______________________________

6. ______________________________

7. ______________________________

8. ______________________________

9. ______________________________

10. ______________________________

11. ______________________________

Name______________________ Date______________________

ANSWERS TO SECTION 9.5 EXERCISES (text p. 353)

Exercise 1, p. 353

For each of the following situations allocate the total cost to the proper fiscal periods. Assume that the company commenced business on January 1, 19-1, and has a fiscal year-end of December 31.

1. A truck was purchased on January 1, 19–1, for $18 000. It was expected to last for five full years, at the end of which it would have a trade-in value of $3 000. Use the straight-line method of depreciation.

19–1	19–2	19–3	19–4	19–5

2. A used vehicle was bought on November 1, 19–1, for $5 800. It was expected to last for four full years, at the end of which it would have a resale value of $1 000. Use the straight-line method of depreciation.

19–1	19–2	19–3	19–4	19–5

3. A building was purchased on May 1, 19–2, for the sum of $113 000. It was expected to last for 25 years, at which time it would have a resale value of $5 000. Use the straight-line method of depreciation.

19–1	19–2	19–3	19–4	19–5

4. A new machine was bought on January 1, 19–1, for $54 000. It is depreciated using the declining-balance method at the rate of 20 per cent.

19–1	19–2	19–3	19–4	19–5

5. A new building was bought on July 1, 19–1, for $282 000. It is depreciated using the declining-balance method at a rate of 5 per cent.

19–1	19–2	19–3	19–4	19–5

Name__________________________ Date____________________

ANSWERS TO SECTION 9.5 EXERCISES (cont.)

Exercise 2, p. 353

1.

Year	Straight-line Depreciation	
	Depreciation	Balance
1		
2		
3		
4		
5		

2.

Year	Declining-balance Depreciation	
	Depreciation	Balance
1		
2		
3		
4		
5		

Name____________________ Date________________

ANSWERS TO SECTION 9.5 EXERCISES (cont.)

Exercise 3, p. 354

The simplified general ledger of Salk Company at the end of its annual fiscal period appears below.

1. **Using the additional information that is provided, record the year-end adjusting entries directly in the T-accounts.**
2. **Prepare an adjusted trial balance.**

1.

Bank	
400	

Accounts Receivable	
8 285	

Supplies	
1 900	

Prepaid Insurance	
1 800	

Land	
50 000	

Buildings	
70 000	

Accum. Deprec. Bldgs.	
	6 750

Equipment	
96 500	

Accum. Deprec. Equip.	
	24 000

Accounts Payable	
	3 200

J. Salk, Capital	
	144 985

J. Salk, Drawings	
30 000	

Revenue	
	140 700

Bank Charges Expense	
450	

Delivery Expense	
1 500	

(Ledger continues on next page.)

Name________________________ Date________________

ANSWERS TO SECTION 9.5 EXERCISES (cont.)

Exercise 3 (cont.)

Light and Heat Expense	
1 300	

Miscellaneous Expense	
490	

Telephone Expense	
390	

Wages Expense	
56 620	

Supplies Used	

Insurance Expense	

Depreciation – Buildings	

Depreciation – Equipment	

Additional Information

1. Inventory of supplies at the year-end is $850.
2. Unexpired insurance at the year-end is $625.
3. Depreciation is calculated on a straight-line basis. The building is expected to last 40 years, at which time it will be worth $25 000. The equipment is expected to last 15 years, after which it will be worth $6 500.

ANSWERS TO SECTION 9.5 EXERCISES (cont.)

Exercise 3 (cont.)

2.

Salk Company

Adjusted Trial Balance

— date —

ACCOUNTS	DEBIT	CREDIT

Name______________________ Date______________________

ANSWERS TO SECTION 9.5 EXERCISES (cont.)

Exercise 4, p. 355

Fram Associates — Work Sheet — Year Ended December 31, 19—

ACCOUNTS	TRIAL BALANCE DEBIT	TRIAL BALANCE CREDIT	ADJUSTMENTS DEBIT	ADJUSTMENTS CREDIT	INCOME STATEMENT DEBIT	INCOME STATEMENT CREDIT	BALANCE SHEET DEBIT	BALANCE SHEET CREDIT
Bank	5 080.20							
Accounts Receivable	17 491.–							
Supplies	2 635.–							
Prepaid Insurance	1 800.–							
Equipment	10 200.–							
Accum. Deprec. Equipment		6 022.08						
Automobiles	32 500.–							
Accum. Deprec. Automobiles		16 575.–						
Accounts Payable		4 802.50						
GST Payable		940.20						
GST Recoverable	516.80							
C. Fram, Capital		21 821.04						
C. Fram, Drawings	48 000.–							
Consulting Fees		154 326.–						
Automobile Expense	32 756.04							
General Expense	1 575.–							
Rent Expense	10 000.–							
Telephone Expense	1 567.–							
Wages Expense	40 365.78							
	204 486.82	204 486.82						

Name________________ Date____________

ANSWERS TO CHAPTER 9.6 COMPUTER REVIEW QUESTIONS (text p. 362)

Using a Computer: A Spreadsheet for the Expanded Work Sheet

1. ____________________
2. ____________________
3. ____________________
4. ____________________
5. ____________________

ANSWERS TO SECTION 9.6 COMPUTER EXERCISES (text p. 362)

Because the computer sections of this chapter have no manual application, in interests of saving space, we have deleted the applicable pages from the Workbook. The Workbook continues below at page 231.

Communicate It (text p. 363)

Name____________________ Date____________________

ANSWERS TO CHAPTER 9 EXERCISES (text p. 364)

Exercise 1, p. 364

1. d. ______
2. d. ______
3. e. ______
4. a. ______
5. a. ______

Exercise 2, p. 365

ACCOUNT Supplies NO.

DATE		PARTICULARS	P.R.	DEBIT	CREDIT	D/C	BALANCE

ACCOUNT Supplies Expense NO.

DATE		PARTICULARS	P.R.	DEBIT	CREDIT	D/C	BALANCE

Exercise 3, p. 365

1. ______
2. ______
3. Insurance Expense ______
   Prepaid Insurance ______
4. ______
5. 1) ______
   2) ______
   3) ______
   TOTAL ______
6. ______
7. Insurance Expense ______
   Prepaid Insurance ______
8. 1) Genuine ______
   ______
   2) Regal ______
   ______
   3) Standard ______
   TOTAL ______

Name______ Date______

ANSWERS TO CHAPTER 9 EXERCISES (cont.)

Exercise 4, p. 366

Karen Denby, Real Estate — Work Sheet — Year Ended September 30,19–4

ACCOUNTS	TRIAL BALANCE		ADJUSTMENTS		INCOME STATEMENT		BALANCE SHEET	
	DEBIT	CREDIT	DEBIT	CREDIT	DEBIT	CREDIT	DEBIT	CREDIT
Bank	3 800 –							
Accounts Receivable	10 900 –							
Supplies	500 –							
Prepaid Insurance	1 000 –							
Land	50 000 –							
Building	70 000 –							
Accum. Deprec. Building		6 825 –						
Furniture and Equipment	15 000 –							
Accum. Deprec. Furn. & Equip.		5 400 –						
Automotive Equipment	17 000 –							
Accum. Deprec. Auto Equip.		8 670 –						
Accounts Payable		400 –						
Bank Loan		100 000 –						
Karen Denby, Capital		35 005 –						
Karen Denby, Drawings	30 000 –							
Commissions Revenue		96 600 –						
Advertising Expense	4 700 –							
Bank Charges	8 100 –							
Car Expense	8 000 –							
Commissions Expense	18 000 –							
Light & Heat Expense	2 200 –							
Miscellaneous Expense	200 –							
Postage Expense	600 –							
Telephone Expense	900 –							
Wages Expense	12 000 –							
	252 900 –	252 900 –						

Name________________ Date________________

ANSWERS TO CHAPTER 9 EXERCISES (cont.)

Exercise 5, p. 367

Tom's Plastering — Work Sheet — Year Ended October 31, 19–3

ACCOUNTS	TRIAL BALANCE		ADJUSTMENTS		INCOME STATEMENT		BALANCE SHEET	
	DEBIT	CREDIT	DEBIT	CREDIT	DEBIT	CREDIT	DEBIT	CREDIT
Bank	1 412.01							
Accounts Receivable	7 545.–							
Supplies	1 416.70							
Small Tools	1 903.–							
Prepaid Insurance	2 107.80							
Equipment	9 500.–							
Accum. Deprec. Equip.		3 200.–						
Truck	19 500.–							
Accum. Deprec. Truck		8 000.–						
Accounts Payable		2 407.35						
GST Payable		702.–						
GST Recoverable	480.00							
Bank Loan		10 000.–						
Tom Michaud, Capital		17 510.28						
Tom Michaud, Drawings	35 534.–							
Revenue		120 365.–						
Bank Interest & Charges	1 325.15							
Materials Used	25 369.20							
Miscellaneous Expense	756.32							
Rent Expense	6 000.–							
Telephone Expense	864.32							
Truck Expense	8 325.40							
Utilities Expense	4 563.26							
Wages Expense	35 582.47							
	162 184.63	162 184.63						

Name__________ Date__________

ANSWERS TO CHAPTER 9 EXERCISES (cont.)

Exercise 5 (cont.)

Income Statement

Name________________ Date________________

ANSWERS TO CHAPTER 9 EXERCISES (cont.)

Exercise 5 (cont.)

Balance Sheet

ANSWERS TO CHAPTER 9 EXERCISES (cont.)

Exercise 6, p. 368, Comprehensive Exercise

Oakville Journal — Work Sheet — Year Ended December 31, 19—

ACCOUNTS	TRIAL BALANCE		ADJUSTMENTS		INCOME STATEMENT		BALANCE SHEET	
	DEBIT	CREDIT	DEBIT	CREDIT	DEBIT	CREDIT	DEBIT	CREDIT
Bank	2 000 –							
Accounts Receivable	15 317 20							
Supplies and Materials	23 795 16							
Prepaid Insurance	4 200 –							
Land	75 000 –							
Buildings	105 000 –							
Accum. Deprec. Buildings		7 500 –						
Equipment	95 700 –							
Accum. Deprec. Equip.		22 710 –						
Automotive Equipment	75 325 –							
Accum. Deprec. Auto. Equip.		30 000 –						
Accounts Payable		9 216 42						
GST Payable		1 280 –						
GST Recoverable	750 –							
Bank Loan		100 000 –						
Mortgage Payable		110 000 –						
R. Lucht, Capital		61 148 91						
R. Lucht, Drawings	50 000 –							
Revenue – Advertising		218 946 –						
Revenue – Circulation		91 315 –						
Bank Interest & Charges	12 150 –							
Bldg Maintenance Expense	3 220 –							
Car Expense	4 960 50							
Light & Heat Expense	11 350 –							
Miscellaneous Expense	5 940 13							
Mortgage Interest Expense	5 500 –							
Postage Expense	1 240 –							
Office Salaries Expense	34 319 15							
Sales Promotion Expense	2 750 –							
Telephone Expense	2 946 –							
Truck Expense	26 334 19							
Wages Expense	94 319 –							
	652 116 33	652 116 33						

Name______________ Date______________

ANSWERS TO CHAPTER 9 EXERCISES (cont.)

Exercise 6 (cont.)

Income Statement

ANSWERS TO CHAPTER 9 EXERCISES (cont.)

Exercise 6 (cont.)

Balance Sheet

Name____________________ Date________________

ANSWERS TO CHAPTER 9 EXERCISES (cont.)

Exercise 6 (cont.)

Adjusting and Closing Entries

GENERAL JOURNAL

Note: *For this exercise, do not separate journal entries with blank lines.*

DATE	PARTICULARS	P.R.	DEBIT	CREDIT

Name____________________ Date____________________

ANSWERS TO CHAPTER 9 EXERCISES (cont.)

Exercise 6 (cont.)

GENERAL JOURNAL

DATE		PARTICULARS	P.R.	DEBIT	CREDIT

GENERAL LEDGER

Account	Debit	Credit
Bank	2 000	
Accounts Receivable	15 317.20	
Supplies & Materials	23 795.16	
Prepaid Insurance	4 200	
Land	75 000	
Buildings	105 000	
Accum. Depr. Buildings		7 500
Equipment	95 700	
Accum. Depr. Equip.		22 710
Automotive Equipment	75 325	
Accum. Depr. Auto. Equip.		30 000
Accounts Payable		9 216.42
GST Payable		1 280
GST Recoverable	750	
Bank Loan		100 000
Mortgage Payable		110 000
R. Lucht, Capital		61 148.91
R. Lucht, Drawings	50 000	
Revenue – Advertising		218 946
Revenue – Circulation		91 315

Name____________________ Date________________

ANSWERS TO CHAPTER 9 EXERCISES (cont.)

Exercise 6 (cont.)

GENERAL LEDGER (cont.)

Account	Debit	Credit
Bank Interest and Charges	12 150	
Building Maintenance Expense	3 220	
Car Expense	4 960.50	
Light and Heat Expense	11 350	
Miscellaneous Expense	5 940.13	
Mortgage Interest Expense	5 500	
Postage Expense	1 240	
Office Salaries Expense	34 319.15	
Sales Promotion Expense	2 750	
Telephone Expense	2 946	
Truck Expense	26 334.19	
Wages Expense	94 319	
Depreciation of Buildings		
Depreciation of Equipment		
Depreciation of Auto. Equipment		
Supplies & Materials Expense		
Insurance Expense		
Income Summary		

Name________________________ Date________________

ANSWERS TO CHAPTER 9 EXERCISES (cont.)

Exercise 6 (cont.)

Post-Closing Trial Balance

ACCOUNTS	DEBIT	CREDIT

Name____________________ Date____________

ANSWERS TO CHAPTER 9 EXERCISES (cont.)

Note: For this exercise, do not separate journal entries with blank lines.

Exercise 7, p. 370

GENERAL JOURNAL   PAGE ____

DATE 19—		PARTICULARS	P.R.	DEBIT	CREDIT

Exercise 8, p. 370 **For Further Thought** *(Use more paper if necessary.)*

1. ____________________

2. ____________________

3. ____________________

4. ____________________

5. ____________________

6. ____________________

7. ____________________

Name ____________ Date ____________

ANSWERS TO CHAPTER 9 EXERCISES (cont.)

Exercise 9, p. 370 **Cases for Further Thought** *(Use more paper if necessary.)*

1. ______

2. ______

3. ______

CASE STUDIES (text p. 371)

Case 1 *A Balancing Act*, p. 371 *(Use more paper if necessary.)*

1. ______

2. ______

3. ______

Case 2 *A Mix-Up in Year-End Accounting*, p. 374 *(Use more paper if necessary.)*

(Note: Three of the accounts in the unadjusted general ledger shown on page 375 have wrong balances. Equipment should read $27 375, not $24 375. Automobile should be $18 012, not $19 780. F. Oke, Capital should be $52 330, not $39 586.)

1. ______

2. ______

3. ______

4. ______

5. ______

Name______ Date______

CASE STUDIES (cont.)

Case 2 (cont.)

6.

Challenge Case 3 *Can You Meet This Deadline?*, p. 375

Stetsko and Company

Work Sheet

Six Months Ended June 30,

ACCOUNTS	TRIAL BALANCE		ADJUSTMENTS		INCOME STATEMENT		BALANCE SHEET	
	DEBIT	CREDIT	DEBIT	CREDIT	DEBIT	CREDIT	DEBIT	CREDIT

Name____________________ Date______________

CASE STUDIES (cont.)

Co-operative Learning

Case 4 *A Better Way of Depreciating a Truck?*, p. 377

The comparative depreciation schedule is shown below:

Year	*Distance Travelled*	*Depreciation Straight-line*	*Depreciation Km travelled*

CAREER Jeff Rushton / Certified Management Accountant

ANSWERS TO DISCUSSION QUESTIONS (text p. 379)

1.

2.

3.

Name__________ Date__________

Chapter 10 Subsidiary Ledger Accounting

ANSWERS TO SECTION 10.1 REVIEW QUESTIONS (text p. 385)

Subsidiary Ledger Theory

1.

2.

3.

4.

5.

6.

7.

8.

9.

10.

11.

12.

13.
    1.
    2.
    3.

14.

15.

Name________________ Date________________

ANSWERS TO SECTION 10.1 EXERCISES (text p. 385)

Exercise 1, p. 385

1. Most office duties are handled by____________employees under the supervision of a few ____________ employees.
2. The bookkeeping for____________and____________accounts is ideally suited to a division of work.
3. The accounts of customers and the accounts of creditors are taken out of the____________and placed in separate groups.
4. These new groups of accounts are arranged____________.
5. The ledger of customers' accounts in known as the____________.
6. The ledger of creditors' accounts is known as the____________.
7. The main ledger is now called the____________.
8. Two accounts are opened in the general ledger to replace those that were removed. These are called ____________and ____________.
9. The balance of the Accounts Receivable account is____________the total of all the customers' accounts in the accounts receivable ledger.
10. Each of the two new ledgers is known as a____________.
11. Each of the two____________accounts in the general ledger is known as a ____________.
12. At the end of every month, the subsidiary ledgers must be____________with their respective control accounts.

Name____________ Date____________

ANSWERS TO SECTION 10.1 EXERCISES (cont.)

Exercise 2, p. 386

1. The total value of the accounts receivable accounts is ______________.

2. The total value of the accounts payable accounts is ______________.

3. a.

Proctor's Pet Store

General Ledger Trial Balance

June 30, 19—

ACCOUNTS	DEBIT	CREDIT

Name______________________ Date______________________

ANSWERS TO SECTION 10.1 EXERCISES (cont.)

Exercise 2 (cont.)

3. b.

Proctor's Pet Store

Accounts Receivable Listing

June 30, 19—

3. c.

Proctor's Pet Store

Accounts Payable Listing

June 30, 19—

Name________________ Date____________

ANSWERS TO SECTION 10.1 EXERCISES (cont.)

Exercise 3, p. 387

1.
2.
3.
4.
5.
6.
7.

ANSWERS TO SECTION 10.2 REVIEW QUESTIONS (text p. 394)

Subsidiary Ledger Systems

1.
2.
3.
4.
5.
6.
7.
8.

Name____________________ Date__________

ANSWERS TO SECTION 10.2 REVIEW QUESTIONS (cont.)

9. ______

10. ______

11. ______

12. ______

13. ______

14. ______

ANSWERS TO SECTION 10.2 EXERCISES (text p. 394)

Exercise 1, p. 394

1. ______
2. ______
3. ______
4. ______
5. ______
6. ______
7. ______
8. ______
9. ______
10. ______

Name______ Date______

ANSWERS TO SECTION 10.2 EXERCISES (cont.)

Exercise 2, p. 394

ACCOUNTS PAYABLE SYSTEM

Name____________________________ Date____________________

ANSWERS TO SECTION 10.2 EXERCISES (cont.)

Exercise 3, p. 395

1., 2. **ACCOUNTS RECEIVABLE LEDGER**

ACCOUNT Adams Bros., 12 Mountain Avenue

DATE		PARTICULARS	P.R.	DEBIT	CREDIT	D/C	BALANCE
19—							
June	30	Inv. No. 480		67.20		DR	67.20
	30	507		94.20		DR	161.40

ACCOUNT Cozo & Son, 620 Main Street

DATE		PARTICULARS	P.R.	DEBIT	CREDIT	D/C	BALANCE
19—							
June	30	Inv. No. 512		75.65		DR	75.65

ACCOUNT A. G. Farmer, 120A Blackwell Ave.

DATE		PARTICULARS	P.R.	DEBIT	CREDIT	D/C	BALANCE
19—							
June	30	Inv. No. 514		315.62		DR	315.62

Name____________________ Date________________

ANSWERS TO SECTION 10.2 EXERCISES (cont.)

Exercise 3 (cont.)

1., 2. (cont.)

ACCOUNT S. P. Handy Ltd., 75 Porter Ave.

DATE		PARTICULARS	P.R.	DEBIT	CREDIT	D/C	BALANCE
19—							
June	30	Inv. No. 484		216.25		DR	216.25
	30	Inv. No. 511		200.22	216.25	DR	416.47

ACCOUNT R. Mortimer, 60 Hawley Crescent

DATE		PARTICULARS	P.R.	DEBIT	CREDIT	D/C	BALANCE
19—							
June	30	Inv. No. 470		516.25		DR	516.25
	30	496		621.90		DR	1138.15
	30	505		608.36		DR	1746.51

ACCOUNT Renforth Sales, 192 Dale Place

DATE		PARTICULARS	P.R.	DEBIT	CREDIT	D/C	BALANCE
19—							
June	30	Inv. No. 510		137.62		DR	137.62

ACCOUNT Vista Limited, 2001 Central Ave.

DATE		PARTICULARS	P.R.	DEBIT	CREDIT	D/C	BALANCE
19—							
June	30	Inv. No. 515		50.–		DR	50.–

Name________________ Date________________

ANSWERS TO SECTION 10.2 EXERCISES (cont.)

Exercise 3 (cont.)

1., 2. (cont.)

ACCOUNT

DATE		PARTICULARS	P.R.	DEBIT	CREDIT	D/C	BALANCE

3.

Quick Distributing Co.

Accounts Receivable Trial Balance

July 6, 19—

Name____________________ Date________________

ANSWERS TO SECTION 10.2 EXERCISES (cont.)

Exercise 4, p. 396

1., 2.

ACCOUNTS PAYABLE LEDGER

ACCOUNT Daiton Enterprises, 106 Fleet Street, Barbary

DATE		PARTICULARS	P.R.	DEBIT	CREDIT	D/C	BALANCE
19— Sep.	30	Purchase Inv. No. 516			430 74	CR	430 74

ACCOUNT Gordon & Associates, 700 King Street, Oak City

DATE		PARTICULARS	P.R.	DEBIT	CREDIT	D/C	BALANCE
19— Sep.	30	Purchase Inv. No. B7407			216 92	CR	216 92

ACCOUNT Henderson Associates, Box 65, Welton

DATE		PARTICULARS	P.R.	DEBIT	CREDIT	D/C	BALANCE
19— Sep.	30	Purchase Inv. No. 16421			507 –	CR	507 –
	30	16907			615 –	CR	1122 –

Name____________________ Date____________________

ANSWERS TO SECTION 10.2 EXERCISES (cont.)

Exercise 4 (cont.)

ACCOUNT Kohler, R.. M., 141 Nixon Avenue, Barbary

DATE		PARTICULARS	P.R.	DEBIT	CREDIT	D/C	BALANCE
19— Sep.	30	Purchase Inv. No. 615			1 0 4 70	CR	1 0 4 70

ACCOUNT North State Packaging, 1500 Middle Road, Lennox

DATE		PARTICULARS	P.R.	DEBIT	CREDIT	D/C	BALANCE
19— Sep.	30	Purchase Inv. No. 901			7 4 87	CR	7 4 87

ACCOUNT Orenson & Company, 560 The Eastway, Dayson

DATE		PARTICULARS	P.R.	DEBIT	CREDIT	D/C	BALANCE
19— Sep.	30	Purchase Inv. No. 1604			1 0 4 6 26	CR	1 0 4 6 26
	30	1809			5 1 6 15	CR	1 5 6 2 41

Name____________________ Date________________

ANSWERS TO SECTION 10.2 EXERCISES (cont.)

Exercise 4 (cont.)

ACCOUNT Riggs, J. B., 75 Baxter Road, Estwing

DATE		PARTICULARS	P.R.	DEBIT	CREDIT	D/C	BALANCE
19— Sep.	30	Purchase Inv. No. 74621			502 –	CR	502 –

ACCOUNT Smithers, P. R., 106 Farr Street, Wibbling

DATE		PARTICULARS	P.R.	DEBIT	CREDIT	D/C	BALANCE
19— Sep.	30	Purchase Inv. No. 74			57 05	CR	57 05

ACCOUNT Union Advertising, 7900 Primeau Avenue, Marks County

DATE		PARTICULARS	P.R.	DEBIT	CREDIT	D/C	BALANCE
19— Sep.	30	Purchase Inv. No. 16352			436 21	CR	436 21
	30	17201			702 16	CR	1138 37
	30	17306			518 90	CR	1657 27

Name________________ Date____________

ANSWERS TO SECTION 10.2 EXERCISES (cont.)

Exercise 4 (cont.)

ACCOUNT

DATE	PARTICULARS	P.R.	DEBIT	CREDIT	D/C	BALANCE

3. *Magnetic Controls Company*

Accounts Payable Trial Balance

October 7, 19—

ANSWERS TO SECTION 10.2 EXERCISES (cont.)

Exercise 5 (cont.)

Blue Bell Company
Accounts Receivable Trial Balance
— at beginning —

Blue Bell Company
Accounts Payable Trial Balance
— at beginning —

Name____________________ Date______________

ANSWERS TO SECTION 10.2 EXERCISES (cont.)

Exercise 5 (cont.)

GENERAL JOURNAL PAGE ____

DATE		PARTICULARS	P.R.	DEBIT	CREDIT

Name____________________ Date______________

ANSWERS TO SECTION 10.2 EXERCISES (cont.)

Exercise 5 (cont.)

GENERAL JOURNAL PAGE ____

DATE		PARTICULARS	P.R.	DEBIT	CREDIT

Name________________ Date____________

ANSWERS TO SECTION 10.2 EXERCISES (cont.)

Exercise 5 (cont.)

ACCOUNTS RECEIVABLE LEDGER

Aube	
300	

Crozier	
200	

Elyk	
150	

Isola	
500	

Perrier	
300	

Tams	
250	

ACCOUNTS PAYABLE LEDGER

Ace Co.	
	225

Delta Co.	
	150

Galaxy Co.	
	75

Meteor Co.	
	300

Sun Co.	
	400

Venus Co.	
	300

Name________________ Date________________

ANSWERS TO SECTION 10.2 EXERCISES (cont.)

Exercise 5, p. 398

GENERAL LEDGER

Account	Debit	Credit
Bank	500	
Accounts Receivable	1 700	
Supplies	70	
Equipment	4 000	
Automobiles	10 000	
Bank Loan		1 000
Accounts Payable		1 450
C. Chen, Capital		14 550
C. Chen, Drawings	200	
Revenue		12 400
Advertising Expense	500	
General Expense	130	
Light and Heat Expense	1 500	
Rent Expense	1 800	
Wages Expense	9 000	

Name____________________ Date____________

ANSWERS TO SECTION 10.2 EXERCISES (cont.)

Exercise 5 (cont.)

Blue Bell Company

General Ledger Trial Balance

— at end —

ACCOUNTS	DEBIT	CREDIT

Name____________________ Date______________

ANSWERS TO SECTION 10.2 EXERCISES (cont.)

Exercise 5 (cont.)

Blue Bell Company

Accounts Receivable Trial Balance

— at end —

Blue Bell Company

Accounts Payable Trial Balance

— at end —

Name____________________ Date____________

ANSWERS TO SECTION 10.3 REVIEW QUESTIONS (text p. 403)

Customer's Statement of Account

1. ______________________________

2. ______________________________

3. ______________________________

4. ______________________________

5. ______________________________

6. ______________________________

7. ______________________________

8. ______________________________

9. ______________________________

Name ______________ Date ______________

ANSWERS TO SECTION 10.3 EXERCISES (text p. 403)

Exercise 1, p. 403

BIWAY SUPPLY COMPANY

4000 HUNTERS TRAIL
PRINCE EDWARD, ALBERTA

Phone
123-4567
Fax
123-5568

In Account With *R. Kott*
30 Beechwood Crescent
Baton Place, Manitoba

DATE		REFERENCE	CHARGES		CREDITS		BALANCE	

2% Interest Charged on Overdue Accounts

Exercise 2, p. 403

1. ______________________________

2. ______________________________

3. ______________________________

Name ______________ Date ______________

ANSWERS TO SECTION 10.3 EXERCISES (cont.)

Exercise 3, p. 404

ANSWERS TO SECTION 10.4 COMPUTER REVIEW QUESTIONS (text p. 410)

How Accountants Use Computers: Software for Subsidiary Ledgers

1.
2.
3.
4.
5.
6.
7.
8.

ANSWERS TO SECTION 10.4 COMPUTER EXERCISES (text p. 411)

1. 1.

   2.

   3.

   4.

   5.

   6.

   7.

Name ______________________ Date ______________

ANSWERS TO SECTION 10.4 COMPUTER EXERCISES (cont.)

2. WORK OF THE ACCOUNTS RECEIVABLE CLERK USING SIMPLY ACCOUNTING

3. WORK OF THE ACCOUNTS PAYABLE CLERK USING SIMPLY ACCOUNTING

Name________________ Date________________

ANSWERS TO SECTION 10.4 COMPUTER EXERCISES (cont.)

Communicate It (text p. 411)

____
____
____
____
____
____

ANSWERS TO CHAPTER 10 EXERCISES (text p. 412)

Exercise 1, p. 412 Using Your Knowledge

For each part of each statement below, place a "T" (for true) or an "F" (for false) in the spaces provided. Assume that the system described in the chapter is used. Ignore GST and PST.

1. An entire journal entry, for a $500 purchase invoice for supplies, is not recorded. As a result:

- **a.** The general ledger still balances. ☐
- **b.** Two accounts in the general ledger have incorrect balances. ☐
- **c.** The accounts payable ledger does not agree with its control account. ☐
- **d.** The total in the accounts payable ledger is $500 more than the balance in the control account. ☐

2. A cheque for $400 received from a customer is posted to the customer's account as a credit of $40. As a result:

- **a.** The general ledger does not balance. ☐
- **b.** The accounts receivable ledger does not agree with its control account. ☐
- **c.** The total of the accounts receivable ledger is greater than the balance in the control account. ☐
- **d.** The accounts receivable ledger equals the control account but contains one or more errors. ☐

Name______________________ Date______________________

ANSWERS TO CHAPTER 10 EXERCISES (cont.)

Exercise 1 (cont.)

3. Cash in the amount of $208 received from a customer is recorded correctly in the journal and general ledger, but is credited to the customer's account as $280. To correct this error the accountant should:

a. Credit the customer's account $72. ☐

b. Debit the customer's account $72. ☐

c. Debit the control account $72. ☐

d. Credit the control account $72. ☐

4. A sales transaction for $800 is entered in the general journal as follows:

Revenue	$800	
Accounts Receivable		$800

As a result of this entry:

a. The general ledger trial balance does not balance. ☐

b. The accounts receivable ledger disagrees with the control account by $800. ☐

c. The balance in the Revenue account is incorrect by $800. ☐

d. The balance in the Revenue account is incorrect by $1 600. ☐

5. A purchase invoice for $250 is posted in the accounts payable ledger as a debit. As a result:

a. The accounts payable ledger does not equal the control account. ☐

b. The difference between the accounts payable ledger and the control account is $250. ☐

c. The difference between the accounts payable ledger and the control account is $500. ☐

d. The general ledger balances. ☐

6. A debit of $1 200 is not posted to a customer's account in the accounts receivable ledger. As a result:

a. The Revenue account and the Accounts Receivable account are both incorrect. ☐

b. The general ledger remains in balance. ☐

c. The balance of the control account is greater than the total of the accounts receivable ledger by $1 200. ☐

d. The balance of the control account is smaller than the total of the accounts receivable ledger by $1 200. ☐

Name______________________ Date__________

ANSWERS TO CHAPTER 10 EXERCISES (cont.)

Exercise 2, p. 413

Error No.	*Control Account Balance* $13 500	*Accounts Receivable Subsidiary Ledger Balance* $13 125
1.		
2.		
3.		
4.		
5.		
True Balance		

Exercise 3, p. 414

Analysis of errors:

	Changes to control account figure	*Changes to subsidiary ledger figure*
1.	________	________
2.	________	________
3.	________	________
4.	________	________
5.	________	________
6.	________	________
7.	________	________
Total Net Corrections	________	________

1. The correct total for the subsidiary ledger and the control is:

Balance before corrections	$32 456
Net corrections to ledger	________
Corrected balance	________

2.

Correct control account figure	________
Total corrections required	________
Figure before corrections	________

Name________________________ Date________________

ANSWERS TO CHAPTER 10 EXERCISES (cont.)

Exercise 4, p. 414

Source Document	In the Subsidiary Ledger: Which subsidiary ledger is affected?		In the Subsidiary Ledger: Will the account be increased or decreased?		In the Subsidiary Ledger: Will the account be debited or credited?		In the General Ledger: The accounting entry will be — Bank		Accounts Receivable		Accounts Payable		Asset or Expense		Revenue	
	A/R	A/P	Increase	Decrease	Dr	Cr	Dr	Cr	Dr	Cr	Dr	Cr	Dr	Cr	Dr	Cr
purchase invoice																
cash receipt on account																
sales invoice																
cheque copy on account																

Name____________________ Date______________

ANSWERS TO CHAPTER 10 EXERCISES (cont.)

Exercise 5, p. 415 **Comprehensive Exercise**

(Note: The following transaction is missing from page 417 of the text:

15 *Cash Receipt*
From Blue Cab Company, $1 920.00 on account.

Include this transaction as part of the exercise.)

GENERAL JOURNAL PAGE 76

DATE		PARTICULARS	P.R.	DEBIT	CREDIT

Name____________________ Date________________

ANSWERS TO CHAPTER 10 EXERCISES (cont.)

Exercise 5 (cont.)

GENERAL JOURNAL PAGE 77

DATE	PARTICULARS	P.R.	DEBIT	CREDIT

Name________________ Date________________

ANSWERS TO CHAPTER 10 EXERCISES (cont.)

Exercise 5 (cont.) GENERAL LEDGER

ACCOUNT Bank **No.** 101

DATE		PARTICULARS	P.R.	DEBIT	CREDIT	D/C	BALANCE
19— Mar.	31	Forwarded	–			DR	1748 –

ACCOUNT Accounts Receivable **No.** 105

DATE		PARTICULARS	P.R.	DEBIT	CREDIT	D/C	BALANCE
19— Mar.	31	Forwarded	–			DR	7220 –

ACCOUNT Supplies **No.** 110

DATE		PARTICULARS	P.R.	DEBIT	CREDIT	D/C	BALANCE
19— Mar.	31	Forwarded	–			DR	2750 –

Name__________ Date__________

ANSWERS TO CHAPTER 10 EXERCISES (cont.)

Exercise 5 (cont.)

ACCOUNT Office Equipment **No. 115**

DATE		PARTICULARS	P.R.	DEBIT	CREDIT	D/C	BALANCE
19— Mar.	31	Forwarded	–			DR	20800 –

ACCOUNT Accumulated Depreciation – Office Equipment **No. 116**

DATE		PARTICULARS	P.R.	DEBIT	CREDIT	D/C	BALANCE
19— Mar.	31	Forwarded	–			CR	2400 –

ACCOUNT Automobile **No. 120**

DATE		PARTICULARS	P.R.	DEBIT	CREDIT	D/C	BALANCE
19— Mar.	31	Forwarded	–			DR	29500 –

ACCOUNT Accumulated Depreciation – Automobile **No. 121**

DATE		PARTICULARS	P.R.	DEBIT	CREDIT	D/C	BALANCE
19— Mar.	31	Forwarded	–			DR	4800 –

ACCOUNT Accounts Payable **No. 205**

DATE		PARTICULARS	P.R.	DEBIT	CREDIT	D/C	BALANCE
19— Mar.	31	Forwarded	–			CR	6264 70

Name____________________ Date_______________

ANSWERS TO CHAPTER 10 EXERCISES (cont.)

Exercise 5 (cont.)

ACCOUNT GST Payable **No.** 206

DATE		PARTICULARS	P.R.	DEBIT	CREDIT	D/C	BALANCE
19— Mar.	31	Forwarded	–			CR	185 –

ACCOUNT GST Recoverable **No.** 207

DATE		PARTICULARS	P.R.	DEBIT	CREDIT	D/C	BALANCE
19— Mar.	31	Forwarded	–			DR	102 –

ACCOUNT R. Bragg, Capital **No.** 301

DATE		PARTICULARS	P.R.	DEBIT	CREDIT	D/C	BALANCE
19— Mar.	31	Forwarded	–			CR	47 374 15

ACCOUNT R. Bragg, Drawings **No.** 302

DATE		PARTICULARS	P.R.	DEBIT	CREDIT	D/C	BALANCE
19— Mar.	31	Forwarded	–			DR	12 000 –

ACCOUNT Fees Income **No.** 401

DATE		PARTICULARS	P.R.	DEBIT	CREDIT	D/C	BALANCE
19— Mar.	31	Forwarded	–			CR	31 650 –

Name____________________ Date____________________

ANSWERS TO CHAPTER 10 EXERCISES (cont.)

Exercise 5 (cont.)

ACCOUNT Car Expense **No.** 505

DATE		PARTICULARS	P.R.	DEBIT	CREDIT	D/C	BALANCE
19— Mar.	31	Forwarded	–			DR	3 2 9 5 60

ACCOUNT Light and Heat Expense **No.** 510

DATE		PARTICULARS	P.R.	DEBIT	CREDIT	D/C	BALANCE
19— Mar.	31	Forwarded	–			DR	9 5 0 20

ACCOUNT Miscellaneous Expense **No.** 515

DATE		PARTICULARS	P.R.	DEBIT	CREDIT	D/C	BALANCE
19— Mar.	31	Forwarded	–			DR	3 7 5 40

ACCOUNT Rent Expense **No.** 520

DATE		PARTICULARS	P.R.	DEBIT	CREDIT	D/C	BALANCE
19— Mar.	31	Forwarded	–			DR	3 0 0 0 –

ACCOUNT Telephone Expense **No.** 525

DATE		PARTICULARS	P.R.	DEBIT	CREDIT	D/C	BALANCE
19— Mar.	31	Forwarded	–			DR	5 1 6 15

Name________________ Date________________

ANSWERS TO CHAPTER 10 EXERCISES (cont.)

Exercise 5 (cont.)

ACCOUNT Wages Expense **No.** 530

DATE		PARTICULARS	P.R.	DEBIT	CREDIT	D/C	BALANCE
19— Mar.	31	Forwarded	–			DR	10 4 1 6 50

ACCOUNTS RECEIVABLE LEDGER

ACCOUNT Blue Cab Company 16 Fox Street

DATE		PARTICULARS	P.R.	DEBIT	CREDIT	D/C	BALANCE
19— Mar.	31	Forwarded Invoice #74	–			DR	1 9 2 0 –

ACCOUNT Champion Store 175 Main Street

DATE		PARTICULARS	P.R.	DEBIT	CREDIT	D/C	BALANCE
19— Mar.	31	Forwarded Invoice #75	–			DR	7 5 0 –

ACCOUNT Oasis Restaurant 325 Second Street

DATE		PARTICULARS	P.R.	DEBIT	CREDIT	D/C	BALANCE
19— Mar.	31	Forwarded Invoice #76	–			DR	1 5 5 0 –

ACCOUNT Village Restaurant 400 Main Street

DATE		PARTICULARS	P.R.	DEBIT	CREDIT	D/C	BALANCE
19— Mar.	31	Forwarded Invoice #77	–			DR	3 0 0 0 –

Name________________________ Date________________

ANSWERS TO CHAPTER 10 EXERCISES (cont.)

Exercise 5 (cont.)

ACCOUNTS PAYABLE LEDGER

ACCOUNT M. Ball, Consultant 430 Red Road, Bigtown

DATE		PARTICULARS	P.R.	DEBIT	CREDIT	D/C	BALANCE
19— Mar.	31	Forwarded	–			CR	1515 –

ACCOUNT R. & R. Supply 151 King Street

DATE		PARTICULARS	P.R.	DEBIT	CREDIT	D/C	BALANCE
19— Mar.	31	Forwarded	–			CR	2740 –

ACCOUNT Stirling Company 46 River Road

DATE		PARTICULARS	P.R.	DEBIT	CREDIT	D/C	BALANCE
19— Mar.	31	Forwarded	–			CR	759 50

ACCOUNT Tom's Garage 705 Victoria Street

DATE		PARTICULARS	P.R.	DEBIT	CREDIT	D/C	BALANCE
19— Mar.	31	Forwarded	–			CR	1250 20

Name________________ Date____________

ANSWERS TO CHAPTER 10 EXERCISES (cont.)

Exercise 5 (cont.)

6.

R. Bragg

General Ledger Trial Balance

April 30, 19—

ACCOUNTS	DEBIT	CREDIT

Name ______________________ Date ______________________

ANSWERS TO CHAPTER 10 EXERCISES (cont.)

Exercise 5 (cont.)

7.

R. Bragg

Accounts Receivable Trial Balance

April 30, 19—

8.

R. Bragg

Accounts Payable Trial Balance

April 30, 19—

Name ______________________ Date ______________________

ANSWERS TO CHAPTER 10 EXERCISES (cont.)

Exercise 6, p. 417 **For Further Thought** *(Use more paper if necessary.)*

1. ______

2. ______

3. ______

4. ______

5. ______

6. ______

7. ______

8. ______

9. ______

10. ______

11. ______

12. ______

13. ______

14. ______

15. ______

Name______ Date______

Chapter 10 Subsidiary Ledger Accounting

CASE STUDIES (text p. 418)

Case 1 *Gaining Control over Accounts Receivable*, p. 419 *(Use more paper if necessary.)*

1. __________

2. __________

3. __________

Case 2 *Looking After Number One: Good or Bad?*, p. 419 *(Use more paper if necessary.)*

1. __________

2. __________

Challenge Case 3 *Would You Loan Money to Either of These Companies?*, p. 420
(Use more paper if necessary.)

1. __________

2. __________

3. __________

Name__________ Date__________

CASE STUDIES (cont.)

Challenge Case 3 (cont.)

4.

5.

CAREER Graham Murray / Accounting Teacher

ANSWERS TO DISCUSSION QUESTIONS (text p. 422)

1.

2.

3.

Name Date

ANSWERS TO SECTION 11.1 REVIEW QUESTIONS (text p. 428)

The Merchandising Business

1. _____

2. _____

3. _____

4. _____

5. _____

6. _____

7. _____

8. _____

9. _____

10. _____

11. _____

12. _____
    1. _____
    2. _____
    3. _____
    4. _____

13. _____

14. _____

15. _____

16. _____
    1. _____
    2. _____

Name__________ Date__________

ANSWERS TO SECTION 11.1 EXERCISES (text p. 248)

Exercise 1, p. 428 (Workbook Exercise)

Complete the chart by filling in the blank spaces.

	Selling price	*Cost price*	*Gross profit*	*Cost of goods sold as a % of selling price*	*Gross profit as a % of selling price*
Easy	$ 250	$	$ 100	%	%
	$	$ 85	$ 40	%	%
	$ 80	$ 56	$	%	%
	$	$ 75	$ 75	%	%
	$ 300	$ 195	$	%	%
	$ 225	$	$ 63	%	%
More difficult	$	$ 54	$	%	40 %
	$ 500	$	$	70 %	%
	$ 200	$	$	65 %	%
	$	$ 120	$	%	52 %

Exercise 2, p. 429

1.

	Year 1	*Year 2*	*Year 3*
Beginning inventory	100 units	units	units
Merchandise purchased	units	900 units	units
Goods available for sale	800 units	units	units
Merchandise sold	units	1 000 units	800 units
Ending inventory	300 units	units	50 units

2. On the income statement for Year 3:

Cost of Goods Sold

Beginning Inventory ______________

Purchases ______________

Goods Available for Sale ______________

Deduct: Ending Inventory ______________

Cost of Goods Sold ______________

Name______________________________ Date____________________

ANSWERS TO SECTION 11.1 EXERCISES (cont.)

Exercise 3, p. 429

	Sales	*Beginning Inventory*	*Purchases*	*Ending Inventory*	*Cost of Goods Sold*	*Gross Profit*
1.	$125 000	32 000	74 250	33 500		
2.	$750 585	85 600	410 360	88 300		
3.	$288 635	65 550	110 357	60 548		
4.	$174 000	33 800	82 640	33 500		
5.	$255 324	48 500	150 650	50 300		

Exercise 4, p. 429

Cost of Goods Sold Calculation

Beginning Inventory ________

Purchases ________

Total merchandise available for sale ________

Deduct Ending Inventory ________

Cost of Goods Sold ________

Exercise 5, p. 430

1. Beginning inventory figure: ________

2. Ending inventory figure: ________

3. Selling price of the goods sold: ________

4. Beginning Inventory ________

Purchases ________

Cost of merchandise available for sale ________

Deduct: Ending Inventory ________

Cost of Goods Sold ________

5. Gross profit: ________

6. Total operating expenses: ________

7. Net profit: ________

Name________________________ Date________________

ANSWERS TO SECTION 11.2 REVIEW QUESTIONS (text p. 433)

Accounting Procedures for a Merchandising Business

1. ______

2. ______

3. ______
   1. ______
   2. ______

4. ______

5. ______

6. ______

7. ______

8. ______

9. ______

10. ______

11. ______

12. a. Real ______
    b. Nominal ______
    c. Nominal ______
    d. Nominal ______

Students may have to review Chapter 9 to be sure of the meanings of "real" and "nominal."

Name______ Date______

ANSWERS TO SECTION 11.2 EXERCISES (text p. 433)

Exercise 1, p. 433

GENERAL JOURNAL PAGE ____

DATE		PARTICULARS	P.R.	DEBIT	CREDIT

Name ________________________ Date ____________

ANSWERS TO SECTION 11.2 EXERCISES (cont.)

Exercise 2, p. 434

1. The final inventory figure appears on the__________ and on the__________.
2. Neither the __________ nor the __________ is known during the accounting period.
3. The cost of goods sold figure is__________ using a__________.
4. Merchandise inventory is kept in two accounts. These are the__________ and the __________.
5. The__________ normally shows the merchandise inventory figure as of the __________.
6. At the fiscal year-end, the inventory is counted and valued at__________.
7. The Merchandise Inventory account is adjusted __________.
8. The__________ is the only accounting entry made to the Merchandise Inventory account.
9. Merchandise purchased during the fiscal period is debited to the__________.
10. The "Purchases" account is a short form of__________.
11. If merchandise is purchased on account, the account debited is__________.
12. If a tire company purchases office supplies, the account debited is__________.
13. For a merchandising business, the sales account is the __________.
14. When a business using the periodic inventory method sells goods, there is no accounting entry to record the__________.
15. The Freight-in account is used to accumulate the__________.

Exercise 3, p. 434

Opening Inventory	*Purchases*	*Freight-in*	*Closing Inventory*	*Cost of Goods Sold*
$20 000	40 000	5 000	25 000	
$29 000	50 000	1 000	30 000	
$12 000		1 000	15 000	50 000
	90 000	8 000	39 000	101 000
$50 000	100 000		60 000	100 000
$75 000	200 000	5 000		200 000

Name__________ Date__________

ANSWERS TO SECTION 11.3 REVIEW QUESTIONS (text p. 440)

Work Sheet for a Merchandising Business

1. ________________________________
2. ________________________________
3. ________________________________
4. ________________________________
5. ________________________________
6. ________________________________
7. ________________________________
8. ________________________________
9. ________________________________
10. ________________________________
11. ________________________________
12. ________________________________
13. ________________________________
14. ________________________________

Name____________________ Date____________

ANSWERS TO SECTION 11.3 EXERCISES (text p. 441)

Exercise 1, p. 441

Work Sheet — Bok Trading Company — Year Ended Dec. 31, 19—

ACCOUNTS	TRIAL BALANCE		ADJUSTMENTS		INCOME STATEMENT		BALANCE SHEET	
	DEBIT	CREDIT	DEBIT	CREDIT	DEBIT	CREDIT	DEBIT	CREDIT
Bank	500 –							
Accounts Receivable	17 910 –							
Merchandise Inventory	39 600 –							
Supplies	2 500 –			(2) 1 200 –				
Prepaid Insurance	1 800 –			(3) 1 150 –				
Equipment	27 850 –							
Accum. Deprec. – Equip.		5 200 –		(4) 2 600 –				
Accounts Payable		7 400 –		(1) 350 –				
GST Payable		550 –						
GST Recoverable	390 –							
PST Payable		628 –						
R. Bok, Capital		63 712 –						
R. Bok, Drawings	10 000 –							
Sales		94 310 –						
Purchases	41 500 –		(1) 300 –					
Freight–in	950 –							
Light and Heat Expense	2 750 –							
Miscellaneous Expense	350 –		(1) 50 –					
Rent Expense	4 800 –							
Telephone Expense	1 500 –							
Wages Expense	19 400 –							
	171 800 –	171 800 –						
Supplies Expense			(2) 1 200 –					
Insurance Expense			(3) 1 150 –					
Depreciation of Equipment			(4) 2 600 –					

Name________ Date________

ANSWERS TO SECTION 11.3 EXERCISES (cont.)

Exercise 1 (cont.)

2.

Bok Trading Company

Income Statement

Year Ended December 31, 19—

Name______________________ Date______________________

ANSWERS TO SECTION 11.3 EXERCISES (cont.)

Exercise 1 (cont.)

3.

Bok Trading Company

Balance Sheet

December 31, 19—

ANSWERS TO SECTION 11.3 EXERCISES (cont.)

Exercise 1 (cont.)

4.

GENERAL JOURNAL

DATE		PARTICULARS	P.R.	DEBIT	CREDIT

Name________________________ Date________________

ANSWERS TO SECTION 11.3 EXERCISES (cont.)

Exercise 2, p. 442

Work Sheet — Small Engine Sales and Service — Year Ended December 31, 19—

ACCOUNTS	TRIAL BALANCE		ADJUSTMENTS		INCOME STATEMENT		BALANCE SHEET	
	DEBIT	CREDIT	DEBIT	CREDIT	DEBIT	CREDIT	DEBIT	CREDIT
Bank	520 –							
Accounts Receivable	12 260 –							
Merchandise Inventory	36 050 –							
Supplies	1 975 –							
Parts and Materials	10 350 –							
Prepaid Insurance	1 150 –							
Equipment	18 600 –							
Accum. Deprec. – Equipment		12 505 –						
Truck	18 000 –							
Accum. Deprec. – Truck		14 975 –						
Accounts Payable		5 360 –						
GST Payable		850 –						
GST Recoverable	420 –							
PST Payable		980 –						
H. Rohr, Capital		29 010 –						
H. Rohr, Drawings	25 000 –							
Revenue – Sales		80 362 –						
Revenue – Service		66 215 –						
Bank Charges	410 –							
Freight–in	862 –							
Light and Heat Expense	2 240 –							
Miscellaneous Expense	650 –							
Purchases	52 795 –							
Rent Expense	3 600 –							
Telephone Expense	1 250 –							
Truck Expense	5 825 –							
Wages Expense	18 300 –							
	210 257 –	210 257 –						

Name__________ Date__________

ANSWERS TO SECTION 11.3 EXERCISES (cont.)

Exercise 2 (cont.)

2.

Small Engine Sales and Service

Income Statement

Year Ended December 31, 19—

Name________________ Date________________

ANSWERS TO SECTION 11.3 EXERCISES (cont.)

Exercise 2 (cont.)

3.

Small Engine Sales and Service

Balance Sheet

December 31, 19—

Name________________ Date________________

ANSWERS TO SECTION 11.3 EXERCISES (cont.)

Omit the blank lines between journal entries when doing this exercise.

Exercise 2 (cont.)

4.

GENERAL JOURNAL

PAGE ____

DATE		PARTICULARS	P.R.	DEBIT	CREDIT

Name______________________ Date______________

ANSWERS TO SECTION 11.3 EXERCISES (cont.)

Exercise 2 (cont.)

4. (cont.)

GENERAL JOURNAL

DATE		PARTICULARS	P.R.	DEBIT	CREDIT

5.

GENERAL LEDGER

Account	Debit	Credit
Bank	520	
Accounts Receivable	12 260	
Merchandise Inventory	36 050	
Supplies	1 975	
Parts and Materials	10 350	
Prepaid Insurance	1 150	
Equipment	18 600	
Accumulated Deprec. Equip.		12 505
Truck	18 000	
Accumulated Depreciation – Truck		14 975
Accounts Payable		5 360
GST Payable		850
GST Recoverable	420	
PST Payable		980
H. Rohr, Capital		29 010

Name________________ Date____________

ANSWERS TO SECTION 11.3 EXERCISES (cont.)

Exercise 2 (cont.)

5. GENERAL LEDGER (cont.)

H. Rohr, Drawings	
25 000	

Revenue – Sales	
	80 362

Revenue – Service	
	66 215

Bank Charges Expense	
410	

Freight-in	
862	

Light and Heat Expense	
2 240	

Miscellaneous Expense	
650	

Purchases	
52 795	

Rent Expense	
3 600	

Telephone Expense	
1 250	

Truck Expense	
5 825	

Wages Expense	
18 300	

Supplies Expense	

Parts and Materials Expense	

Insurance Expense	

Depreciation – Equipment	

Depreciation – Truck	

Income Summary	

Name____________________ Date____________

ANSWERS TO SECTION 11.3 EXERCISES (cont.)

Exercise 2 (cont.)

6.

Small Engine Sales and Service
Post-Closing Trial Balance
December 31, 19—

ACCOUNTS	DEBIT	CREDIT

Name________________________ Date________________

ANSWERS TO SECTION 11.3 EXERCISES (cont.)

For this exercise, omit the blank lines between journal entries.

Exercise 3, p. 443

1. GENERAL JOURNAL PAGE ____

DATE		PARTICULARS	P.R.	DEBIT	CREDIT

Name____________________ Date____________

ANSWERS TO SECTION 11.3 EXERCISES (cont.)

Exercise 3 (cont.)

2. **GENERAL LEDGER**

Account	Debit	Credit
Bank	3 250.00	
Accounts Receivable	33 930.10	
Merchandise Inventory	43 700.00	
Supplies	3 400.50	
Prepaid Insurance	2 090.00	
Land	35 000.00	
Building	95 000.00	
Accum. Deprec. – Building		17 620.00
Equipment	53 400.00	
Accum. Deprec. – Equipment		31 527.00
Trucks	76 000.00	
Accum. Deprec. – Trucks		57 752.00
Accounts Payable		40 820.20
GST Payable		1 350.00
GST Recoverable	720.00	
PST Payable		1 560.00
T. Barbini, Capital		159 180.05
T. Barbini, Drawings	36 000.00	

Name____________________ Date________________

ANSWERS TO SECTION 11.3 EXERCISES (cont.)

Exercise 3 (cont.)

2. GENERAL LEDGER (cont.)

Sales	
	232 250.00

Advertising Expense	
2 570.00	

Freight-in	
3 705.00	

Light and Heat Expense	
12 316.00	

Miscellaneous Expense	
1 750.00	

Purchases	
80 702.50	

Telephone Expense	
1 250.00	

Wages Expense	
57 275.15	

Supplies Expense	

Insurance Expense	

Depreciation of Building	

Depreciation of Equipment	

Depreciation of Trucks	

Income Summary	

Name____________________ Date________________

ANSWERS TO SECTION 11.3 EXERCISES (cont.)

Exercise 3 (cont.)

3.

Barbini Stone Products

Post-Closing Trial Balance

December 31, 19—

ACCOUNTS	DEBIT	CREDIT

Name______________________ Date______________

ANSWERS TO SECTION 11.4 REVIEW QUESTIONS (text p. 451)

Merchandise Returns and Allowances

1.
2.
3.
4.
5.
6.
7.
   1.
   2.
   3.
8.
9.
10.
11.
12.
13.
14.
15.

Name ____________________ Date ____________________

ANSWERS TO SECTION 11.4 EXERCISES (text p. 451)

Exercise 1, p. 451

1. ____________________
2. ____________________
3. ____________________
4. ____________________
5. ____________________
6. ____________________
7. ____________________

Exercise 2, p. 453

Name____________________ Date____________________

ANSWERS TO SECTION 11.4 EXERCISES (cont.)

Exercise 3, p. 453

1. ____________ 4. ____________

2. ____________ 5. ____________

3. ____________ 6. ____________

7. ____

Exercise 4, p. 454

____

Exercise 5, p. 454

Tonk Traders

Partial Income Statement

Year Ended December 31, 19—

Name________________________ Date____________________

ANSWERS TO SECTION 11.5 REVIEW QUESTIONS (text p. 457)

Perpetual Inventory

1. ______________________________

2. ______________________________

3. ______________________________

4. ______________________________

5. ______________________________

6. ______________________________

7. ______________________________

8. ______________________________

9. ______________________________

10. ______________________________

11. ______________________________

12. ______________________________

ANSWERS TO SECTION 11.5 EXERCISES (text p. 458)

Exercise 1, p. 458

1. Competition forces department stores to use the perpetual inventory system. ☐
2. The periodic inventory system produces information that cannot be produced by the perpetual inventory system. ☐
3. The copies of receiving reports are the source documents for data entry to increase the perpetual inventory. ☐
4. Deductions from the perpetual inventory are made only through the cash register in a computer perpetual inventory system. ☐
5. In a computer inventory system, each inventory item is given a special code number. ☐

ANSWERS TO SECTION 11.5 EXERCISES (cont.)

Exercise 1 (cont.)

6. There is no reason to take a physical inventory in a computer perpetual inventory system. ☐
7. Any differences between the book figures and the manual count figures in a perpetual inventory system require a correction to the book figures. ☐
8. Given the unique code for an item, the computer can give back any information about the item that is stored in its memory. ☐
9. In a computer inventory system, goods are ordered when the quantity on hand becomes less than the maximum required. ☐
10. A computer inventory system provides management with immediate feedback, making it unnecessary to solve problems. ☐

Explanations For "F" Responses:

____

____

____

____

____

____

____

____

____

____

Exercise 2, p. 458

1. Additions to inventory are usually made from copies of______________.
2. ______________forces department stores to use the perpetual inventory system.
3. In a computer inventory system, each inventory item is given a______________.
4. A computer inventory system provides management with______________ feedback that it can use to______________problems.
5. Given the unique code for an item, the computer can give back any information about the item that is ______________in its______________.
6. A computer-produced inventory status report makes it possible to compare the inventory on hand with suggested______________and______________quantities.
7. The______________ inventory system provides information that cannot be produced by the ______________inventory system.

Name______________ Date______________

ANSWERS TO SECTION 11.5 EXERCISES (cont.)

Exercise 2 (cont.)

8. Deductions from inventory are usually made from copies of____________________ or through____________________in a modern store.
9. Any differences between the____________figures and the actual figures require an ____________to the book figures.
10. Even in a computer inventory system, a____________of the stock is necessary.

Exercise 3, p. 459

1.

INVENTORY CONTROL CARD

STOCK NO. 730-0320
DESCRIPTION SCHAEFER CHEEK BLOCK MAXIMUM 30
LOCATION: ROW 16 BIN 3 MINIMUM 10

DATE	REFERENCE		UNIT COST	RECEIVED	SHIPPED	BALANCE
Feb 20	Forward		15.50			28
26	SO	904			5	23

INVENTORY CONTROL CARD

STOCK NO. 713-3011
DESCRIPTION BARTON CAM CLEAT MAXIMUM 50
LOCATION: ROW 20 BIN 14 MINIMUM 20

DATE	REFERENCE		UNIT COST	RECEIVED	SHIPPED	BALANCE
Feb 24	Forward		9.20			37
28	SO	910			10	27

Name____________________ Date________________

ANSWERS TO SECTION 11.5 EXERCISES (cont.)

Exercise 3 (cont.)

2. Inventory values at cost:

#730-0320 ______________________

#713-3011 ______________________

Exercise 4, p. 460

1.

THE WALTON COMPANY

INCOME STATEMENT

YEARS ENDED DECEMBER 31, 19–8 AND 19–9

	19–8	19–9
Sales	$100 000	$120 000
Cost of Goods Sold		
Opening Inventory	$ 20 000	$ 25 000
Purchases		
Goods Available for Sale		$ 63 000
Less Closing Inventory	25 000	
Cost of Goods Sold		
Gross Income	$ 65 000	
Expenses		$ 37 000
Net Income	$ 33 000	$ 42 000

2. **a.** ______________________

b. ______________________

3. ______________________

1. ______________________

2. ______________________

Name______________________ Date______________________

ANSWERS TO SECTION 11.5 EXERCISES (cont.)

Exercise 5, p. 461

Shown below are some of the accounts (in T-account form) from the ledger of Master Trading Company. Master Trading Company has a computer accounting system and is able to keep its inventory and cost of goods accounts up to the minute. There is no account for Purchases. Assume that the Bank account has a balance of $40 000.

Bank	
40 000	

Sales	

Merchandise Inventory	
50 000	

Cost of Goods Sold	

Record the journal entries for the following transactions directly into the ledger accounts above. Ignore freight-in, GST, and PST.

Transactions

1. Purchased merchandise for cash at a cost of $10 000.
2. Sold goods for cash. The goods, recorded in the inventory at $6 000, are sold for $11 000. ***(Note:** There are two aspects of this transaction to record.)*
3. Sold goods for cash. The goods, recorded in the inventory at $9 000, are sold for $15 000. ***(Note:** There are two aspects of this transaction to record.)*
4. Purchased merchandise for cash at a cost of $3 000.

Name________________________ Date________________

ANSWERS TO SECTION 11.6 COMPUTER REVIEW QUESTIONS (text p. 467)

Using a Computer: A Spreadsheet for Merchandising Decisions

1. ______

2. ______

3. ______

4. ______

______

5. ______

ANSWERS TO SECTION 11.6 COMPUTER EXERCISES (text p. 467)

***(Note:** Because the computer sections of this chapter have no manual application, in the interest of saving paper, we have deleted as many of the applicable pages as we can from the Woorkbook. Pages 321 and 322 do not appear.)*

Name ______ Date ______

ANSWERS TO SECTION 11.6 COMPUTER EXERCISES (cont.)

Communicate It (text p. 469)

ANSWERS TO CHAPTER 11 EXERCISES (text p. 471)

Exercise 1, p. 471 **Using Your Knowledge**

GENERAL JOURNAL

DATE		PARTICULARS	P.R.	DEBIT	CREDIT

Name______________________ Date______________

ANSWERS TO CHAPTER 11 EXERCISES (cont.)

Exercise 2, p. 471

GENERAL JOURNAL

DATE		PARTICULARS	P.R.	DEBIT	CREDIT

Name________________ Date________________

ANSWERS TO CHAPTER 11 EXERCISES (cont.)

Exercise 2 (cont.)

GENERAL JOURNAL

DATE		PARTICULARS	P.R.	DEBIT	CREDIT

Exercise 3, p. 472

Indicate whether each of the following statements is true or false by placing a "T" or an "F" in the box indicated. Explain the reason for each "F" response in the space provided at the end of the exercise.

1. A "wholesaler" is a "merchandiser." Therefore, a "merchandiser" is a "wholesaler".
2. Some of the goods found in the inventory of a hardware store are also goods found in the inventory of a building supply store.
3. Merchandise inventory is on the balance sheet under Prepaid Expenses.
4. The cost of goods sold figure normally includes the cost of goods that are lost, stolen, or broken.
5. The merchandise inventory of a drug store is calculated by counting all of the goods on hand and multiplying by the selling prices marked on the goods.
6. An item that cost $40 and sold for $80 produced a gross profit of 50 per cent of the selling price.
7. The difference between the selling price and the cost price of the goods for a fiscal period is also the net income figure before any operating expenses are deducted.
8. The goods not sold represent the ending inventory.
9. The goods sold at selling prices represent the revenue figure.
10. The perpetual inventory system has not been commonly used because of the amount of work required to keep track of the many individual items in the inventory.

Name______________________________ Date____________________

ANSWERS TO CHAPTER 11 EXERCISES (cont.)

Exercise 3 (cont.)

11. A used car business could easily use the perpetual inventory system because the number of items in its inventory is quite small. ☐

12. XYZ department store uses the periodic inventory method. It must take a physical inventory at least once a year. ☐

13. A perpetual inventory results in a "calculated" inventory figure. The inventory quantities shown on a perpetual inventory listing should be checked by actually inspecting the inventory from time to time. This would make clear whether or not any goods had been stolen. ☐

14. If the beginning inventory was 10 000 units and the ending inventory was 12 000 units, the business sold more units than it purchased. ☐

15. The merchandise inventory figures can be found during the fiscal period from the Merchandise Inventory account. ☐

16. The Purchases account is used to accumulate all purchases during the period. ☐

17. When a business that uses the periodic method sells goods, no accounting entry is made to reduce the merchandise inventory. If it were made, this entry would be: Debit Cost of Goods Sold and Credit Merchandise Inventory. ☐

18. The Freight-in account is used to accumulate all transportation charges during the fiscal period. ☐

19. Freight-in is considered to be a cost of the goods acquired. ☐

20. On the work sheet, the Purchases figure in the trial balance is extended to the Income Statement section, Debit column. ☐

21. On the work sheet, the Merchandise Inventory figure in the trial balance is extended to the Balance Sheet section, Debit column. ☐

22. Both the beginning and the ending inventory figures are shown on the income statement of a merchandising company. ☐

23. The Merchandise Inventory account is automatically adjusted by the closing entries. ☐

24. A credit invoice is issued by the vendor and received by the buyer. ☐

Name____________________________ Date____________________

ANSWERS TO CHAPTER 11 EXERCISES (cont.)

Exercise 3 (cont.)

25. The accounting entry for a credit note issued is either:

		DR	CR
a.	Accounts Receivable	$$$$	
	Sales		$$$$
	or		
b.	Accounts Receivable	$$$$	
	Sales Returns and Allowances		$$$$

☐

Explanations for "F" Responses:

Name____________________ Date____________

ANSWERS TO CHAPTER 11 EXERCISES (cont.)

Exercise 4, p. 473

Master Trading Company

Income Statement

Year Ended December 31, 19—

Name________________________ Date______________

ANSWERS TO CHAPTER 11 EXERCISES (cont.)

Exercise 5, p. 474

		#460	#911
1.	Quantity on hand to start		
	Receipts and shipments		
	Quantity on hand at end		

2. Inventory value for item #460

____

Exercise 6, p. 475

***(Note:** The key to this exercise is that the gross profit figure is 40 per cent of the sales figure.)*

Sutton Hardware Store

Estimated Income Statement

Month Ended January 31, 19—

Name________________ Date________________

ANSWERS TO CHAPTER 11 EXERCISES (cont.)

Exercise 7, p. 476

Unaudited Net Income ____________

1. Add cost of new equipment ____________
   Deduct depreciation on new equipment ____________
2. No change
3. Add overcharge on repairs to auto ____________
4. Deduct supplies used ____________
5. Deduct inventory deduction ____________

Adjusted Net Income figure ____________

Exercise 8, p. 476

1. ____________________
2. ____________________
3. ____________________
4. ____________________
5. ____________________
6. ____________________
7. ____________________

Exercise 9, p. 476 For Further Thought *(Use more paper if necessary.)*

1. ____________________
2. ____________________
3. ____________________
4. ____________________

Name____________________ Date____________________

ANSWERS TO CHAPTER 11 EXERCISES (cont.)

Exercise 9 (cont.)

5.

6.

7.

8.

9.

10.

11.

12.

13.

14.

15.

16.

17.

18.

Exercise 10, p. 477 A Case for Further Thought

1.

Name ______ Date ______

CASE STUDIES (text p. 477)

Case 1 *Analyzing Income Statements for Two Merchandising Companies*, p. 478
(Use more paper if necessary.)

1.

2.

3. **a.**
b.

Case 2 *Why Have Gross Profits Declined?* p. 479 *(Use more paper if necessary.)*

1.

2.

3.

4.

Challenge Case 3 *A Scheme To Save Income Tax?*, p. 481 *(Use more paper if necessary.)*

1.

2.

3.

4.

Name ______________________ Date ______________________

ANSWERS TO SECTION 12.1 REVIEW QUESTIONS (text p. 498)

The Synoptic Journal

1. ______

2. ______

3. ______

4. ______

5. ______

6. ______

7. ______

8. ______

9. ______

10. ______

11. ______

12. ______

Name______ Date______

ANSWERS TO SECTION 12.1 EXERCISES (text p. 498)

Exercise 1, p. 498

1. A non-routine transaction is one that is out of the ordinary. ☐
2. The synoptic journal is ideally suited to a large company. ☐
3. A synoptic journal is a multi-columnar journal. ☐
4. In the synoptic journal, there would be a special column for Sales Tax Payable because it is a frequently occurring item. ☐
5. The headings in a synoptic journal are always the same as those shown in the textbook. ☐
6. The main advantage of the synoptic journal is time saved in journalizing transactions. ☐
7. An advantage of the synoptic journal is that it is not necessary to balance the accounting entry for every transaction. ☐
8. The synoptic journal is balanced at the end of every month and at the end of every page. ☐
9. The accuracy of the synoptic journal is checked by cross-balancing. ☐
10. The synoptic journal should be cross-balanced before the final totals are inked in and the journal ruled off. ☐
11. It is customary to forward the totals from one page of the synoptic journal to the next. ☐
12. The total of the Other Accounts debit section is posted as a debit to the general ledger. ☐
13. The postings from the synoptic journal are dated the last day of the month. ☐
14. No cross-referencing is necessary when using a synoptic journal. ☐
15. A two-journal system provides a different route for non-routine transactions. ☐
16. A debit amount can be entered in a credit column if it is circled. ☐
17. Every entry in the synoptic journal takes only one line. ☐

NOTE: RECORD EXPLANATIONS ON PAGE 338.

Name________________________________ Date______________________

ANSWERS TO SECTION 12.1 EXERCISES (cont.)

Exercise 2, p. 499

1.

SYNOPTIC JOURNAL

DATE		CUSTOMER / SUPPLIER	NO.	BANK		ACCOUNTS RECEIVABLE		
				DR	CR	DR	CR	
								1
								2
								3
								4
								5
								6
								7
								8
								9
								10
								11
								12
								13
								14
								15
								16
								17
								18
								19
								20
								21
								22
								23
								24
								25
								26
								27
								28
								29
								30
								31
								32
								33
								34
								35
								36

Name____________________ Date______________

ANSWERS TO SECTION 12.1 EXERCISES (cont.)

Exercise 2 (cont.)

MONTH OF ________________ 19— PAGE 19

	ACCOUNTS PAYABLE		SALES OR REVENUE CR	PURCHASES DR	PST PAYABLE CR	OTHER ACCOUNTS			
	DR	CR				ACCOUNT	PR	DR	CR
1									
2									
3									
4									
5									
6									
7									
8									
9									
10									
11									
12									
13									
14									
15									
16									
17									
18									
19									
20									
21									
22									
23									
24									
25									
26									
27									
28									
29									
30									
31									
32									
33									
35									
35									
36									

Name ______________________ Date ________________

ANSWERS TO SECTION 12.1 EXERCISES (cont.)

Exercise 1 (cont.)

Explanations for "F" Responses for Exercise 1 on text p. 498:

Exercise 2 (cont.)

SYNOPTIC JOURNAL POSTING SUMMARY

ACCOUNTS	DEBIT	CREDIT

Name ______________________ Date ______________

ANSWERS TO SECTION 12.1 EXERCISES (cont.)

Exercise 3, p. 501

Shown below and on the next page, in simplified form, are the synoptic journal and the T-account general ledger of Plastic Products, owned by Jean Webb.

1. **Post the synoptic journal to the general ledger. Ignore dates and cross-references. Use check marks to indicate that postings are completed.**

2. **Take off a general ledger trial balance.**

1. SYNOPTIC JOURNAL **Month of June 19 —** **Page** 16

			BANK		ACCOUNTS RECEIVABLE		ACCOUNTS PAYABLE		SALES	PURCHASES	PST PAYL.	OTHER ACCOUNTS			
DATE		PARTICULARS	DR	CR	DR	CR	DR	CR	CR	DR	CR	ACCOUNT	P.R.	DR	CR
Jun	20	Forwarded	1800	1450	2150	1970	1270	1350	1750	1460	160				
	23	Laine	55						50		5				
	23	Moors		60								Rent		60	
	24	Park			110				100		10				
	25	Reid	80			80									
	25	Ruel		250			250								
	25	Sacerty		20								Telephone		20	
	26	Bass						150		150					
	26	Clayton						300		300					
	27	Delski		40								Wages		40	
	27	Eady						90				Car Exp.		90	
	27	Green		70								Freight-in		70	
	27	Hock	400			400									
	30	Klaus		230			230								
	30	McCoy	88						80		8				
	30	Nagy			77				70		7				
	30	Perry			44				40		4				
			2423	2120	2381	2450	1750	1890	2090	1910	194			280	

Name________________________ Date__________________

ANSWERS TO SECTION 12.1 EXERCISES (cont.)

Exercise 3 (cont.)

GENERAL LEDGER

Account	Debit	Credit
Bank	70	
Accounts Receivable		
Mdse Inventory	900	
Supplies	100	
Equipment	2 000	
Bank Loan		1 000
Accounts Payable		150
PST Payable		300
J. Webb, Capital		3 020
J. Webb, Drawings	500	
Sales		4 500
Bank Charges	40	
Car Expense	500	
Freight-in	100	
General Expense	90	
Purchases	2 000	
Rent Expense	300	
Telephone Expense	50	
Utilities Expense	1 220	
Wages Expense	750	

Name________________________ Date________________

ANSWERS TO SECTION 12.1 EXERCISES (cont.)

Exercise 3 (cont.)

2.

ACCOUNTS	DEBIT	CREDIT

ANSWERS TO SECTION 12.1 EXERCISES (cont.)

Exercise 4, p. 503 **SYNOPTIC JOURNAL**

DATE	CUSTOMER / SUPPLIER	NO.	BANK DR	BANK CR	ACCOUNTS RECEIVABLE DR	ACCOUNTS RECEIVABLE CR	
19—							
							1
							2
							3
							4
							5
							6
							7
							8
							9
							10
							11
							12
							13
							14
							15
							16
							17
							18
							19
							20
							21
							22
							23
							24
							25
							26
							27
							28
							29
							30
							31
							32
							33
							34
							35
							36
							37

Name____________________ Date________________

ANSWERS TO SECTION 12.1 EXERCISES (cont.)

Exercise 4 (cont.)

PAGE 73

	ACCOUNTS PAYABLE		SALES OR REVENUE CR	PURCHASES DR	PST PAYABLE CR	OTHER ACCOUNTS			
	DR	CR				ACCOUNT	PR	DR	CR
1									
2									
3									
4									
5									
6									
7									
8									
9									
10									
11									
12									
13									
14									
15									
16									
17									
18									
19									
20									
21									
22									
23									
24									
25									
26									
27									
28									
29									
30									
31									
32									
33									
34									
35									
36									
37									

Name____________________ Date________________

ANSWERS TO SECTION 12.1 EXERCISES (cont.)

Exercise 4 (cont.)

GENERAL LEDGER

ACCOUNT Bank **No.** 101

DATE		PARTICULARS	P.R.	DEBIT	CREDIT	DR/CR	BALANCE
19— Jun	30	Forwarded				DR	12 400 –

ACCOUNT Accounts Receivable **No.** 105

DATE		PARTICULARS	P.R.	DEBIT	CREDIT	DR/CR	BALANCE
19— Jun	30	Forwarded				DR	5 365 25

ACCOUNT Merchandise Inventory **No.** 110

DATE		PARTICULARS	P.R.	DEBIT	CREDIT	DR/CR	BALANCE
19— Jun	30	Forwarded				DR	46 090 20

ACCOUNT Supplies **No.** 115

DATE		PARTICULARS	P.R.	DEBIT	CREDIT	DR/CR	BALANCE
19— Jun	30	Forwarded				DR	1 395 –

ACCOUNT Store Equipment **No.** 120

DATE		PARTICULARS	P.R.	DEBIT	CREDIT	DR/CR	BALANCE
19— Jun	30	Forwarded				DR	40 906 –

ACCOUNT Accumulated Depreciation — Store Equipment **No.** 121

DATE		PARTICULARS	P.R.	DEBIT	CREDIT	DR/CR	BALANCE
19— Jun	30	Forwarded				CR	14 726 –

Name____________________ Date____________

ANSWERS TO SECTION 12.1 EXERCISES (cont.)

Exercise 4 (cont.)

GENERAL LEDGER (cont.)

ACCOUNT Delivery Equipment **No.** 130

DATE		PARTICULARS	P.R.	DEBIT	CREDIT	DR/CR	BALANCE
19—							
Jun	30	Forwarded				DR	39 500 –

ACCOUNT Accumulated Depreciation — Delivery Equipment **No.** 131

DATE		PARTICULARS	P.R.	DEBIT	CREDIT	DR/CR	BALANCE
19—							
Jun	30	Forwarded				CR	20 145 –

ACCOUNT Accounts Payable **No.** 201

DATE		PARTICULARS	P.R.	DEBIT	CREDIT	DR/CR	BALANCE
19—							
Jun	30	Forwarded				CR	6 265 35

ACCOUNT PST Payable **No.** 205

DATE		PARTICULARS	P.R.	DEBIT	CREDIT	DR/CR	BALANCE
19—							
Jun	30	Forwarded				CR	240 –

ACCOUNT Loan Payable — Federal Finance **No.** 210

DATE		PARTICULARS	P.R.	DEBIT	CREDIT	DR/CR	BALANCE
19—							
Jun	30	Forwarded				CR	8 550 85

ACCOUNT F. Dunn, Capital **No.** 301

DATE		PARTICULARS	P.R.	DEBIT	CREDIT	DR/CR	BALANCE
19—							
Jun	30	Forwarded				CR	87 952 08

Name________________ Date________________

ANSWERS TO SECTION 12.1 EXERCISES (cont.)

Exercise 4 (cont.)

GENERAL LEDGER (cont.)

ACCOUNT F. Dunn, Drawings **No.** 302

DATE		PARTICULARS	P.R.	DEBIT	CREDIT	DR/CR	BALANCE	
19—								
Jun	30	Forwarded				DR	6 000	–

ACCOUNT Sales **No.** 401

DATE		PARTICULARS	P.R.	DEBIT	CREDIT	DR/CR	BALANCE	
19—								
Jun	30	Forwarded				CR	53 714	50

ACCOUNT Delivery Expense **No.** 505

DATE		PARTICULARS	P.R.	DEBIT	CREDIT	DR/CR	BALANCE	
19—								
Jun	30	Forwarded				DR	5 258	–

ACCOUNT Freight-in **No.** 510

DATE		PARTICULARS	P.R.	DEBIT	CREDIT	DR/CR	BALANCE	
19—								
Jun	30	Forwarded				DR	956	23

ACCOUNT General Expense **No.** 515

DATE		PARTICULARS	P.R.	DEBIT	CREDIT	DR/CR	BALANCE	
19—								
Jun	30	Forwarded				DR	2 953	10

ACCOUNT Purchases **No.** 520

DATE		PARTICULARS	P.R.	DEBIT	CREDIT	DR/CR	BALANCE	
19—								
Jun	30	Forwarded				DR	14 120	–

Name____________________ Date__________

ANSWERS TO SECTION 12.1 EXERCISES (cont.)

Exercise 4 (cont.)

GENERAL LEDGER (cont.)

ACCOUNT Rent Expense **No.** 525

DATE		PARTICULARS	P.R.	DEBIT	CREDIT	DR/CR	BALANCE
19— Jun	30	Forwarded				DR	2 400 –

ACCOUNT Wages Expense **No.** 530

DATE		PARTICULARS	P.R.	DEBIT	CREDIT	DR/CR	BALANCE
19— Jun	30	Forwarded				DR	14 250 –

ACCOUNTS RECEIVABLE LEDGER

ACCOUNT R. Lai

DATE		PARTICULARS	P.R.	DEBIT	CREDIT	DR/CR	BALANCE
19— Jun	30	Forwarded #1407				DR	2 072 15

ACCOUNT G. Langford

DATE		PARTICULARS	P.R.	DEBIT	CREDIT	DR/CR	BALANCE
19— Jun	30	Forwarded #1431				DR	316 20

Name____________________ Date________________

ANSWERS TO SECTION 12.1 EXERCISES (cont.)

Exercise 4 (cont.)

ACCOUNTS RECEIVABLE LEDGER (cont.)

ACCOUNT R. Potts

DATE		PARTICULARS	P.R.	DEBIT	CREDIT	DR/CR	BALANCE
19— Jun	30	Forwarded #1436				DR	2 976 90

ACCOUNTS PAYABLE LEDGER

ACCOUNT City Hardware Supply

DATE		PARTICULARS	P.R.	DEBIT	CREDIT	DR/CR	BALANCE
19— Jun	30	Forwarded #1742				CR	2 742 10

ACCOUNT Clix Oil Company

DATE		PARTICULARS	P.R.	DEBIT	CREDIT	DR/CR	BALANCE

ACCOUNT Joe Jay Transport

DATE		PARTICULARS	P.R.	DEBIT	CREDIT	DR/CR	BALANCE

ACCOUNT Special Steel Products

DATE		PARTICULARS	P.R.	DEBIT	CREDIT	DR/CR	BALANCE
19— Jun	30	Forwarded #147				CR	3 523 25

Name____________________ Date______________

ANSWERS TO SECTION 12.1 EXERCISES (cont.)

Exercise 4 (cont.)

GENERAL LEDGER TRIAL BALANCE

ACCOUNTS	DEBIT	CREDIT

Name________________ Date________________

ANSWERS TO SECTION 12.1 EXERCISES (cont.)

Exercise 4 (cont.)

5.

SUBSIDIARY LEDGER TRIAL BALANCES

Crest Hardware

Accounts Receivable Trial Balance

July 31, 19—

Crest Hardware

Accounts Payable Trial Balance

July 31, 19—

Name____________________ Date________________

ANSWERS TO SECTION 12.2 REVIEW QUESTIONS (text p. 513)

The Five-Journal System

1. ______

2. ______

3. ______
   1. ______
   2. ______

4. ______

5. ______

6. ______

7. ______

8. ______

9. ______

10. ______

11. ______

12. ______

13. ______

Name______ Date______

ANSWERS TO SECTION 12.2 EXERCISES (text p. 513)

Exercise 1, p. 513

CASH PAYMENTS JOURNAL MONTH OF ________

DATE		PARTICULARS	OTHER ACCOUNTS DR			WAGES DR	PURCHASES DR	ACCOUNTS PAYABLE DR	REF. NO.	BANK CR
			ACCOUNT	P.R.	AMOUNT					

Name ________________ Date ________________

ANSWERS TO SECTION 12.2 EXERCISES (cont.)

Exercise 2, p. 514

1. ______________ 7. ______________ 13. ______________
2. ______________ 8. ______________ 14. ______________
3. ______________ 9. ______________ 15. ______________
4. ______________ 10. ______________ 16. ______________
5. ______________ 11. ______________ 17. ______________
6. ______________ 12. ______________ 18. ______________

Exercise 3, p. 514

SALES JOURNAL MONTH OF ________ 19___ PAGE 18

DATE		PARTICULARS	GST PAYABLE CR	PST PAYABLE CR	SALES CR	REF. NO.	ACCOUNTS RECEIVABLE DR

Name ______________________ Date ______________

ANSWERS TO SECTION 12.2 EXERCISES (cont.)

Exercise 3 (cont.)

CASH RECEIPTS JOURNAL MONTH OF ________ 19___ Page 27

DATE	PARTICULARS	OTHER ACCOUNTS CR			GST PAYABLE CR	PST PAYABLE CR	SALES CR	ACCOUNTS RECEIVABLE CR	REF. NO.	BANK DR
		ACCOUNT	P.R.	AMOUNT						

Name ____________________ Date ____________________

ANSWERS TO SECTION 12.2 EXERCISES (cont.)

Exercise 3 (cont.)

CASH PAYMENTS JOURNAL MONTH OF ________ 19__ Page 36

DATE	PARTICULARS	OTHER ACCOUNTS DR			WAGES DR	GST RECOVERABLE DR	SUPPLIES DR	ACCOUNTS PAYABLE DR	REF. NO.	BANK CR
		ACCOUNT	P.R.	AMOUNT						

Name________________________ Date________________

ANSWERS TO SECTION 12.2 EXERCISES (cont.)

Exercise 3 (cont.)

PURCHASES JOURNAL MONTH OF ______ 19__ Page 14

DATE	PARTICULARS	OTHER ACCOUNTS DR			DELIVERY EXPENSE DR	GST RECOVERABLE DR	PURCHASES DR	SUPPLIES DR	REF. NO.	ACCOUNTS PAYABLE CR
		ACCOUNT	P.R.	AMOUNT						

Name______________ Date______________

ANSWERS TO SECTION 12.2 EXERCISES (cont.)

Exercise 3 (cont.) GENERAL JOURNAL PAGE 17

DATE		PARTICULARS	P.R.	DEBIT	CREDIT
19—					

Exercise 4, p. 516 **Workbook Exercise**

Husky Hardware is a business owned by C. D. Mould. The accounting system for this business contains five journals and three ledgers. The subsidiary ledgers are posted daily directly from the source documents. There is a sales tax of 8 per cent on all sales.

The three ledgers of Husky Hardware are set out below. These three ledgers are also set up for you in the Workbook.

Husky Hardware
General Ledger Trial Balance
June 30, 19—

		Debit	Credit
100	Bank	$26 142.00	
105	Accounts Receivable	4 212.00	
110	Merchandise Inventory	40 951.20	
115	Supplies	3 000.00	
120	Store Equipment	26 750.00	
121	Accumulated Depreciation — Store Equipment		$5 000.00
125	Delivery Equipment	35 000.00	
126	Accumulated Depreciation — Delivery Equipment		12 000.00
200	Accounts Payable		50 639.40
205	Sales Tax Payable		1 085.20
300	C.D. Mould, Capital		61 643.60
305	C.D. Mould, Drawings	58 763.40	
400	Sales		198 000.00
500	Purchases	95 000.00	
505	Miscellaneous Expense	2 077.10	
510	Rent	18 000.00	
515	Wages	18 472.50	
		$328 368.20	$328 368.20

Name________________ Date________________

ANSWERS TO SECTION 12.2 EXERCISES (cont.)

Exercise 4 (cont).

Husky Hardware
Accounts Receivable Trial Balance
June 30, 19—

J. Barkley, 260 Western Avenue	No. 490	$950.40	
	No. 496	151.20	
	No. 503	615.60	$1 717.20
T. Fairley, 300 Centre Road	No. 501		577.80
S. Harvey, 466 Keeley Street	No. 502		783.00
R. Taylor, 588 Truway Drive	No. 498		1 134.00
			$4 212.00

Husky Hardware
Accounts Payable Trial Balance
June 30, 19—

Household Utensils Company, 487 Faith Avenue	No. 52	$10 675.00
J. & A. Hardware Supply, 600 Young Street	No. 596	5 052.50
Learner Bros., 5012 Direct Avenue	No. 141	30 672.00
Specialty Manufacturing Co., Barbary	No. 163	4 239.90
		$50 639.40

1. Journalize the transactions listed below in the five journals of Husky Hardware. (The five journals are provided for you following the transactions.) Use the page numbers shown. Ignore GST.

Cash Receipts Journal	Page 42
Cash Payments Journal	Page 93
Sales Journal	Page 56
Purchases Journal	Page 85
General Journal	Page 16

TRANSACTIONS

July

2 *Cheque Copy*

No. 187, to D.C. Harper, for the rent for the month, $3 000.00.

Purchase Invoice

From Household Utensils Company, No. 87, for the purchase of merchandise, $1 845.00.

3 *Sales Invoices*

No. 504, to S. Harvey, $500.00 plus sales tax.

No. 505, to R. Taylor, $260.00 plus sales tax.

No. 506, to T. Fairley, $420.00 plus sales tax.

No. 507, to J. Barkley, $640.00 plus sales tax.

4 *Cash Receipt*

From the owner, C.D. Mould, for the purpose of increasing his investment in the company, $10 000.00.

Name________________ Date________________

ANSWERS TO SECTION 12.2 EXERCISES (cont.)

Exercise 4 (cont).

5 *Purchase Invoice*

From Learner Bros., No. 206, for supplies, $356.00.

Cheque Copy

No. 188, to Supply House, for the cash purchase of merchandise, $1 470.00.

Cash Register Slips

For the cash sales for the week, $8 221.00 plus sales tax.

8 *Cash Receipt*

From T. Fairley, paying invoice No. 501, $577.80.

9 *Sales Invoices*

No. 508, to L. Peck, 12 Semore St., $410.00 plus sales tax.

No. 509, to S. Harvey, $180.00 plus sales tax.

No. 510, to T. Fairley, $250.00 plus sales tax.

10 *Purchase Invoice*

From J. & A. Hardware Supply, No. 612, for a shipment of hammers, saws, and other tools, $3 150.00.

12 *Cash Register Slips*

For the cash sales for the week, $9 360.00 plus sales tax.

Bank Debit Memo

From Sovereign Bank, bank account decrease for service charge, $102.00.

Cheque Copy

No. 189, to Modern Manufacturing Company, for the cash purchase of merchandise, $2 730.00.

13 *Cash Receipts*

From S. Harvey, paying invoices No. 502 and No. 504, $1 323.00.

From J. Barkley, paying invoices No. 490 and No. 496, $1 101.60.

15 *Cheque Copies*

No. 190, to Learner Bros., on account, $15 000.00.

No. 191, to Household Utensils Company, on account, $5 000.00.

No. 192, to B. Wiley, wages for the first half of the month, $1 250.00.

No. 193, to W. Brown, wages for the first half of the month, $1 500.00.

No. 194, to C.D. Mould, personal withdrawal by owner, $2 000.00.

No. 195, to the Provincial Government, paying sales tax for the previous month, $1 085.20.

Name________________________ Date____________________

ANSWERS TO SECTION 12.2 EXERCISES (cont.)

Exercise 4 (cont.)

17 *Sales Invoices*

No. 511, to V. Parker, 466 Janes Road, $750.00 plus sales tax.

No. 512, to L. Peck, $450.00 plus sales tax.

No. 513, to S. Harvey, $190.00 plus sales tax.

Cash Receipt

From R. Taylor, paying invoice No. 498, $1 134.00.

18 *Non-Routine Transaction*

Bills amounting to $240.80 representing miscellaneous expenses paid out of the owner's pocket. Credit the owner's Drawings account.

19 *Cash Register Slips*

For the cash sales for the week, $8 560.00 plus sales tax.

Cash Receipts

From S. Harvey, paying his account in full, $399.60.

From T. Fairley, paying invoice No. 506, $453.60.

From L. Peck, paying invoice No. 508, $442.80.

22 *Purchase Invoice*

From Maple Feed Company (Maple), No. 996, for the purchase of merchandise, $6 037.50.

23 *Purchase Invoice*

From Household Utensils Company, No. 156, for the purchase of merchandise, $4 126.50.

26 *Cash Register Slips*

For the cash sales for the week, $10 650.00 plus sales tax.

Cheque Copy

No. 196, to Learner Bros., for the cash purchase of merchandise, $2 625.00.

29 *Cheque Copies*

No. 197, to Household Utensils Company, paying invoice No. 52, $5 675.00.

No. 198, to J. & A. Hardware Supply, paying invoice No. 596, $5 052.50.

No. 199, to Specialty Manufacturing Company, paying invoice No. 163, $4 239.90.

Name________________________ Date________________

ANSWERS TO SECTION 12.2 EXERCISES (cont.)

Exercise 4 (cont.)

31 *Cheque Copies*

No. 200, to B. Wiley, wages for the last half of the month, $1 250.00.

No. 201, to W. Brown, wages for the last half of the month, $1 500.00.

No. 202, to C.D. Mould, for personal use, $800.00.

2. Balance and post the journals to the general ledger.

3. Balance the general ledger.

4. Balance the subsidiary ledgers.

SALES JOURNAL PAGE 56

DATE		PARTICULARS	SALES TAX PAYABLE CR	SALES CR	INV. NO.	ACCOUNTS RECEIVABLE DR

Name____________________ Date____________________

ANSWERS TO SECTION 12.2 EXERCISES (cont.)

Exercise 4 (cont.)

PURCHASES JOURNAL

Page 85

DATE		PARTICULARS	OTHER ACCOUNTS DR			PURCHASES DR	SUPPLIES DR	REF. NO.	ACCOUNTS PAYABLE CR
			ACCOUNT	P.R.	AMOUNT				

GENERAL JOURNAL

PAGE 16

DATE		PARTICULARS	P.R.	DEBIT	CREDIT

Name____________________ Date____________

ANSWERS TO SECTION 12.2 EXERCISES (cont.)

Exercise 4 (cont.)

CASH PAYMENTS JOURNAL

Page 93

DATE	PARTICULARS	OTHER ACCOUNTS DR			WAGES DR	PURCHASES DR	ACCOUNTS PAYABLE DR	CHQ. NO.	BANK CR
		ACCOUNT	P.R.	AMOUNT					

Name____________________ Date______________

ANSWERS TO SECTION 12.2 EXERCISES (cont.)

Exercise 4 (cont.)

CASH RECEIPTS JOURNAL

Page 42

DATE	PARTICULARS	OTHER ACCOUNTS CR			ACCOUNTS RECEIVABLE CR	SALES TAX PAYABLE CR	SALES CR	REF. NO.	BANK DR
		ACCOUNT	P.R.	AMOUNT					

Name____________________ Date__________

ANSWERS TO SECTION 12.2 EXERCISES (cont.)

Exercise 4 (cont.)

GENERAL LEDGER

ACCOUNT Bank **No.** 100

DATE		PARTICULARS	P.R.	DEBIT	CREDIT	DR/CR	BALANCE
19—							
June	30	Forwarded				DR	26 142 –

ACCOUNT Accounts Receivable **No.** 105

DATE		PARTICULARS	P.R.	DEBIT	CREDIT	DR/CR	BALANCE
19—							
June	30	Forwarded				DR	4 212 –

ACCOUNT Merchandise Inventory **No.** 110

DATE		PARTICULARS	P.R.	DEBIT	CREDIT	DR/CR	BALANCE
19—							
June	30	Forwarded				DR	40 951 20

ACCOUNT Supplies **No.** 115

DATE		PARTICULARS	P.R.	DEBIT	CREDIT	DR/CR	BALANCE
19—							
June	30	Forwarded				DR	3 000 –

ACCOUNT Store Equipment **No.** 120

DATE		PARTICULARS	P.R.	DEBIT	CREDIT	DR/CR	BALANCE
19—							
June	30	Forwarded				DR	26 750 –

ACCOUNT Accumulated Depreciation — Store Equipment **No.** 121

DATE		PARTICULARS	P.R.	DEBIT	CREDIT	DR/CR	BALANCE
19—							
June	30	Forwarded				CR	5 000 –

Name____________________ Date________________

ANSWERS TO SECTION 12.2 EXERCISES (cont.)

Exercise 4 (cont.)

GENERAL LEDGER (cont.)

ACCOUNT Delivery Equipment — No. 125

DATE		PARTICULARS	P.R.	DEBIT	CREDIT	DR/CR	BALANCE
19—							
June	30	Forwarded				DR	35 000 –

ACCOUNT Accumulated Depreciation — Delivery Equipment — No. 126

DATE		PARTICULARS	P.R.	DEBIT	CREDIT	DR/CR	BALANCE
19—							
June	30	Forwarded				CR	12 000 –

ACCOUNT Accounts Payable — No. 200

DATE		PARTICULARS	P.R.	DEBIT	CREDIT	DR/CR	BALANCE
19—							
June	30	Forwarded				CR	50 639 40

ACCOUNT Sales Tax Payable — No. 205

Date		Particulars	P.R.	Debit	Credit	DR/CR	Balance
19—							
June	30	Forwarded				CR	1 085 20

ACCOUNT C. D. Mould, Capital — No. 300

DATE		PARTICULARS	P.R.	DEBIT	CREDIT	DR/CR	BALANCE
19—							
June	30	Forwarded				CR	61 643 60

Name________________ Date__________

ANSWERS TO SECTION 12.2 EXERCISES (cont.)

Exercise 4 (cont.)

GENERAL LEDGER (cont.)

ACCOUNT C. D. Mould, Drawings — No. 305

DATE		PARTICULARS	P.R.	DEBIT	CREDIT	DR/DC	BALANCE
19— June	30	Forwarded				DR	58 763 40

ACCOUNT Sales — No. 400

DATE		PARTICULARS	P.R.	DEBIT	CREDIT	DR/CR	BALANCE
19— June	30	Forwarded				CR	198 000 –

ACCOUNT Purchases — No. 500

DATE		PARTICULARS	P.R.	DEBIT	CREDIT	DR/CR	BALANCE
19— June	30	Forwarded				DR	95 000 –

ACCOUNT Miscellaneous Expense — No. 505

DATE		PARTICULARS	P.R.	DEBIT	CREDIT	DR/CR	BALANCE
19— June	30	Forwarded				DR	2 077 10

ACCOUNT Rent Expense — No. 510

DATE		PARTICULARS	P.R.	DEBIT	CREDIT	DR/CR	BALANCE
19— June	30	Forwarded				DR	18 000 –

Name____________________ Date_______________

ANSWERS TO SECTION 12.2 EXERCISES (cont.)

Exercise 4 (cont.)

GENERAL LEDGER (cont.)

ACCOUNT Wages Expense **No.** 515

DATE		PARTICULARS	P.R.	DEBIT	CREDIT	DR/CR	BALANCE
19— June	30	Forwarded				DR	18 472 50

ACCOUNTS RECEIVABLE LEDGER

ACCOUNT J. Barkley 260 Western Avenue

DATE		PARTICULARS	P.R.	DEBIT	CREDIT	DR/CR	BALANCE
19— June	30	Forwarded #490 950.40					
		#496 151.20					
		#503 615.60				DR	1 717 20

ACCOUNT T. Fairley 300 Centre Road

DATE		PARTICULARS	P.R.	DEBIT	CREDIT	DR/CR	BALANCE
19— June	30	Forwarded #501				DR	577 80

ACCOUNT S. Harvey 466 Keeley Street

DATE		PARTICULARS	P.R.	DEBIT	CREDIT	DR/CR	BALANCE
19— June	30	Forwarded #502				DR	783 –

Name____________________ Date____________

ANSWERS TO SECTION 12.2 EXERCISES (cont.)

Exercise 4 (cont.)

ACCOUNTS RECEIVABLE LEDGER (cont.)

ACCOUNT V. Parker 466 Janes Road

DATE		PARTICULARS	P.R.	DEBIT	CREDIT	DR/CR	BALANCE

ACCOUNT L. Peck 12 Semore St.

DATE		PARTICULARS	P.R.	DEBIT	CREDIT	DR/CR	BALANCE

ACCOUNT R. Taylor 588 Truway Drive

DATE		PARTICULARS	P.R.	DEBIT	CREDIT	DR/CR	BALANCE
June	30	Forwarded #498				DR	1 134 –

ACCOUNTS PAYABLE LEDGER

ACCOUNT Household Utensils Company 487 Faith Avenue

DATE		PARTICULARS	P.R.	DEBIT	CREDIT	DR/CR	BALANCE
19— June	30	Forwarded #52				CR	10 675 –

ACCOUNT J. & A. Hardware Supply 600 Young Street

DATE		PARTICULARS	P.R.	DEBIT	CREDIT	DR/CR	BALANCE
19— June	30	Forwarded #596				CR	5 052 50

Name________________ Date________________

ANSWERS TO SECTION 12.2 EXERCISES (cont.)

Exercise 4 (cont.)

ACCOUNTS PAYABLE LEDGER (cont.)

ACCOUNT Learner Bros. 5012 Direct Avenue

DATE		PARTICULARS	P.R.	DEBIT	CREDIT	DR/CR	BALANCE
19— June	30	Forwarded #141				CR	30 672 –

ACCOUNT Maple Feed Company Maple

DATE		PARTICULARS	P.R.	DEBIT	CREDIT	DR/CR	BALANCE

ACCOUNT Specialty Manufacturing Barbary

DATE		PARTICULARS	P.R.	DEBIT	CREDIT	DR/CR	BALANCE
19— June	30	Forwarded #163				CR	4 239 90

Name____________________ Date____________

ANSWERS TO SECTION 12.2 EXERCISES (cont.)

Exercise 4 (cont.)

Husky Hardware
General Ledger Trial Balance
July 31, 19—

ACCOUNTS	DEBIT	CREDIT

Husky Hardware
Accounts Receivable Trial Balance
July 31, 19—

Husky Hardware
Accounts Payable Trial Balance
July 31, 19—

Name________________________ Date__________________

ANSWERS TO SECTION 12.3 REVIEW QUESTIONS (text p. 521)

Cash Discounts

1. ____________________

2. ____________________

3. ____________________

4. ____________________

5. ____________________

6. ____________________

7. ____________________

8. ____________________

9. ____________________

10. ____________________

11. ____________________

12. ____________________

13. ____________________

14. ____________________

15. ____________________

16. ____________________

ANSWERS TO SECTION 12.3 EXERCISES (text p. 521)

Exercise 1, p. 521

Date of Invoice	*Amount of Invoice*	*Terms of Sale*	*Amount of Credit Note*	*Date of Credit Note*	*Date Payment Is Made*	*Amount of Payment Required*
Mar. 12	$52.50	2/10, N30	—	—	Mar. 20	
May 18	47.25	Net 30	—	—	May 27	
Sep. 4	115.50	3/15, N/60	—	—	Oct. 10	
Feb. 6	1 050.00	1/20, N/60	$126.00	Feb. 18	Mar. 6	
Oct. 19	588.00	2/10, N/30	42.00	Nov. 5	Nov. 27	
Aug. 27	882.00	2/15, N/60	168.00	Sep. 7	Sep. 10	

Name________________ Date__________

ANSWERS TO SECTION 12.3 EXERCISES (cont.)

Exercise 2, p. 522

Date of Invoice	*Amount of Invoice*	*Terms of Sale*	*Amount of Credit Note*	*Date of Credit Note*	*Date Payment Is Made*	*Amount of Payment Required*
May 14	$147.00	2/10, N/30	—	—		
Apr. 15	315.00	3/20, N/60	$42.00	May 1		
Jun. 3	220.05	2/10, N/60	78.75	Jun. 20		
Nov. 20	59.25	2/15, N/60	36.75	Dec. 2		

Exercise 3, p. 522

IN THE BOOKS OF CIRCLE SUPPLY

GENERAL JOURNAL PAGE _____

	DATE		PARTICULARS	P.R.	DEBIT	CREDIT
1.a.						
1.b.						

IN THE BOOKS OF WATSON CONSTRUCTION

GENERAL JOURNAL PAGE _____

	DATE		PARTICULARS	P.R.	DEBIT	CREDIT
2.a.						
2.b.						

Name______________________ Date______________

ANSWERS TO SECTION 12.3 EXERCISES (cont.)

Exercise 4, p. 523

IN THE BOOKS OF CIRCLE SUPPLY

GENERAL JOURNAL PAGE ____

	DATE		PARTICULARS	P.R.	DEBIT	CREDIT
1.a.						
1.b.						
1.c.						

IN THE BOOKS OF JACKSON AND JACKSON

GENERAL JOURNAL PAGE ____

	DATE		PARTICULARS	P.R.	DEBIT	CREDIT
2.a.						
2.b.						
2.c.						

Name ____________________ Date ____________

ANSWERS TO SECTION 12.4 COMPUTER REVIEW QUESTIONS (text p. 529)

How Accountants Use Computers: Journal Systems

1. ______
2 ______
3. ______
4. ______
5. ______
6. ______
7. ______
8. ______
9. ______
10. ______
11. ______
12. ______

ANSWERS TO SECTION 12.4 COMPUTER EXERCISES (text p. 529)

Exercise 1, p. 529

General Ledger
Enter Transactions
Form GL–8
Use this form to prepare data for the Add Modify Delete Batches function

Page ___ of ___	Initials	Date
Prepared by		
Approved by		

Batch Number ☐ Entry mode: ☐ Normal entry ☐ Quick entry

Archive batch as ☐

Description (30 characters) ☐

A* M D	Entry No.**	Pd.	Line No.**	Source Code***	Date	Reference (12 characters)	Description (30 characters)	Account Department	Debit	Credit
				GL-					.	.
				GL-					.	.
				GL-					.	.
				GL-					.	.
				GL-					.	.
				GL-					.	.
				GL-					.	.
				GL-					.	.
				GL-					.	.
				GL-					.	.
				GL-					.	.
				GL-					.	.
				GL-					.	.
				GL-					.	.
								Totals	.	.

* A = Add
M = Modify
D = Delete

** Entry and line numbers are assigned by the Program

*** To include a comment line press Enter before typing the source code

Entered by ____________ Date ________

Name ____________ Date ____________

General Ledger **Enter Transactions** Form GL–8 Use this form to prepare data for the Add Modify Delete Batches function	Page ____ of ____	Initials	Date
	Prepared by		
	Approved by		

Batch Number [ ]   Entry mode: ☐ Normal entry ☐ Quick entry

Archive batch as [| | | |]

Description (30 characters) [ ]

A* M D	Entry No.**	Pd.	Line No.**	Source Code***	Date	Reference (12 characters)	Description (30 characters)	Account Department	Debit	Credit
				GL-					.	.
				GL-					.	.
				GL-					.	.
				GL-					.	.
				GL-					.	.
				GL-					.	.
				GL-					.	.
				GL-					.	.
				GL-					.	.
				GL-					.	.
				GL-					.	.
				GL-					.	.
				GL-					.	.
				GL-					.	.
								Totals	.	.

* A = Add
M = Modify
D = Delete

** Entry and line numbers are assigned by the Program

*** To include a comment line press Enter before typing the source code

Entered by ____________________ Date __________

Name ____________________ Date ____________

General Ledger **Enter Transactions** Form GL–8 Use this form to prepare data for the Add Modify Delete Batches function	Page ____ of ____	Initials	Date
	Prepared by		
	Approved by		

Batch Number ☐ Entry mode: ☐ Normal entry ☐ Quick entry

Archive batch as ☐

Description (30 characters) ☐

A* M D	Entry No.**	Pd.	Line No.**	Source Code***	Date	Reference (12 characters)	Description (30 characters)	Account Department	Debit	Credit
				GL-					.	.
				GL-					.	.
				GL-					.	.
				GL-					.	.
				GL-					.	.
				GL-					.	.
				GL-					.	.
				GL-					.	.
				GL-					.	.
				GL-					.	.
				GL-					.	.
				GL-					.	.
				GL-					.	.
				GL-					.	.
								Totals	.	.

* A = Add
M = Modify
D = Delete

** Entry and line numbers are assigned by the Program

*** To include a comment line press Enter before typing the source code

Entered by ________________ Date ________

Name ________________ Date ________

General Ledger **Enter Transactions** Form GL–8 Use this form to prepare data for the Add Modify Delete Batches function	Page ___ of ___	Initials	Date
	Prepared by		
	Approved by		

Batch Number ☐ Entry mode: ☐ Normal entry ☐ Quick entry

Archive batch as

Description (30 characters)

A* M D	Entry No.**	Pd.	Line No.**	Source Code***	Date	Reference (12 characters)	Description (30 characters)	Account Department	Debit	Credit
				GL-					.	.
				GL-					.	.
				GL-					.	.
				GL-					.	.
				GL-					.	.
				GL-					.	.
				GL-					.	.
				GL-					.	.
				GL-					.	.
				GL-					.	.
				GL-					.	.
				GL-					.	.
				GL-					.	.
				GL-					.	.
								Totals	.	.

* A = Add
M = Modify
D = Delete

** Entry and line numbers are assigned by the Program

*** To include a comment line press Enter before typing the source code

Entered by ______________ Date ________

Name ______________ Date ______________

General Ledger **Enter Transactions** Form GL–8 Use this form to prepare data for the Add Modify Delete Batches function	Page ___ of ___	Initials	Date
	Prepared by		
	Approved by		

Batch Number ☐ Entry mode: ☐ Normal entry ☐ Quick entry

Archive batch as ☐

Description (30 characters) ☐

A* M D	Entry No.**	Pd.	Line No.**	Source Code***	Date	Reference (12 characters)	Description (30 characters)	Account Department	Debit	Credit
				GL-					.	.
				GL-					.	.
				GL-					.	.
				GL-					.	.
				GL-					.	.
									.	.
									.	.
									.	.
									.	.
									.	.
									.	.
									.	.
									.	.
									.	.
								Totals	.	.

* A = Add
  M = Modify
  D = Delete

** Entry and line numbers are assigned by the Program

*** To include a comment line press Enter before typing the source code

Entered by ______________ Date ________

Name ______________ Date ______________

ANSWERS TO SECTION 12.4 COMPUTER EXERCISES (text p. 529)

Communicate It (text p. 532)

Name________________ Date________________

Chapter 12 Specialized Journals

ANSWERS TO CHAPTER 12 EXERCISES (text, p. 533)

Exercise 1, p. 533 Using Your Knowledge

Indicate whether each of the following statements is true or false by placing a "T" or an "F" in the box provided. Explain the reason for each "F" response in the space provided.

1. The general journal is not normally used if the business has a synoptic journal. ☐
2. There is a special column for every general ledger account in the synoptic journal. ☐
3. The chief disadvantage of the synoptic journal is that you have to post column totals. ☐
4. An accounting entry that takes more than one line cannot be recorded in the synoptic journal. ☐
5. There would be a special column for Rent Expense in the synoptic journal. ☐
6. The synoptic journal is balanced at the end of every page. ☐
7. The date used when formally posting the synoptic journal is the last day of the month. ☐
8. A credit to Sales in the synoptic journal would normally be entered in the Other Accounts credit column. ☐
9. All sales of merchandise are recorded in the sales journal. ☐
10. The cash payments journal is also known as the cash disbursements journal. ☐
11. Additional cash invested in the business by the owner would be recorded in the general journal. ☐
12. A bank debit advice requires an entry in the cash receipts journal. ☐
13. The five journal system inevitably leads to the clerks becoming specialists within the system. ☐
14. The general ledger would not balance if only four of the five journals were posted. ☐
15. A purchase partly for cash and partly on account would be recorded in the purchases journal. ☐

Explanations for "F" responses:

Name________________ Date__________

ANSWERS TO CHAPTER 12 EXERCISES (cont.)

Exercise 1 (cont.)

Exercise 2, p. 533

1.

2.

Exercise 3, p. 533

1.

2.

Exercise 4, p. 534

Name Date

ANSWERS TO CHAPTER 12 EXERCISES (cont.)

Exercise 5, p. 534

1. ______

2. ______

3. ______

4. ______

5. ______

Exercise 6, p. 534

1. IN THE BOOKS OF CIRCLE SUPPLY

GENERAL JOURNAL

DATE		PARTICULARS	P.R.	DEBIT	CREDIT

Name______ Date______

ANSWERS TO CHAPTER 12 EXERCISES (cont.)

Exercise 7, p. 536

ANSWERS TO CHAPTER 12 EXERCISES (cont.)

Exercise 8, p. 537 Short Comprehensive Exercise

CASH RECEIPTS JOURNAL

Page 61

DATE	PARTICULARS	OTHER ACCOUNTS CR			GST PAYABLE CR	PST PAYABLE CR	SALES CR	ACCOUNTS RECEIVABLE CR	REF. NO.	BANK DR
		ACCOUNT	P.R.	AMOUNT						

PURCHASES JOURNAL

Page 74

DATE	PARTICULARS	OTHER ACCOUNTS DR					GST RECOVERABLE DR	PURCHASES DR	REF. NO.	ACCOUNTS PAYABLE CR
		ACCOUNT	P.R.	AMOUNT						

Name________________ Date________________

ANSWERS TO CHAPTER 12 EXERCISES (cont.)

Exercise 8 (cont.)

CASH PAYMENTS JOURNAL

Page 117

DATE	PARTICULARS	OTHER ACCOUNTS DR			GST RECOVERABLE DR	WAGES DR	PURCHASES DR	ACCOUNTS PAYABLE DR	REF. NO.	BANK CR
		ACCOUNT	P.R.	AMOUNT						

Name ____________________ Date ______________

ANSWERS TO CHAPTER 12 EXERCISES (cont.)

Exercise 8 (cont.)

SALES JOURNAL

Page 82

DATE		PARTICULARS	GST PAYABLE CR	PST PAYABLE CR	SALES CR	REF. NO.	ACCOUNTS RECEIVABLE DR

GENERAL JOURNAL

Page 29

DATE		PARTICULARS	P.R.	DEBIT	CREDIT

GENERAL LEDGER

ACCOUNT Bank **No.** 105

DATE		PARTICULARS	P.R.	DEBIT	CREDIT	DR/CR	BALANCE
19— Dec	31	Forwarded	–			DR	16 2 2 5 85

ACCOUNT Accounts Receivable **No.** 110

DATE		PARTICULARS	P.R.	DEBIT	CREDIT	DR/CR	BALANCE
19— Dec	31	Forwarded	–			DR	8 2 3 1 70

Name____________________ Date______________

ANSWERS TO CHAPTER 12 EXERCISES (cont.)

Exercise 8 (cont.)

GENERAL LEDGER (cont.)

ACCOUNT Supplies **No.** 115

DATE		PARTICULARS	P.R.	DEBIT	CREDIT	DR/CR	BALANCE
19— Dec	31	Forwarded	–			DR	312 50

ACCOUNT Merchandise Inventory **No.** 120

DATE		PARTICULARS	P.R.	DEBIT	CREDIT	DR/CR	BALANCE
19— Dec	31	Forwarded	–			DR	37 416 40

ACCOUNT Equipment **No.** 125

DATE		PARTICULARS	P.R.	DEBIT	CREDIT	DR/CR	BALANCE
19— Dec	31	Forwarded	–			DR	26 800 –

ACCOUNT Accumulated Depreciation — Equipment **No.** 126

DATE		PARTICULARS	P.R.	DEBIT	CREDIT	DR/CR	BALANCE
19— Dec	31	Forwarded	–			CR	12 400 –

ACCOUNT Truck **No.** 130

DATE		PARTICULARS	P.R.	DEBIT	CREDIT	DR/CR	BALANCE
19— Dec	31	Forwarded	–			DR	22 200 –

Name__________________ Date____________

ANSWERS TO CHAPTER 12 EXERCISES (cont.)

Exercise 8 (cont.)

GENERAL LEDGER (cont.)

ACCOUNT Accumulated Depreciation — Truck **No.** 131

DATE		PARTICULARS	P.R.	DEBIT	CREDIT	DR/CR	BALANCE
19— Dec	31	Forwarded	–			CR	8 400 –

ACCOUNT Accounts Payable **No.** 205

DATE		PARTICULARS	P.R.	DEBIT	CREDIT	DR/CR	BALANCE
19— Dec	31	Forwarded	–			CR	12 358 50

ACCOUNT Bank Loan **No.** 210

DATE		PARTICULARS	P.R.	DEBIT	CREDIT	DR/CR	BALANCE
19— Dec	31	Forwarded	–			CR	18 000 –

ACCOUNT PST Payable **No.** 215

DATE		PARTICULARS	P.R.	DEBIT	CREDIT	DR/CR	BALANCE
19— Dec	31	Forwarded	–			CR	360 –

Name____________________ Date______________

ANSWERS TO CHAPTER 12 EXERCISES (cont.)

Exercise 8 (cont.)

GENERAL LEDGER (cont.)

ACCOUNT GST Payable **No.** 220

DATE		PARTICULARS	P.R.	DEBIT	CREDIT	DR/CR	BALANCE
19— Dec	31	Forwarded	–			CR	315 –

ACCOUNT GST Recoverable **No.** 225

DATE		PARTICULARS	P.R.	DEBIT	CREDIT	DR/CR	BALANCE
19— Dec	31	Forwarded	–			DR	210 –

ACCOUNT S. Scales, Capital **No.** 305

DATE		PARTICULARS	P.R.	DEBIT	CREDIT	DR/CR	BALANCE
19— Dec	31	Forwarded	–			CR	59 562 95

ACCOUNT S. Scales, Drawings **No.** 310

DATE		PARTICULARS	P.R.	DEBIT	CREDIT	DR/CR	BALANCE

ACCOUNT Sales **No.** 405

DATE		PARTICULARS	P.R.	DEBIT	CREDIT	DR/CR	BALANCE

Name____________________ Date________________

ANSWERS TO CHAPTER 12 EXERCISES (cont.)

Exercise 8 (cont.)

GENERAL LEDGER (cont.)

ACCOUNT Purchases No. 505

DATE		PARTICULARS	P.R.	DEBIT	CREDIT	DR/CR	BALANCE

ACCOUNT Delivery Expense No. 510

DATE		PARTICULARS	P.R.	DEBIT	CREDIT	DR/CR	BALANCE

ACCOUNT General Expense No. 515

DATE		PARTICULARS	P.R.	DEBIT	CREDIT	DR/CR	BALANCE

ACCOUNT Rent Expense No. 520

DATE		PARTICULARS	P.R.	DEBIT	CREDIT	DR/CR	BALANCE

ACCOUNT Telephone Expense No. 525

DATE		PARTICULARS	P.R.	DEBIT	CREDIT	DR/CR	BALANCE

ACCOUNT Wages Expense No. 530

DATE		PARTICULARS	P.R.	DEBIT	CREDIT	DR/CR	BALANCE

Name____________________ Date________________

ANSWERS TO CHAPTER 12 EXERCISES (cont.)

Exercise 8 (cont.)

ACCOUNTS RECEIVABLE LEDGER

ACCOUNT C. Bruk

DATE		PARTICULARS	P.R.	DEBIT	CREDIT	DR/CR	BALANCE
19— Dec	31	Forwarded #325	–			DR	363.40

ACCOUNT M. Howard

DATE		PARTICULARS	P.R.	DEBIT	CREDIT	DR/CR	BALANCE
19— Dec	31	Forwarded #296	–			DR	3 559.25

ACCOUNT J. Joss

DATE		PARTICULARS	P.R.	DEBIT	CREDIT	DR/CR	BALANCE
19— Dec	31	Forwarded #306	–			DR	1 048.80

ACCOUNT S. Pampu

DATE		PARTICULARS	P.R.	DEBIT	CREDIT	DR/CR	BALANCE
19— Dec	31	Forwarded #217	–			DR	155.25

ACCOUNT D. Wilkins

DATE		PARTICULARS	P.R.	DEBIT	CREDIT	DR/CR	BALANCE
19— Dec	31	Forwarded #331	–			DR	3 105.–

Name____________________ Date________________

ANSWERS TO CHAPTER 12 EXERCISES (cont.)

Exercise 8 (cont.)

ACCOUNTS PAYABLE LEDGER

ACCOUNT Smith's Service Station

DATE		PARTICULARS	P.R.	DEBIT	CREDIT	DR/CR	BALANCE

ACCOUNT Stirling Company

DATE		PARTICULARS	P.R.	DEBIT	CREDIT	DR/CR	BALANCE
19—							
Dec	31	Forwarded #245	–			CR	4815 –

ACCOUNT Triangle Electric

DATE		PARTICULARS	P.R.	DEBIT	CREDIT	DR/CR	BALANCE
19—							
Dec	31	Forwarded #4701	–			CR	4280 –

ACCOUNT Universal Vacuums

DATE		PARTICULARS	P.R.	DEBIT	CREDIT	DR/CR	BALANCE
19—							
Dec	31	Forwarded #6508	–			CR	1070 –

ACCOUNT Western Electric

DATE		PARTICULARS	P.R.	DEBIT	CREDIT	DR/CR	BALANCE
19—							
Dec	31	Forwarded #246	–			CR	2193 50

Name____________________ Date______________

ANSWERS TO CHAPTER 12 EXERCISES (cont.)

Exercise 8 (cont.)

Bristol Appliances Company

General Ledger Trial Balance

January 31, 19—

ACCOUNTS	DEBIT	CREDIT

Name______________________ Date______________________

ANSWERS TO CHAPTER 12 EXERCISES (cont.)

Exercise 8 (cont.)

Bristol Appliances Company
Accounts Receivable Trial Balance
January 31, 19—

Bristol Appliances Company
Accounts Payable Trial Balance
January 31, 19—

Exercise 9, p. 539 For Further Thought

1.

2.

3.

4.

5.

6.

7.

8.

9.

10.

11. a.

b.

c.

Name ____________________ Date ____________

ANSWERS TO CHAPTER 12 EXERCISES (cont.)

Exercise 9 (cont.)

d. ______________________________

e. ______________________________

Exercise 10, p. 540 Cases for Further Thought *(Use more paper if necessary.)*

1. ______________________________

   1. ______________ 3. ______________
   2. ______________ 4. ______________

2. ______________________________

3. ______________________________

4. ______________________________

5. ______________________________

6. ______________________________

7. ______________________________

Name______________________ Date______________

ANSWERS TO CHAPTER 12 EXERCISES (cont.)

Exercise 10 (cont.)

8. ______

9. ______

CASE STUDIES (text p. 542)

Case 1 *A Personalized Synoptic Journal?*, p. 542 *(Use more paper if necessary.)*

1. ______

a. ______

b. ______

a. ______

b. ______

2. ______

Case 2 *Squeeze Play*, p. 542 *(Use more paper if necessary.)*

1. ______

2. ______

3. ______

4. ______

Name ______ Date ______

ANSWERS TO CHAPTER 12 EXERCISES (cont.)

CASE STUDIES (cont.)

Challenge Case *No Journal!*, p. 543 *(Use more paper if necessary.)*

1.

2.

3.

4.

5.

6.

CAREER Alfonso Gagliano / Chief Opposition Whip, House of Commons

ANSWERS TO DISCUSSION QUESTIONS (text p. 546) *(Use more paper if necessary.)*

1.

2.

3.

4.

Name__________ Date__________

ANSWERS TO SECTION 13.1 COMPUTER REVIEW QUESTIONS (text p. 554)

Getting Started in ACCPAC® Simply Accounting™

1. ______________________________

2. ______________________________

3. ______________________________

4. ______________________________

5. ______________________________

6. ______________________________

7. ______________________________

8. ______________________________

9. ______________________________

10. ______________________________

11. ______________________________

12. ______________________________

13. ______________________________

14. ______________________________

15. ______________________________

16. ______________________________

17. ______________________________

18. ______________________________

19. ______________________________

20. ______________________________

21. ______________________________

22. ______________________________

23. ______________________________

Name ______________ Date ______________

ANSWERS TO SECTION 13.1 COMPUTER EXERCISES (text p. 555)

1. *(There is no manual application for this exercise.)*

Communicate It (text p. 555)

ANSWERS TO SECTION 13.2 COMPUTER REVIEW QUESTIONS (text p. 562)

Simply Accounting in the Accounting Cycle

1.

2.

3.

4.

5.

6.

7.

8.

9.

11.

12.

13.

14.

15.

Name________________ Date____________

***(Note:** Because the computer accounting sections have no manual application, in the interests of saving paper, we have deleted pages 402 through 405 from the Workbook.)*

ANSWERS TO SECTION 13.3 COMPUTER EXERCISES (text p. 573)

Communicate It (text p. 565)

1.

2.

Name______________________ Date______________

ANSWERS TO SECTION 13.3 COMPUTER REVIEW QUESTIONS (text p. 572)

Payable and Receivable Modules

1. ______

2. ______

3. ______

4. ______

5. ______

6. ______

7. ______

8. ______

9. ______

10. ______

Name______ Date______

*(**Note:** Because the computer accounting sections have no manual application, in the interests of saving paper, we have deleted pages 408 through 413 from the Workbook.)*

ANSWERS TO SECTION 13.3 COMPUTER EXERCISES (cont.)

Communicate It (text p. 574)

Name__________ Date__________

TRAVEL TRAILERS (text p. 575)

Cash Payments Journal

CASH PAYMENTS JOURNAL Page 84

DATE	PARTICULARS	OTHER ACCOUNTS DR			GST RECOVERABLE DR	WAGES DR	DRAWINGS DR	ACCOUNTS PAYABLE DR	REF. NO.	BANK CR
		ACCOUNT	P.R.	AMOUNT						

Name________________ Date________________

Summary Exercise

TRAVEL TRAILERS (cont.)

Cash Payments Journal (cont.) and Cash Receipts Journal

CASH PAYMENTS JOURNAL Page 85

DATE	PARTICULARS	OTHER ACCOUNTS DR			GST RECOVERABLE DR	WAGES DR	DRAWINGS DR	ACCOUNTS PAYABLE DR	REF. NO.	BANK CR
		ACCOUNT	P.R.	AMOUNT						

CASH RECEIPTS JOURNAL Page 37

DATE	PARTICULARS	OTHER ACCOUNTS CR			GST PAYABLE CR	PST PAYABLE CR	SALES CR	ACCOUNTS RECEIVABLE CR	REF. NO.	BANK DR
		ACCOUNT	P.R.	AMOUNT						

Name________________ Date________________

TRAVEL TRAILERS (cont.)

Purchases Journal

PURCHASES JOURNAL — Page 74

DATE	PARTICULARS	OTHER ACCOUNTS DR			GST RECOVERABLE DR	FREIGHT-IN DR	SUPPLIES DR	PURCHASES DR	REF. NO.	ACCOUNTS PAYABLE CR
		ACCOUNT	P.R.	AMOUNT						

Name____________________ Date_______________

TRAVEL TRAILERS (cont.)

Sales Journal

SALES JOURNAL Page *19*

DATE		PARTICULARS	GST PAYABLE CR	PST PAYABLE CR	SALES CR	REF. NO.	ACCOUNTS RECEIVABLE DR

Name____________________ Date____________

TRAVEL TRAILERS (cont.)

General Journal

GENERAL JOURNAL PAGE 5

DATE		PARTICULARS	P.R.	DEBIT	CREDIT

Name______________________ Date______________

TRAVEL TRAILERS (cont.)

General Journal (cont.)

GENERAL JOURNAL PAGE 6

DATE		PARTICULARS	P.R.	DEBIT	CREDIT

Name______________________ Date______________

TRAVEL TRAILERS (cont.)

GENERAL LEDGER

ACCOUNT Bank **No.** 101

DATE		PARTICULARS	P.R.	DEBIT	CREDIT	DR/CR	BALANCE
19— May	31	Forwarded	–			DR	11 751.75

ACCOUNT Accounts Receivable **No.** 110

DATE		PARTICULARS	P.R.	DEBIT	CREDIT	DR/CR	BALANCE
19— May	31	Forwarded	–			DR	2 719.75

ACCOUNT Merchandise Inventory **No.** 115

DATE		PARTICULARS	P.R.	DEBIT	CREDIT	DR/CR	BALANCE
19— May	31	Forwarded	–			DR	125 423.–

ACCOUNT Supplies **No.** 120

DATE		PARTICULARS	P.R.	DEBIT	CREDIT	DR/CR	BALANCE
19— May	31	Forwarded	–			DR	1 151.–

Name____________________ Date________________

TRAVEL TRAILERS (cont.)

General Ledger (cont.)

ACCOUNT Prepaid Insurance **No.** 125

DATE		PARTICULARS	P.R.	DEBIT	CREDIT	DR/CR	BALANCE
19— May	31	Forwarded	–			DR	2 650 –

ACCOUNT Equipment **No.** 130

DATE		PARTICULARS	P.R.	DEBIT	CREDIT	DR/CR	BALANCE
19— May	31	Forwarded	–			DR	34 472 –

ACCOUNT Accumulated Depreciation – Equipment **No.** 131

DATE		PARTICULARS	P.R.	DEBIT	CREDIT	DR/CR	BALANCE
19— May	31	Forwarded	–			CR	6 000 –

ACCOUNT Truck **No.** 140

DATE		PARTICULARS	P.R.	DEBIT	CREDIT	DR/CR	BALANCE
19— May	31	Forwarded	–			DR	38 000 –

ACCOUNT Accumulated Depreciation – Truck **No.** 141

DATE		PARTICULARS	P.R.	DEBIT	CREDIT	DR/CR	BALANCE
19— May	31	Forwarded	–			CR	16 000 –

Name____________________ Date____________

TRAVEL TRAILERS (cont.)

General Ledger (cont.)

ACCOUNT Accounts Payable No. 201

DATE		PARTICULARS	P.R.	DEBIT	CREDIT	DR/CR	BALANCE
19— May	31	Forwarded	–			CR	21 386.09

ACCOUNT Bank Loan No. 205

DATE		PARTICULARS	P.R.	DEBIT	CREDIT	DR/CR	BALANCE
19— May	31	Forwarded	–			CR	120 000.–

ACCOUNT PST Payable No. 210

DATE		PARTICULARS	P.R.	DEBIT	CREDIT	DR/CR	BALANCE
19— May	31	Forwarded	–			CR	3 030.78

ACCOUNT GST Payable No. 212

DATE		PARTICULARS	P.R.	DEBIT	CREDIT	DR/CR	BALANCE
19— May	31	Forwarded	–			CR	2 651.90

Name________________________ Date________________

Summary Exercise

TRAVEL TRAILERS (cont.)

General Ledger (cont.)

ACCOUNT GST Recoverable — No. 215

DATE		PARTICULARS	P.R.	DEBIT	CREDIT	DR/CR	BALANCE
19— May	31	Forwarded	–			DR	1 629 28

ACCOUNT C. Fowler, Capital — No. 305

DATE		PARTICULARS	P.R.	DEBIT	CREDIT	DR/CR	BALANCE
19— May	31	Forwarded	–			CR	40 245 76

ACCOUNT C. Fowler, Drawings — No. 310

DATE		PARTICULARS	P.R.	DEBIT	CREDIT	DR/CR	BALANCE
19— May	31	Forwarded	–			DR	15 000 –

ACCOUNT Sales — No. 405

DATE		PARTICULARS	P.R.	DEBIT	CREDIT	DR/CR	BALANCE
19— May	31	Forwarded	–			CR	189 423 51

Name________________ Date________________

TRAVEL TRAILERS (cont.)

General Ledger (cont.)

ACCOUNT Discounts Earned **No.** 407

DATE		PARTICULARS	P.R.	DEBIT	CREDIT	DR/CR	BALANCE
19— May	31	Forwarded	–			CR	1 0 3 4 20

ACCOUNT Discounts Allowed **No.** 501

DATE		PARTICULARS	P.R.	DEBIT	CREDIT	DR/CR	BALANCE
19— May	31	Forwarded	–			DR	3 5 7 –

ACCOUNT Purchases **No.** 505

DATE		PARTICULARS	P.R.	DEBIT	CREDIT	DR/CR	BALANCE
19— May	31	Forwarded	–			DR	96 5 8 1 75

ACCOUNT Freight-in Expense **No.** 510

DATE		PARTICULARS	P.R.	DEBIT	CREDIT	DR/CR	BALANCE
19— May	31	Forwarded	–			DR	1 1 7 4 72

Name____________________ Date________________

TRAVEL TRAILERS (cont.)

General Ledger (cont.)

ACCOUNT Bank Charges and Interest Expense **No.** 515

DATE		PARTICULARS	P.R.	DEBIT	CREDIT	DR/CR	BALANCE
19— May	31	Forwarded	–			DR	4 5 1 6 50

ACCOUNT Delivery Expense **No.** 520

DATE		PARTICULARS	P.R.	DEBIT	CREDIT	DR/CR	BALANCE
19— May	31	Forwarded	–			DR	5 6 5 0 20

ACCOUNT Depreciation of Equipment **No.** 522

DATE		PARTICULARS	P.R.	DEBIT	CREDIT	DR/CR	BALANCE

ACCOUNT Depreciation of Truck **No.** 523

DATE		PARTICULARS	P.R.	DEBIT	CREDIT	DR/CR	BALANCE

ACCOUNT Insurance Expense **No.** 525

DATE		PARTICULARS	P.R.	DEBIT	CREDIT	DR/CR	BALANCE

Name____________________ Date________________

TRAVEL TRAILERS (cont.)

General Ledger (cont.)

ACCOUNT Light and Heat Expense — **No.** 530

DATE		PARTICULARS	P.R.	DEBIT	CREDIT	DR/CR	BALANCE
19— May	31	Forwarded	–			DR	4 350 40

ACCOUNT Miscellaneous Expense — **No.** 535

DATE		PARTICULARS	P.R.	DEBIT	CREDIT	DR/CR	BALANCE
19— May	31	Forwarded	–			DR	994 58

ACCOUNT Rent Expense — **No.** 540

DATE		PARTICULARS	P.R.	DEBIT	CREDIT	DR/CR	BALANCE
19— May	31	Forwarded	–			DR	6 250 –

ACCOUNT Supplies Expense — **No.** 545

DATE		PARTICULARS	P.R.	DEBIT	CREDIT	DR/CR	BALANCE

ACCOUNT Telephone Expense — **No.** 550

DATE		PARTICULARS	P.R.	DEBIT	CREDIT	DR/CR	BALANCE
19— May	31	Forwarded	–			DR	1 376 20

Name____________________ Date______________

Summary Exercise

TRAVEL TRAILERS (cont.)

General Ledger (cont.)

ACCOUNT Wages Expense **No.** 555

DATE		PARTICULARS	P.R.	DEBIT	CREDIT	DR/CR	BALANCE
19— May	31	Forwarded	–			DR	45 724 11

ACCOUNT Income Summary **No.** 598

DATE		PARTICULARS	P.R.	DEBIT	CREDIT	DR/CR	BALANCE

ACCOUNTS RECEIVABLE LEDGER

ACCOUNT B. Fraser 15 Gray Street

DATE		PARTICULARS	P.R.	DEBIT	CREDIT	DR/CR	BALANCE
19— May	31	Forwarded (of May 10) #634				DR	4 02 50

ACCOUNT W. Hoyle 49 First Street

DATE		PARTICULARS	P.R.	DEBIT	CREDIT	DR/CR	BALANCE
19— May	31	Forwarded (of May 12) #635				DR	86 25

Name____________________ Date________________

TRAVEL TRAILERS (cont.)

Accounts Receivable Ledger (cont.)

ACCOUNT A. Newman 250 Fort Road

DATE		PARTICULARS	P.R.	DEBIT	CREDIT	DR/CR	BALANCE
19— May	31	Forwarded (of Apr 30) #629				DR	287.50

ACCOUNT Schell Brothers 96 Garrison Avenue

DATE		PARTICULARS	P.R.	DEBIT	CREDIT	DR/CR	BALANCE
19— May	31	Forwarded (of May 4) #633				DR	1161.50

ACCOUNT N. Thompson 20 Wilson Avenue

DATE		PARTICULARS	P.R.	DEBIT	CREDIT	DR/CR	BALANCE
19— May	31	Forwarded (of May 1) #630				DR	684.25

ACCOUNT L. Walker 4 Dennis Avenue

DATE		PARTICULARS	P.R.	DEBIT	CREDIT	DR/CR	BALANCE
19— May	31	Forwarded (of May 2) #631				DR	97.75

Name____________________ Date________________

TRAVEL TRAILERS (cont.)

ACCOUNTS PAYABLE LEDGER

ACCOUNT Double-G Industries Manortown

DATE		PARTICULARS	P.R.	DEBIT	CREDIT	DR/CR	BALANCE
19— May	31	Forwarded #420	–			CR	11 315 25

ACCOUNT Maynard's Cartage 49 Larry Lane

DATE		PARTICULARS	P.R.	DEBIT	CREDIT	DR/CR	BALANCE

ACCOUNT Modern Mobile Homes West City

DATE		PARTICULARS	P.R.	DEBIT	CREDIT	DR/CR	BALANCE
19— May	31	Forwarded #2213	–			CR	2 247 –

ACCOUNT National Hardware 64 Venture Street

DATE		PARTICULARS	P.R.	DEBIT	CREDIT	DR/CR	BALANCE
19— May	31	Forwarded #2309	–			CR	2 982 09

Name____________________ Date________________

TRAVEL TRAILERS (cont.)

Accounts Payable Ledger (cont.)

ACCOUNT Parker Manufacturing 10 Bergen Street

DATE		PARTICULARS	P.R.	DEBIT	CREDIT	DR/CR	BALANCE

ACCOUNT Windsor Manufacturing Windsor

Date		Particulars	P.R.	Debit	Credit	DR/DC	Balance
19— May	31	Forwarded #404	–			CR	4 8 4 1 75

Name__________________ Date______________

Summary Exercise

TRAVEL TRAILERS (cont.)

General Ledger Trial Balance

ACCOUNTS	DEBIT	CREDIT

Name ______________________ Date ______________________

TRAVEL TRAILERS (cont.)

Subsidiary Ledger Trial Balances

Summary Exercise

TRAVEL TRAILERS (cont.)

Work Sheet (cont.)

Travel Trailers

Work Sheet

Six months ended June 30, 19—

ACCOUNTS	TRIAL BALANCE		ADJUSTMENTS		INCOME STATEMENT		BALANCE SHEET	
	DR	CR	DR	CR	DR	CR	DR	CR

Name____________________ Date________________

TRAVEL TRAILERS (cont.)

Work Sheet (cont.)

Name______________________________ Date______________________

Summary Exercise

TRAVEL TRAILERS (cont.)

Income Statement

Name ______________________ Date ______________

TRAVEL TRAILERS (cont.)

Balance Sheet

____

____

____

Name______________________ Date______________

Summary Exercise

TRAVEL TRAILERS (cont.)

Post-Closing Trial Balance

ACCOUNTS	DEBIT	CREDIT

Name____________________ Date______________

ANSWERS TO SECTION 14.1 REVIEW QUESTIONS (text p. 586)

Personal Banking

1. ______
   1. ______
   2. ______
   3. ______
   4. ______
   5. ______
2. ______
   1. ______
   2. ______
   3. ______
3. ______
4. ______
5. ______
6. ______
7. ______
8. ______
9. ______
10. ______
11. ______
12. ______
13. ______
14. ______
15. ______
16. ______
17. ______

Name______ Date______

Chapter 14 Cash Control and Banking

ANSWERS TO SECTION 14.1 EXERCISES (text p. 587)

Exercise 1, p. 587

1. Banks provide____________________for both individuals and businesses.
2. One of the essential services provided by banks is the____________________ of money.
3. Another of the essential services provided by banks is the____________________of money.
4. Of the three most common types of personal bank accounts, the____________________ gives the highest rate of interest.
5. A bank statement is provided each month with the____________________.
6. A____________________record of a savings account is provided.
7. It is advisable for the individual to keep a____________________.
8. The____________________is the simplest form of personal bank record.
9. A cheque that the bank will not cash because of insufficient funds is known as an ____________________.
10. A____________________is one for which the bank takes the funds out of the account in advance.
11. A certified cheque will not____________________.
12. A____________________is one that is dated for some time in the future.
13. The usual reason for writing post-dated cheques is in respect of a ____________________, such as for a mortgage.

Exercise 2, p. 587

Indicate whether each of the following statements is true or false by placing a "T" or an "F" in the space indicated. Explain the reason for each "F" response in the space provided.

1. A basic banking account is designed for the person who writes some cheques but not many. ☐
2. You are not allowed to write cheques on a daily interest savings account. Therefore, you can get money out of a daily interest savings account only by closing out the account. ☐
3. The interest rate on a daily interest savings account is always about one point higher than it is on a basic banking account. ☐
4. A passbook record of a savings account can be updated only at the bank. ☐
5. A personal chequing account is not intended to be used for saving money. ☐
6. There is no limit to the number of cheques that can be written on a personal chequing account. ☐
7. A personal bank record is not really necessary because the bank keeps a record of your account. ☐
8. If Joan Arnott's bank balance as shown by the bank is $352, she can write a cheque for that much money with no fear of its bouncing. ☐
9. A cheque is considered to be cash, but it is not assured cash until it has been through the clearing house of the banking system. ☐
10. The purpose of endorsing a cheque is to enable the bank to compare the endorsement with the signature card. ☐

Name____________________ Date____________________

ANSWERS TO SECTION 14.1 EXERCISES (cont.)

Exercise 2 (cont.)

11. When you deposit a cheque, the bank gives you immediate credit for the amount, even though the cheque might bounce. ☐

12. You visit your sister-in-law's bank to cash a cheque for $100 that she has given to you. The bank informs you that there is only $90 in your sister-in-law's account and gives you the $90. ☐

13. You should request cash or a certified cheque when you sell a used car to a stranger. ☐

14. On March 15, 19–1, the bank would not cash a cheque dated March 20, 19–1. ☐

Explanations for "F" Responses:

____

____

____

____

____

Exercise 3, p. 588

GENERAL JOURNAL PAGE ____

DATE		PARTICULARS	P.R.	DEBIT	CREDIT

Name______________________ Date______________

ANSWERS TO SECTION 14.1 EXERCISES (cont.)

Exercise 4, p. 588

GENERAL JOURNAL PAGE ____

DATE		PARTICULARS	P.R.	DEBIT	CREDIT

ANSWERS TO SECTION 14.2 REVIEW QUESTIONS (text p. 591)

Bank Credit Cards

1. ______________________________
2. ______________________________
3. ______________________________
4. 1. ______________________________
   2. ______________________________
   3. ______________________________

ANSWERS TO SECTION 14.2 EXERCISES (text p. 591)

Exercise 1, p. 591

1. Today's society is often referred to as a ______________ society.
2. Credit cards sponsored by the chartered banks are ______________ and ______________.
3. Bank credit cards can be used in most ______________.
4. During or at the end of the day, the credit card slips are prepared for inclusion in the ______________.
5. The merchant does not get full value for the ______________ of the credit card slips.
6. Each month the bank charges the merchant a ______________.

Name ______________ Date ______________

ANSWERS TO SECTION 14.2 EXERCISES (cont.)

Exercise 2, p. 592

Indicate whether each of the following statements is true or false by placing a "T" or an "F" in the space indicated. Explain the reason for each "F" response in the space provided.

1. Small retail outlets do not offer their own company credit cards because they prefer not to sell on credit. ☐
2. Carrying a bank credit card is like having plastic money. ☐
3. The use of credit cards slows things down at the cash register. ☐
4. During or at the end of the day, the bank credit card slips are included in the bank deposit. ☐
5. The two common bank credit cards are VISA and MasterCard. ☐
6. Bank credit card services would probably not have become widely available without the development of the computer. ☐
7. The merchant never has to worry about collecting the money if a customer offers a credit card in payment. ☐
8. When accounting for the day's bank credit card sales, the debit is to Accounts Receivable (credit card centre). ☐

Explanations for "F" Responses:

____

____

____

____

Exercise 3, p. 592

1. ________________________________
2. ________________________________
3. ________________________________
4. ________________________________
5. ________________________________
6. ________________________________
7. ________________________________
8. ________________________________
9. ________________________________
10. ________________________________

Name____________________ Date____________

ANSWERS TO SECTION 14.2 EXERCISES (cont.)

Exercise 4, p. 593

1. ______ 7. ______
2. ______ 8. ______
3. ______ 9. ______
4. ______ 10. ______
5. ______ 11. ______
6. ______

ANSWERS TO SECTION 14.3 REVIEW QUESTIONS (text p. 603)

Banking for a Business

1. ______
2. ______
3. ______
4. ______
5. ______
6. ______
7. ______
8. ______
9. ______

Name ______ Date ______

ANSWERS TO SECTION 14.3 REVIEW QUESTIONS (cont.)

10. ______________________________

11. ______________________________

12. ______________________________

13. ______________________________

14. ______________________________

15. ______________________________

16. ______________________________

17. ______________________________

18. ______________________________

19. ______________________________

ANSWERS TO SECTION 14.3 EXERCISES (text p. 605)

Exercise 1, p. 605

1. The ______________ of a business represent the money taken in from business operations.
2. It is customary for a business that ______________ to receive payment from its customers by way of cheques through the mail.
3. Cheques received in the mail are ______________ by the mail clerk before being deposited in the bank.
4. Sales slips are ______________ to ensure that all slips are accounted for.
5. In a business where goods are sold for cash, the cash is ______________ at the end of the day.
6. A electronic cash register that is connected to a central computer is known as a ______________
7. A small quantity of money used to start the cash register activity for the day is known as a ______________
8. Cash registers can be used for transactions other than just ______________
9. As transactions occur during the day, the details are stored inside the cash register on a paper tape known as the ______________ or the ______________.
10. At the end of each day, the daily balance form, the cash, and the vouchers are forwarded to the ______________.
11. Cash ______________ are more common than cash ______________.
12. Businesses are required by the banks to use a ______________.
13. All cheques received by the business are endorsed ______________ before being deposited.
14. Business deposit slips are prepared in ______________.
15. When preparing the cash for deposit, bills are sorted by ______________.

Name ______________ Date ______________

ANSWERS TO SECTION 14.3 EXERCISES (cont.)

Exercise 2, p. 606

1. CASH PROOF AND SALES SUMMARY DATE

PART 1. CHARGE SLIPS	Sales	GST	PST	Accounts Receivable	Cash
Charge Sales Slips					
Less Credit Slips					
Net Charge Sales					
PART 2. CASH SALES					
Cash Sales Slips					
Less Refunds					
Net Cash Sales					
CASH SHORT OR OVER ☐ ☐					
COLUMN TOTALS					

ACCOUNTING ENTRY

2. GENERAL JOURNAL

DATE		PARTICULARS	P.R.	DEBIT	CREDIT

 Name__________ Date__________

ANSWERS TO SECTION 14.3 EXERCISES (cont.)

Exercise 3, p. 607

CASH PROOF AND ACCOUNTING SUMMARY DATE

	TO LINE NO.	TOTALS
CASH REGISTER TOTALS		
Cash Sales less Refunds (Incl. Tax)	—	1 4 2 4 85
Visa Sales less Returns (Incl. Tax)	2	9 0 6 20
Charge Sales (Incl. Tax)	3	5 6 4 65
Received on Account	8	2 9 5 –
Returns for Credit (Incl. Tax)	9	9 4 30
Paid Outs	—	4 0 –
Sales less Returns (Before Tax)	10	2 4 3 6 –
GST Payable (Net)	11	1 7 0 52
PST Payable (Net)	12	1 9 4 88
CASH PROOF		
Total Cash Received less Paid Outs	—	1 6 7 9 85
Cash by Actual Count	1	
Cash Short	7	
Cash Over	13	
PAID OUTS BREAKDOWN		
Account ______	4	
Account ______	5	
Account ______	6	
Total Paid Outs		4 0 –

ACCOUNTING ENTRY

LINE NO.	ACCOUNTS	DEBIT	CREDIT
1	Cash		
2	Visa Total to Bank>>>>>>>>>>>>>>>>>		
3	Accounts Receivable (Charge Sales)		
4	Asset or Expense ______		
5	Asset or Expense ______		
6	Asset or Expense ______		
7	Cash Short or Over		
8	Accounts Receivable (Received on Account)		
9	Accounts Receivable (Returned for Credit)		
10	Sales		
11	GST Payable		
12	PST Payable		
13	Cash Short or Over		
	BALANCING TOTAL		

CASHIER'S SIGNATURE

Name______ Date______

ANSWERS TO SECTION 14.3 EXERCISES (cont.)

Exercise 4, p. 607

1. ____________
2. ____________
3. ____________
4. ____________

Exercise 5, p. 608

Cheques

CREDIT ACCOUNT NO.	DATE
NAME	
PARTICULARS	**AMOUNT**
TOTAL CHEQUES (CARRY FORWARD)	

CURRENT ACCOUNT DEPOSIT

Commercial Bank

CREDIT ACCOUNT NO.	DATE
NAME	
DEPOSITED BY	
COINS	
SUB-TOTAL TELLER	
VISA	
U.S. CHEQUES	
U.S. CASH	
TOTAL CHEQUES (BROUGHT FORWARD)	
U.S. CHEQUES (PLUS / MINUS)	
GRAND TOTAL	

CURRENT ACCOUNT DEPOSIT

Name____________________ Date____________

ANSWERS TO SECTION 14.4 REVIEW QUESTIONS (text p. 614)

Accounting Controls for Cash

1. ______

2. ______

3. ______

4. ______

5. ______

6. ______

7. ______

8. ______

9. ______

10. ______

11. ______

12. ______

13. ______

14. ______

ANSWERS TO SECTION 14.4 EXERCISES (text p. 614)

Exercise 1, p. 614 **Cases for Further Thought** *(Use more paper if necessary.)*

1. ______

2. ______

Name______ Date______

ANSWERS TO SECTION 14.4 EXERCISES (cont.)

Exercise 1 (cont.)

3.

4.

5.

6.

7.

8.

9.

10.

11.

12.

Name ______________________ Date ______________

ANSWERS TO SECTION 14.4 EXERCISES (cont.)

Exercise 2, p. 616

1. __________

2. 1. __________
   2. __________

Exercise 3, p. 618

1. __________
2. __________
3. __________
4. __________
5. __________
6. __________

Name__________ Date__________

ANSWERS TO SECTION 14.5 REVIEW QUESTIONS (text p. 622)

Petty Cash Fund

1. ______________________________
2. ______________________________
3. ______________________________
4. ______________________________
5. ______________________________
6. ______________________________
7. ______________________________

ANSWERS TO SECTION 14.5 EXERCISES (text p. 622)

Exercise 1, p. 622

GENERAL JOURNAL PAGE ____

DATE		PARTICULARS	P.R.	DEBIT	CREDIT

Exercise 2, p. 622

GENERAL JOURNAL PAGE ____

DATE		PARTICULARS	P.R.	DEBIT	CREDIT

Name______________________ Date______________

ANSWERS TO SECTION 14.5 EXERCISES (cont.)

Exercise 3, p. 622

Summary of Charges		
ACCOUNTS	GST	AMOUNTS

GENERAL JOURNAL PAGE ____

DATE		PARTICULARS	P.R.	DEBIT	CREDIT

Name________________ Date____________

ANSWERS TO SECTION 14.5 EXERCISES (cont.)

Exercise 4, p. 623

Summary of Charges		
ACCOUNTS	GST	AMOUNTS

GENERAL JOURNAL PAGE ____

DATE		PARTICULARS	P.R.	DEBIT	CREDIT

Name________________ Date__________

ANSWERS TO SECTION 14.5 EXERCISES (cont.)

Exercise 5, p. 623

Indicate whether each of the following statements is true or false by placing a "T" or an "F" in the space indicated. Explain the reason for each "F" response in the space provided.

1. The Petty Cash account in the general ledger must never change. ☐
2. A petty cash voucher must be prepared for every payment out of the fund. ☐
3. The petty cash fund is used for the purpose of cutting down on the number of cheques issued. ☐
4. The accounting entry to replenish the petty cash fund is made by the keeper of the fund. ☐
5. The petty cash box is locked and put away in a safe place outside business hours. ☐
6. The keeper of the petty cash fund must never borrow from it. ☐
7. The petty cash summary is organized by general ledger accounts. ☐
8. A payment out of petty cash can only be charged to an expense account or an asset account. ☐
9. The keeper of the fund is expected to make up any shortage in the petty cash fund. ☐
10. If an auditor were to check the petty cash fund, the procedure would be to total all of the cash and vouchers in the box and check this total against the balance in the Petty Cash account. ☐

Explanations for "F" Responses:

____

____

____

____

____

ANSWERS TO SECTION 14.6 REVIEW QUESTIONS (text p. 625)

Accounting Controls for Expenditures

1. ______________________________
2. ______________________________
3. ______________________________
4. ______________________________
5. ______________________________
6. ______________________________

Name______________________ Date______________

Chapter 14 Cash Control and Banking

ANSWERS TO SECTION 14.6 EXERCISES (text p. 625)

Exercise 1, p. 625

1. Poor accounting controls can result in the payment of bills that were____________________sent to the business.

2. The voucher system is a method of processing__________________________.

3. The__________________________ is effective because it controls expenditures through a rigid set of verification procedures.

4. Any document used in the voucher system as part of the verification process is a____________________.

5. The purchasing department formally orders goods when it issues a____________________________.

6. A____________________________contains detailed information about goods received from suppliers.

7. The_______________________________is a combination file folder and voucher approval form.

Exercise 2, p. 628

1. ____
2. ____
3. ____
4. ____
5. ____
6. ____
7. ____
8. ____
9. ____
10. ____
11. ____
12. ____

Name____________________________ Date____________________

ANSWERS TO SECTION 14.6 EXERCISES (cont.)

Exercise 3, p. 628

1.

Voucher Approval Form

Supplier ______		Voucher No. ______	
Address ______		Purchase Order Checked	
______		Description	
______		Price	
Invoice Date ______		Terms	
Invoice Amount ______		Goods or Services Rec'd	
Discount ______		Calculations Checked	
Net Amount ______		Accounting Distribution	
Payment Date ______		Approved for Payment	

2.

ACCOUNTING DISTRIBUTION

Debits:	Purchases				
	Supplies				
	______				Cheque Number
	______				______
	______				Cheque Date
Credit:	Voucher Payable				______
	Discounts Earned				

*(**Note:** The discount is taken on the amount of the purchase before GST is added.)*

Exercise 4, p. 629

1. ______

a. ______

b. ______

2. ______

______

______

3. ______

______

______

______

ANSWERS TO SECTION 14.7 COMPUTER REVIEW QUESTIONS (text p. 633)

Using a Computer: A Spreadsheet for Bank Reconciliation

1. ______________________________

2. ______________________________

3. ______________________________

4. ______________________________

5. ______________________________

ANSWERS TO SECTION 14.7 COMPUTER EXERCISES (text p. 634)

1. ______________________________

Extending Your Computer Skills (text p. 635)

	G	H	I	J	K	L	M
39							
40							
41							
42							
43							
44							
45							
46							
47							
48							
49							
50							
51							

Communicate It (text p. 635)

____

Name______________ Date______________

ANSWERS TO CHAPTER 14 EXERCISES (text p. 637)

Exercise 1, p. 637 **Using Your Knowledge**

Rough Work

SUMMARY					

Name____________________ Date________________

ANSWERS TO CHAPTER 14 EXERCISES (cont.)

Exercise 2, p. 638

1. **From the audit strip given below and on page 638 of the text:**

1. **Compute the summary totals that would be produced by the machine;**
2. **Work out the accounting entry for these totals if the Paid Out is for supplies. Ignore date.**

		137.00	MDS
		9.59	GST
		10.96	PST
		157.55	TOTL
		160.00	CASH
CASL	166	2.45	CHNG
		175.00	MDS
		12.25	GST
		14.00	PST
VISA	167	201.25	TOTL
		100.00	RECD
RECD	168	100.00	TOTL
		356.25	MDS
		24.94	GST
		28.50	PST
VISA	169	409.69	TOTL
		REFUND	
		128.00–	MDS
		8.96–	GST
		10.24–	PST
		147.20–	TOTL
CASL	170	147.20–	CASH
		50.00	P.O.
P.O.	171	50.00	TOTL
		150.00	MDS
		10.50	GST
		12.00	PST
		172.50	TOTL
		180.00	CASH
CASL	172	7.50	CHNG
		70.00	MDS
		4.90	GST
		5.60	PST
CHRG	173	80.50	TOTL

Name________________________ Date________________

ANSWERS TO CHAPTER 14 EXERCISES (cont.)

Exercise 2 (cont.)

1. **SUMMARY**

CASL	174	(Cash sales including tax)
VISA	175	(Visa sales including tax)
P.O.	176	(Paid outs)
CHRG	177	(Charge sales including tax)
RECD	178	(Received on account)
CRDT	179	(Returned for credit)
GST	180	(Net goods and services tax)
PST	181	(Net provincial sales tax)
MDS	182	(Sales less returns)
CASH	183	(Net cash received)

2. **GENERAL JOURNAL**

DATE		PARTICULARS	P.R.	DEBIT	CREDIT

*(**Note:** Students can calculate the amount of GST paid when supplies were purchased by dividing $50 by 1.07.)*

Name____________________ Date________________

ANSWERS TO CHAPTER 14 EXERCISES (cont.)

Exercise 3, p. 639

Name________________ Date________________

ANSWERS TO CHAPTER 14 EXERCISES (cont.)

Exercise 3 (cont.)

GENERAL JOURNAL PAGE ____

DATE		PARTICULARS	P.R.	DEBIT	CREDIT

Exercise 4, p. 642 (Workbook Exercise)

From the following records, prepare the bank reconciliation statement for Madison Company as of October 31, 19–. Record the necessary accounting entries in the books of the business.

a. Previous bank reconciliation statement

Madison Company
Bank Reconciliation Statement
September 30, 19—

Balance per Bank Statement		2 102.69	Balance per General Ledger		1 652.95
Deduct: Outstanding Cheques			Deduct: Service Charge	$12.50	
#519	$20.00		Loan Interest	36.25	48.75
#526	37.50				
#528	105.00				
#529	2.70				
#531	5.19				
#532	74.10				
#533	112.02				
#534	56.94				
#535	85.04	498.49			
True Balance		1 604.20	True Balance		1 604.20

ANSWERS TO CHAPTER 14 EXERCISES (cont.)

Exercise 4 (cont.)

b. Partial cash payments journal

Page 174

Date			Ch. No.	Bank Cr		
19—						
Oct	1		536		19	05
	1		537		164	02
	2		538		73	74
	3		539		27	60
	3		540		1	95
	4		541		365	12
	5		542		92	06
	8		543		74	09
	8		544		19	65
	10		545		74	02
	11		546		76	75
	12		547		56	21
	12		548		42	96
	15		549		33	21
	17		550		24	02
	19		551		88	61
	22		552		58	36
	22		553		19	05
	23		554		91	50
	24		555		13	30
	24		556		17	50
	26		557		8	61
	29		558	1	047	65
	29		559		319	02
	30		560		1	75
	31		561		2	50
	31		562		19	41
				2	831	71

c. Partial cash receipts journal

Page 147

Date			Bank Dr				Amount of Deposit		
19—									
Oct	3			16	50				
	3			25	02				
	3			516	95			558	47
	8			104	20				
	8			756	12				
	8			56	12				
	8			96	02		1	012	46
	11			33	40			33	40
	15			17	50				
	15			12	09			29	59
	22			19	06				
	22			502	00			521	06
	24			12	06				
	24			13	50				
	24			91	02				
	24			16	51			133	09
	29			56	93				
	29			83	16				
	29			102	52				
	29			127	06				
	29			31	50			401	17
	31			167	75				
	31			138	44			306	19
			2	995	43		2	995	43

Name____________________ Date______________

ANSWERS TO CHAPTER 14 EXERCISES (cont.)

Exercise 4 (cont.)

d. October general journal entry affecting Bank

GENERAL JOURNAL — PAGE 64

DATE		PARTICULARS	P.R.	DEBIT	CREDIT
19—					
Oct	4	Bank Charges	54	12.50	
		Bank Interest	56	36.25	
		Bank			48.75
		To record charges picked up from September			
		bank statement			

e. Bank statement for October

Cheques				Deposits	Date		Balance
					Sept.	30	2 102.69
37.50	(526)				Oct.	30	2 065.19
				558.47		3	2 623.66
2.70	(529)	85.04	(535)			4	2 535.92
19.05	(536)					5	2 516.87
74.10	(532)	105.00	(528)			8	2 337.77
73.74	(538)			1 012.46		9	3 276.49
5.19	(531)	27.60	(539)			10	3 243.70
56.94	(534)					11	3 186.76
74.09	(543)	112.02	(533)	33.40		15	3 034.05
96.02	(N.S.F. cheque of J. Marble)					15	2 938.03
164.02	(537)					16	2 774.01
33.21	(549)	19.65	(544)	29.59		17	2 750.74
365.12	(541)					18	2 385.62
76.75	(546)			521.06		22	2 829.93
1.95	(540)	58.36	(552)			23	2 769.62
42.96	(548)					24	2 726.66
				133.09		25	2 859.75
88.61	(551)					26	2 771.14
91.50	(554)					29	2 679.64
13.30	(555)			401.17		30	3 067.51
8.61	(557)	1 047.65	(558)			31	2 011.25
15.20	(Int)	30.20	(Service Charges)			31	1 965.85
43.50	(Discount Fee)					31	1 922.35

Name____________________ Date________________

ANSWERS TO CHAPTER 14 EXERCISES (cont.)

Exercise 4 (cont.)

f. General ledger account showing October figures

ACCOUNT Bank **No.** 101

Date		Particulars	P.R.	Debit	Credit	DR/DC	Balance
19— Sep	30	—				DR	1 652 95
Oct	4		J64		48 75		
	31		CP174		2 831 71		
	31		CR147	2 995 43		DR	1 767 92

Madison Company

Bank Reconciliation Statement

October 31, 19—

Name__________ Date__________

ANSWERS TO CHAPTER 14 EXERCISES (cont.)

Exercise 4 (cont.)

GENERAL JOURNAL PAGE ____

DATE	PARTICULARS	P.R.	DEBIT	CREDIT

Exercise 5, p. 642

For each of the following groups, indicate which statement is NOT true by recording the appropriate letter in the space indicated.

1. **a.** Cash means dollars bills and coins only. ☐
   b. The principal objective of a business is to earn a profit.
   c. The usual method of establishing a petty cash fund is to issue a cheque made out to Petty Cash.
   d. The imprest system of petty cash involves entrusting the cash to an individual.
   e. The vouchers and the cash in the petty cash box should add up to the balance of the Petty Cash account.

2. **a.** The cheque made out to Petty Cash is usually handed over to the person responsible for the petty cash fund. ☐
   b. Outside of office hours, the petty cash box is usually kept in the company safe.
   c. For every expenditure out of the petty cash fund, there must be a bill or sales slip from a store.
   d. When a payment is being made out of the petty cash fund, no accounting entries are made immediately.
   e. The petty cash fund must be replenished when the amount of cash in the box gets low.

Name________________________ Date________________

ANSWERS TO CHAPTER 14 EXERCISES (cont.)

Exercise 5 (cont.)

3. **a.** The first step to replenishing the petty cash fund is to prepare a summary of the vouchers in the petty cash box. ☐

b. The petty cashier submits the summary of charges, together with the bills and vouchers, in order to obtain a cheque.

c. The summary and the vouchers together are accepted as the source document for the replenishing cheque.

d. The accounting entry to record the replenishing cheque is as follows: debit Petty Cash; credit Bank.

e. The accounting entry to replenish the petty cash fund is one of the two accounting entries that affect petty cash.

4. **a.** Banks provide essential services for both businesses and individuals. ☐

b. The processing of cheques and bank credit card vouchers is known as the electronic transfer of funds.

c. Banks are able to meet the needs of most customers by having a variety of accounts and services.

d. The interest rate for a daily interest savings account is higher than it is for a pure savings* account.

e. You must put some money in the bank account to "open" it.

5. **a.** The bank statement given to the customer once a month is identical to the bank's own record. ☐

b. Except for breakdowns, electronic tellers may be used at any time.

c. It is difficult to borrow money if your credit rating is poor.

d. Writing cheques that bounce can be damaging to your credit rating.

e. The true bank balance is the one shown by the bank's record.

6. **a.** Placing only your signature on the back of a cheque made out to you is an "open" endorsement. ☐

b. Banks require the payee (the person to whom the cheque is issued) to guarantee the cheque by signing it on the back.

c. If the balance in the issuer's account is not large enough to cover the amount of a cheque, the bank will dishonour it.

d. A cheque that has not bounced is a dishonoured cheque.

e. The bank has the right to take the amount of a dishonoured cheque out of your account without contacting you.

7. **a.** The accounting entry to record a dishonoured cheque is the exact opposite of the accounting entry that was made when the cheque was deposited. ☐

b. You must phone the bank to find out if a cheque that you received is certified.

c. You can be sure of a cheque not bouncing if it is certified.

d. The funds to pay a certified cheque are taken out of the bank account at the time the cheque is certified.

e. A post–dated cheque is one that is dated for some time in the future.

8. **a.** The usual reason for issuing a post–dated cheque is to meet a series of payments, such as for a mortgage. ☐

b. A certified cheque is marked GUARANTEED by the bank.

c. A cheque written on January 15 but dated for March 1 is a post–dated cheque.

d. You should ask for a certified cheque when you are dealing with a stranger and when the amount of money is large.

e. The bank does not cash cheques bearing a future date.

*An account on which cheques may not be written.

Name________________________ Date________________

ANSWERS TO CHAPTER 14 EXERCISES (cont.)

Exercise 5 (cont.)

9. **a.** Bank credit cards can be obtained from large department stores and similar chains. ☐
b. Most smaller retail outlets do not offer their own company credit cards.
c. VISA and MasterCard are bank credit cards sponsored by major banks.
d. The consumer is usually given 21 days from the statement date to make payment.
e. Bank credit cards may be used to obtain a cash advance.

10. **a.** A listing of cheques received in the mail is prepared because the cheques have to be deposited in the bank. ☐
b. The listing of the cheques in part (**a**) is prepared by a member of the accounting department who knows the system.
c. Sales slips are prenumbered so that all slips can be accounted for.
d. In a business where there are "cash" receipts, it is necessary to prove the cash at the end of each day.
e. There is a greater chance for a cash shortage than there is for a cash overage.

11. **a.** A point–of–sale terminal is a stand–alone electronic cash register. ☐
b. A "float" is a small sum of money set aside to be used as a starting fund for the cash register each day.
c. The detailed audit tape is locked inside the cash register.
d. At the end of each day, the cash register can be made to produce summary totals for the day.
e. A modern cash register can itself produce most of the figures needed to prove the cash.

12. **a.** At the end of each day, the cash, vouchers, and daily balance form are forwarded to the accounting department. ☐
b. A cash shortage is entered as a debit to an expense account.
c. A current bank account is designed especially for the use of businesses.
d. With a current account, the paid cheques are returned to the depositor at the end of each month.
e. Cash is said to be proved when there is no shortage or overage.

13. **a.** Businesses endorse all cheques FOR DEPOSIT ONLY. ☐
b. All cheques for deposit must be endorsed.
c. For businesses, deposit slips are prepared in duplicate.
d. Every business requires internal control to ensure accuracy and honesty.
e. The person who records transactions or prepares accounting records should not also be the one to control or handle the assets physically.

14. **a.** Cash is the single item most likely to be stolen. ☐
b. The total cash receipts for the day should be deposited on that day and intact.
c. Since both the bank and the business keep a record of the same funds, the two balances should always agree unless an error has been made.
d. Every bank account should be reconciled once a month.
e. An outstanding cheque is a cheque that is issued and recorded by the company but not cashed by the bank.

Name____________________ Date______________

ANSWERS TO CHAPTER 14 EXERCISES (cont.)

Exercise 6, p. 644 **Cases for Further Thought** *(Use more paper if necessary.)*

1.

2.

3.

4.

5.

6.

7.

8.

9.

CASE STUDIES (text p. 645)

Case 1 *Cola Profits Go Flat*, p. 646 *(Use more paper if necessary.)*

1.
   a.
   b.
   c.
   d.

2.

3.

Name Date

CASE STUDIES (cont.)

Case 2 *Service Charges: Are They Always Fair?*, p. 647 *(Use more paper if necessary.)*

1.

2.

3.

4.

5.

Challenge Case 3 *Trials of a Young Entrepreneur*, p. 648 *(Use more paper if necessary.)*

1.

2.

3.

4.

5.

6.

7.

8.

Name____________________ Date______________

CASE STUDIES (cont.)

Group Discussion Case 4 *The Good Life on Plastic Money*, p. 649 *(Use more paper if necessary.)*

1. ______________________________

2. ______________________________

3. ______________________________

4. ______________________________

5. ______________________________

CAREER Janice Fukakusa / Senior Manager, Corporate Finance, Royal Bank

ANSWERS TO DISCUSSION QUESTIONS (text p. 651)

1. ______________________________

2. ______________________________

3. ______________________________

4. ______________________________

5. ______________________________

Name______________________ Date______________________

ANSWERS TO SECTION 15.1 REVIEW QUESTIONS (text p. 653)

Users of Financial Statements

1. ______________________________
2. ______________________________
3. ______________________________
4. ______________________________
____
5. ______________________________
6. ______________________________
7. ______________________________
____
8. ______________________________
____
9. ______________________________
____

ANSWERS TO SECTION 15.2 REVIEW QUESTIONS (text p. 662)

Comparing Financial Data

1. ______________________________
2. ______________________________
3. ______________________________
4. ______________________________
____
5. ______________________________
6. ______________________________
7. ______________________________
____
____
8. ______________________________
9. ______________________________
10. ______________________________
11. ______________________________
____
12. ______________________________
____

Name______________________ Date______________

ANSWERS TO SECTION 15.2 EXERCISES (text p. 662)

Exercise 1, p. 662

1.

GORRY AND ASSOCIATES
INCOME STATEMENT DATA
19–1 to 19–5

	Year 1	*Year 2*	*Year 3*	*Year 4*	*Year 5*
Sales					
Cost of Goods Sold					
Gross Profit					
Operating Expenses					
Net Income					

2. ______________________________

Exercise 2, p. 662

1.

SURREY INDUSTRIES
INCOME STATEMENT DATA
19–1 to 19–5

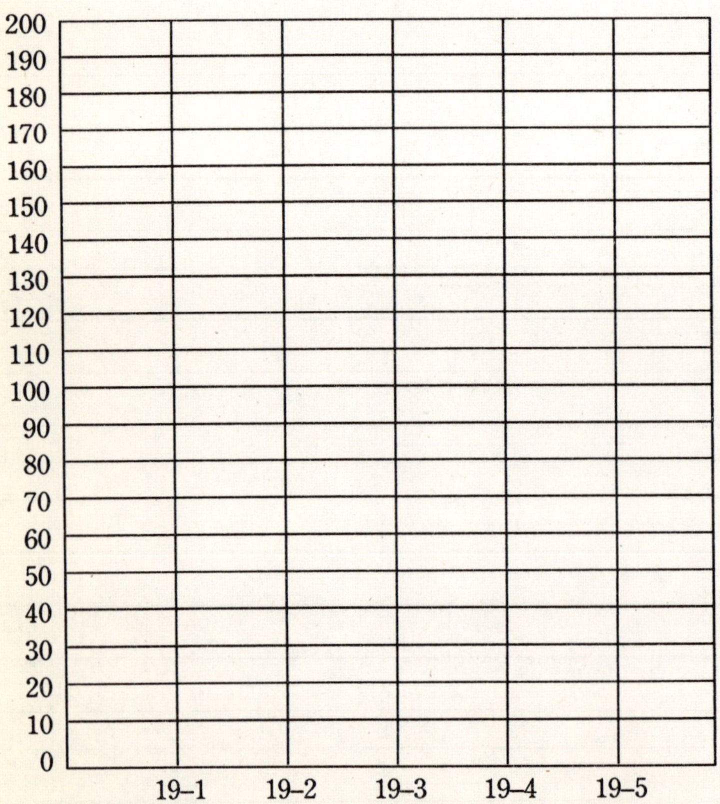

2. ______________________________

Name______________________ Date______________

ANSWERS TO SECTION 15.2 EXERCISES (cont.)

Exercise 3, p. 663

1.

GOODENOUGH COMPANY
BALANCE SHEET DATA
19–1 to 19–5

	19–1	*19–2*	*19–3*	*19–4*	*19–5*
Current Assets	$50 000	$55 500	$59 500	$64 000	$68 500
Current Liabilities	35 000	38 000	40 000	42 500	45 000
Working Capital					

2.

GOODENOUGH COMPANY
BALANCE SHEET DATA
19–1 to 19–5

	19–1	*19–2*	*19–3*	*19–4*	*19–5*
Current Assets					
Current Liabilities					
Working Capital					

3.

GOODENOUGH COMPANY
BALANCE SHEET DATA
19–1 to 19–5

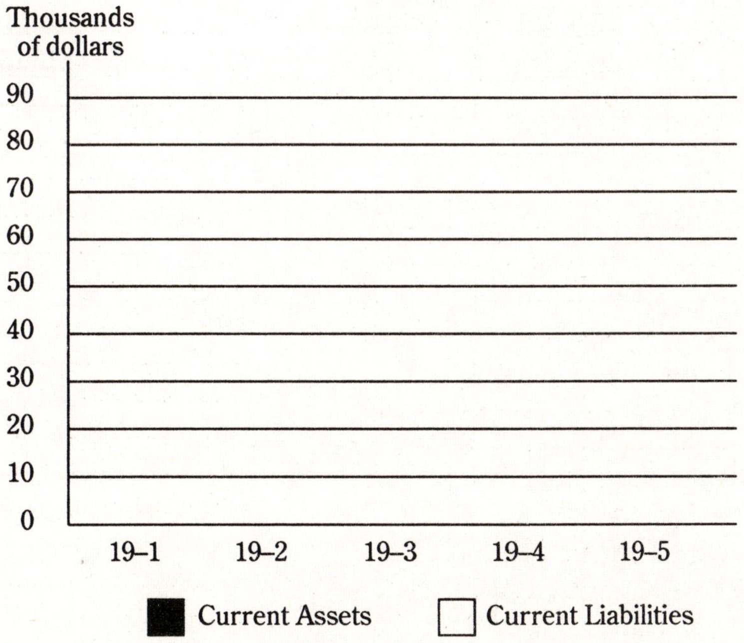

ANSWERS TO SECTION 15.2 EXERCISES (cont.)

Exercise 4, p. 663

1.

COMPARATIVE BALANCE SHEETS
ROSE COMPANY AND LILY COMPANY
DECEMBER 31, 19–6

	Rose Company $	*Rose Company* %	*Lily Company* $	*Lily Company* %
ASSETS				
Bank	$ 41 474		$ 34 971	
Accounts Receivable	44 371		24 008	
Merchandise Inventory	106 780		42 464	
Plant & Equipment	183 538		26 725	
Automobiles	25 675		8 390	
Total Assets	$401 838		$136 558	
LIABILITIES AND EQUITY				
Accounts Payable and Other Debts	$ 86 480		$ 13 940	
Bank Loan	50 000			
Mortgage Payable	120 000			
Total Liabilities	$256 480		$ 13 940	
Owner's Equity				
Beginning Capital	$114 728		$118 539	
Net Income	105 630		29 079	
	$220 358		$147 618	
Drawings	75 000		25 000	
Ending Capital	$145 358		$122 618	
Total Liabilities and Equity	$401 838		$136 558	

Name____________________ Date____________

ANSWERS TO SECTION 15.2 EXERCISES (cont.)

1. (cont.)

COMPARATIVE INCOME STATEMENTS
ROSE COMPANY AND LILY COMPANY
YEAR ENDED DECEMBER 31, 19–6

	Rose Company $	Rose Company %	Lily Company $	Lily Company %
Sales	$767 830		$332 879	
Cost of Goods Sold				
Beginning Inventory	$ 98 200		$ 44 224	
Purchases	561 280		208 740	
Cost of Goods Available	$659 480		$252 964	
Less Ending Inventory	106 780		42 464	
Cost of Goods Sold	$552 700		$210 500	
Gross Profit	$215 130		$122 379	
Operating Expenses				
Bank Interest Expense	$ 7 000		$ 1 000	
Depreciation – Equipment	5 500		6 600	
Depreciation – Automobiles	10 000		3 500	
Mortgage Interest Expense	11 250			
Rent Expense			24 000	
Wages Expense	35 750		47 500	
Other Expense	40 000		10 700	
Total Operating Expenses	$109 500		$93 300	
Net Income	$105 630		$29 079	

2. a. ______________________________

b. ______________________________

Name______________________ Date______________________

ANSWERS TO SECTION 15.2 EXERCISES (cont.)

Exercise 5, p. 664

1.

PLAYFAIR COMPANY
COMPARATIVE BALANCE SHEET
DECEMBER 31, 19–4 AND 19–3

	19–4	*19–3*	*Increase or Decrease (–)*	*% Change*
ASSETS				
Current Assets				
Bank	$ 9 090	$ 5 500		
Accounts Receivable	65 220	35 700		
Merchandise Inventory	67 096	42 100		
Prepaid Expenses	3 540	3 500		
Total Current Assets	$144 946	$86 800		
Fixed Assets				
Land	$ 50 000	$ 50 000		
Buildings (Net)	135 000	138 000		
Equipment (Net)	141 000	160 000		
Automobiles (Net)	25 000	30 000		
Total Fixed Assets	$351 000	$378 000		
Total Assets	$495 946	$464 800		
LIABILITIES AND OWNER'S EQUITY				
Current Liabilities				
Accounts Payable	$ 97 936	$ 52 750		
Bank Loan	50 000	50 000		
Total Current Liabilities	$147 936	$102 750		
Long-Term Liability				
Mortgage Payable	$ 70 000	$ 75 000		
Total Liabilities	$217 936	$177 750		
T. Jennings, Capital				
Capital, January 1	$287 050	$277 700		
Net Income	90 960	84 350		
	$378 010	$362 050		
Drawings	100 000	75 000		
Capital, December 31	$278 010	$287 050		
Total Liabilities & Equity	$495 946	$464 800		

Name____________________ Date________________

ANSWERS TO SECTION 15.2 EXERCISES (cont.)

Exercise 5 (cont.)

2. ______
   1. ______
   2. ______
   3. ______
   4. ______

ANSWERS TO SECTION 15.3 REVIEW QUESTIONS (text p. 670)

Simple Ratios and Percentages

1. ______
   a. ______ d. ______
   b. ______ e. ______
   c. ______ f. ______
2. ______
3. ______
4. ______
5. ______
6. ______

ANSWERS TO SECTION 15.3 EXERCISES (text p. 671)

Exercise 1, p. 671 **Schooner Company**

1. Ratio or Percentage		**2. Comment** *(Use more paper if necessary.)*
a. Current ratio	______	______
b. Quick ratio	______	______
c. Debt ratio	______	______
Equity ratio	______	______
d. Rate of return on net sales	______	______
e. Rate of return on owner's equity	______	______

ANSWERS TO SECTION 15.3 EXERCISES (cont.)

Exercise 2, p. 672 The Cloverdale Company

1. Ratio or Percentage **2. Comment** *(Use more paper if necessary.)*

a. Current ratio ________ ________________________________

b. Quick ratio ________ ________________________________

c. Debt ratio ________ ________________________________

Equity ratio ________ ________________________________

d. Rate of return on net sales ________ ________________________________

e. Rate of return on owner's equity ________ ________________________________

Exercise 3, p. 674 Company A, Company B

1. *Ratio*	*Company A*	*Company B*
a. Current ratio	________	________
b. Quick ratio	________	________
c. Debt ratio	________	________
d. Equity ratio	________	________
e. Rate of return on net sales	________	________
f. Rate of return on owner's equity	________	________

2. ____

Name________________________ Date________________

ANSWERS TO SECTION 15.4 REVIEW QUESTIONS (text p. 677)

Additional Ratios, Percentages, and Statistics

1.

2.

3.

4.

5.

6.

ANSWERS TO SECTION 15.4 EXERCISES (text p. 677)

Exercise 1, p. 677 Saturn Sales Company

Description	*Ratio*	*Opinion*
1. Current ratio		
2. Quick ratio		
3. Collection period		
4. Inventory turnover		
5. Rate of return on net sales		
6. Rate of return on owner's equity		
7. Debit ratio		
8. Equity ratio		
9. Times interest earned		

Name____________________ Date________________

ANSWERS TO SECTION 15.4 EXERCISES (text p. 678)

Exercise 2, p. 678

CALVINO COMPANY
INCOME STATEMENT
YEAR ENDED DECEMBER 31, 19–8

Revenue	
Sales	$170 000
Cost of Goods Sold	
Opening Inventory	
Purchases	$128 500
Goods Available for Sale	
Closing Inventory	
Cost of Goods Sold	$129 000
Gross Profit	
Operating Expenses	
Net Income	

CALVINO COMPANY
BALANCE SHEET
DECEMBER 31, 19–8

ASSETS	
Current Assets	
Bank	$ 3 700
Accounts Receivable	
Merchandise Inventory	10 500
Total Current Assets	
Plant and Equipment	
Land	$ 35 000
Buildings and Equipment	
Total Plant and Equipment	
Total Assets	
LIABILITIES AND OWNER'S EQUITY	
Current Liabilities	
Bank Loan	$ 15 000
Accounts Payable	
Total Current Liabilities	
Owner's Equity	
Beginning Capital	$134 750
Add Net Income	
Deduct Drawings	
Ending Capital	
Total Liabilities and Owner's Equity	

Name____________________ Date____________

ANSWERS TO SECTION 15.4 EXERCISES (cont.)

Exercise 3, p. 680 **Pluto Company and Neptune Company**

1. **Key Ratios and Statistics**

Description	*Pluto*	*Neptune*
Current ratio		
Quick ratio		
Collection period		
Inventory turnover		
Rate of return on net sales		
Rate of return on owner's equity		
Debt ratio		
Equity ratio		
Times interest earned		

2.

3.

Exercise 4, p. 682 **Analysis Calculations**

	19–3	*19–4*

Name________________ Date________________

ANSWERS TO SECTION 15.5 COMPUTER REVIEW QUESTIONS (text p. 687)

Using a Computer: Spreadsheet Models For Financial Analysis

1. ______________________________

2. ______________________________

3. ______________________________

4. ______________________________

5. ______________________________
____

6. ______________________________

ANSWERS TO SECTION 15.5 COMPUTER EXERCISES (text p. 688)

***(Note:** There are no manual applications for these exercises.)*

Name______________________ Date______________

ANSWERS TO CHAPTER 15 EXERCISES (text p. 689)

Exercise 1, p. 689 Using Your Knowledge

1. The condensed financial statements of Magnus Company for the years 19–5 and 19–6 are shown below and on page 690 of your text.
   1. Complete the Net Change column of the comparative balance sheet.
   2. Complete the Per Cent columns of the comparative income statement.

MAGNUS COMPANY
COMPARATIVE BALANCE SHEET
DECEMBER 31, 19–5 AND 19–6

	19–5	*19–6*	*Net Change*
ASSETS			
Bank	$ 13 000	$ 960	
Accounts Receivable	29 500	35 200	
Merchandise Inventory	37 450	38 950	
Prepaid Expenses	3 700	2 600	
Land	64 500	64 500	
Buildings	90 000	166 500	
Equipment	75 000	146 400	
Automobiles	30 000	21 000	
Total Assets	$343 150	$476 110	
LIABILITIES AND EQUITY			
Bank Loan	$ 40 000	$200 000	
Accounts Payable	26 500	18 700	
Mortgage Payable	125 300	112 770	
Owner's Equity	151 350	144 640	
Total Liabilities and Equity	$343 150	$476 110	

Name________________ Date________________

ANSWERS TO CHAPTER 15 EXERCISES (cont.)

Exercise 1 (cont.)

2. MAGNUS COMPANY
COMPARATIVE INCOME STATEMENT
YEARS ENDED DECEMBER 31, 19–5 AND 19–6

	19–5 Amount	19–5 Per Cent	19–6 Amount	19–6 Per Cent
Sales	$289 500		$309 120	
Cost of Goods Sold	142 750		155 700	
Gross Profit	$146 750		$153 420	
Operating Expenses				
Advertising Expense	$ 1 500		$ 1 500	
Car Expense	4 000		4 050	
Depreciation – Building	4 250		8 500	
Depreciation – Equipment	18 000		29 280	
Depreciation – Automobiles	9 000		9 000	
Power Expense	3 500		3 950	
Interest and Bank Charges	16 530		36 530	
Supplies Used	1 000		1 100	
Wages Expense	36 700		38 900	
Total Operating Expenses	$ 94 480		$132 810	
Net Income	$ 52 270		$ 20 610	

(Note: The Per Cent column does not indicate increase or decrease.)

3. a. ______
   b. ______
   c. ______
   d. ______

4. ______

5. ______

Name______ Date______

ANSWERS TO CHAPTER 15 EXERCISES (cont.)

Exercise 2, p. 691

On page 691 of your text and the following page of your Workbook is the partially completed common-size comparative income statement for two companies in the same line of business. You are preparing this analysis with a view to making an investment in one of the two companies.

1. Complete the common-size income statement on the following page of your Workbook, (calculations to one decimal place).

2. Answer the following questions:
   - **a.** Which company has the larger net income?
   - **b.** Which company has the larger net income percentage?
   - **c.** Which company has the larger investment in inventory?
   - **d.** Which company has the larger gross income percentage?
   - **e.** Which company does not own its own building?
   - **f.** What are the three clues to question **e**?
   - **g.** If the owner's average equities are $80 000 for Company A, and $30 000 for Company B, calculate the respective returns on owner's investment.
   - **h.** Which company gives the greater return on owners' investment?
   - **i.** Which company has the greater interest-bearing debt?
   - **j.** How much is Company B disadvantaged by not owning its own building?
   - **k.** Listed below are factors that favour Company A or Company B. For each one, indicate the company favoured on the following page of your Workbook.
     - **i.** greater net income
     - **ii.** higher gross income percentage
     - **iii.** greater return on owners' investment
     - **iv.** more established, owns own building
     - **v.** lower inventory
     - **vi.** lower expense
     - **vii.** greater potential to reduce expenses
     - **viii.** greater share of market (sales)
     - **ix.** lower interest-bearing debts.
   - **l.** In which company would you choose to invest? **Give reasons.**

Name________________________ Date________________

ANSWERS TO CHAPTER 15 EXERCISES (cont.)

Exercise 2 (cont.)

1. (cont.)

COMMON-SIZE COMPARATIVE INCOME STATEMENT
YEAR ENDED DECEMBER 31, 19–3

	Dollars		Percentage of Sales	
	Co. A	*Co. B*	*Co. A*	*Co. B*
Sales	$200 000	$150 000	**100.0**	**100.0**
Cost of Goods Sold				
Opening Inventory	$ 50 000	$ 25 000		
Purchases	123 000	81 200		
Goods Available for Sale	$173 000	$106 200		
Less Closing Inventory	57 000	24 000		
Cost of Goods Sold	$116 000	$ 82 200		
Gross Profit	$ 84 000	$ 67 800		
Operating Expenses				
Advertising Expense	$ 5 000	$ 4 000		
Bank Interest Expense	900	10 000		
Depreciation — Building	10 000	—		
Depreciation — Equipment	4 500	3 000		
General Expense	1 900	1 500		
Insurance Expense	500	400		
Postage Expense	750	350		
Property Tax Expense	2 000	—		
Rent Expense	—	18 000		
Telephone Expense	450	300		
Wages Expense	13 740	9 500		
Total Operating Expenses	$ 39 740	$ 47 050		
Net Income	$ 44 260	$ 20 750		

2. a. ________ f. ________

b. ________ g. ________

c. ________ h. ________

d. ________ i. ________

e. ________ j. ________

Name________ Date________

ANSWERS TO CHAPTER 15 EXERCISES (cont.)

Exercise 2 (cont.)

2. (cont.)

k.

		Favours Co. A	Favours Co. B
i.	greater net income		
ii.	higher gross income percentage		
iii.	greater return on owner's investment		
iv.	more established, owns own building		
v.	lower inventory		
vi.	lower expense		
vii.	greater potential to reduce expenses		
viii.	greater share of market (sales)		
ix.	fewer interest-bearing debts		

l. Both companies seem to be financially healthy. Company B is handicapped slightly by not owning its own building.

A firm decision regarding which company to invest in is not possible without knowing the asking prices. If the asking price for both companies is approximately the same, then Company A is favoured. But if there is a significant difference in the two asking prices, for example, twice as much for Company A, then Company B might be a better choice.

Exercise 3, p. 692

SPARTA COMPANY
INCOME STATEMENT
YEAR ENDED DECEMBER 31, 19–3

Sales	
Cost of Goods Sold	
Beginning Inventory	
Purchases	
Goods Available for Sale	
Less Ending Inventory	21 000
Cost of Goods Sold	$170 000
Gross Profit	
Operating Expenses	$114 375
Net Income	

Name______________________ Date__________________

ANSWERS TO CHAPTER 15 EXERCISES (cont.)

Exercise 3 (cont.)

SPARTA COMPANY
BALANCE SHEET
YEAR ENDED DECEMBER 31, 19–3

ASSETS	
Current Assets	
Bank	
Accounts Receivable	35 000
Merchandise Inventory	21 000
Total Current Assets	
Fixed Assets	
Land	$ 50 000
Plant and Equipment	
Total Fixed Assets	$120 000
Total Assets	
LIABILITIES AND EQUITY	
Current Liabilities	
Accounts Payable	
Bank Loan	20 000
Total Current Liabilities	$ 32 000
Owner's Equity	
Beginning Capital	$130 000
Net Income	
Drawings	
Ending Capital	
Total Liabilities and Equity	

Name__________________ Date__________

ANSWERS TO CHAPTER 15 EXERCISES (cont.)

Exercise 4, p. 694 Comprehensive Exercise

1.

ANSON COMPANY
COMPARATIVE INCOME STATEMENT
YEARS ENDED DECEMBER 31, 19–7 AND 19–8

	19–7	*19–8*	*Net Change*
ASSETS			
Current Assets			
Bank	$ 4 000	$509 000	
Merchandise Inventory	50 000	50 000	
Total Current Assets	$ 54 000	$559 000	
Fixed Assets			
Land	$380 000	$ 80 000	
Buildings	80 000	76 000	
Equipment	90 000	72 000	
Total Fixed Assets	$550 000	$228 000	
Total Assets	$604 000	$787 000	
LIABILITIES AND EQUITY			
Current Liabilities			
Bank Loan	$ 20 000	—	
Accounts Payable	42 000	$ 12 000	
Total Current Liabilities	$ 62 000	$ 12 000	
Owner's Equity			
R. Anson, Capital	$542 000	$775 000	
Total Liabilities and Equity	$604 000	$787 000	

2.

a. ____________________
b. ____________________
c. ____________________
d. ____________________
e. ____________________
f. ____________________

Name____________________ Date____________________

ANSWERS TO CHAPTER 15 EXERCISES (cont.)

Exercise 4 (cont.)

g. Challenge

Increases **1.** ______

2. ______

Total Increases ______

Decreases **1.** ______

2. ______

3. ______

4. ______

Total Decreases ______

Net Increase ______

Exercise 5, p. 696

Exercise 6, p. 696

Name__________ Date__________

ANSWERS TO CHAPTER 15 EXERCISES (cont.)

Exercise 7, p. 697 **For Further Thought** *(Use more paper if necessary.)*

1. ______

2. ______

3. ______

4. ______

5. ______

6. ______

7. ______

8. ______

  1. ______

  2. ______

9. ______

10. ______

  1. ______

  2. ______

  3. ______

  4. ______

  5. ______

11. ______

Name______ Date______

ANSWERS TO CHAPTER 15 EXERCISES (cont.)

Exercise 8, p. 697 **Cases for Further Thought** *(Use more paper if necessary.)*

1.

2.

3.

4.

CASE STUDIES (text p. 699)

Case 1 *Do I have a deal for you!*, p. 699 *(Use more paper if necessary.)*

1.

2.

3.

4.

5.

Name________________ Date__________

CASE STUDIES (cont.)

Case 2 *Is the Manager Competent?*, p. 700 *(Use more paper if necessary.)*

1.

HANNA IMPORTING
INCOME STATEMENT
YEARS 19–1 AND 19–2

	19–1 (Hanna)	*19–2 (Ans)*	*Net Change*
Sales	$315 000	$480 000	
Cost of Goods Sold			
Opening Inventory	$ 80 000	$ 85 000	
Purchases	195 000	285 000	
Goods Available for Sale	$275 000	$370 000	
Less Closing Inventory	85 000	55 000	
Cost of Goods Sold	$190 000	$315 000	
Gross Profit	$125 000	$165 000	
Operating Expenses			
Advertising Expense	$ 2 000	$ 7 000	
Bad Debts Expense	300	2 500	
Bank Interest Expense	10 000	5 000	
Car Expense	3 000	3 100	
Depreciation of Car	1 500	1 500	
Delivery Expense	9 000	8 000	
Depreciation — Delivery Truck	3 600	—	
Light and Heat Expense	1 700	2 000	
Miscellaneous Expense	300	350	
Rent Expense	13 000	16 500	
Telephone Expense	400	500	
Wages and Salaries Expense	24 500	55 000	
Loss on Sale of Truck		2 000	
Total Operating Expenses	$ 69 300	$103 450	
Net Income	$ 55 700	$ 61 550	

2. *Key Ratios and Statistics for 19–2*
(for data available)

____

____

____

3. **a.** ______________________________

b. ______________________________

c. ______________________________

d. ______________________________

e. ______________________________

Name______________________ Date______________________

CASE STUDIES (cont.)

Case 2 (cont.)

4. ______________________________

5. ______________________________

Challenge Case 3 *To Lend or Not To Lend*, p. 701 *(Use more paper if necessary.)*

1. Part A

Key Ratios and Statistics	*19–6*	*19–7*	*19–8*
Working capital			
Current ratio			
Quick ratio			
Collection period			
Inventory turnover			
Debt ratio			
Equity ratio			
Times interest earned ratio			
Rate of return on net sales			
Rate of return on owner's equity			

2. ______________________________

Name ______________________ Date ______________________

CASE STUDIES (cont.)

Challenge Case 3 (cont.)

Part B

3.

ESTIMATED INCOME STATEMENT
19–9 FISCAL YEAR

4. Super Challenge

ESTIMATED BALANCE SHEET
19–9 FISCAL YEAR

Name____________________ Date______________

CASE STUDIES (cont.)

Challenge Case 3 (cont.)

5. Super Challenge

The key ratios and statistics developed from the estimated statements are as follows:

RATIOS AND STATISTICS	
Working capital	________
Current ratio	________
Quick ratio	________
Collection period	________
Inventory turnover	________
Debt ratio	________
Equity ratio	________
Times interest earned	________
Rate of return on net sales	________
Rate of return on owner's equity	________

The bank manager's thoughts might be as follows:

1. ________

2. ________

4. ________

5. ________

7. ________

Name________________ Date________________

ANSWERS TO SECTION 16.1 REVIEW QUESTIONS (text p. 708)

Gross Pay

1. ______

2. ______

3. ______

4. ______

5. ______
   1. ______
   2. ______
   3. ______
   4. ______
   5. ______

6. ______

7. ______

8. ______

9. ______

10. ______

11. ______

12. ______

13. ______

14. ______

(*Note: Whenever you are asked to work out payments to wage employees, the following rules apply.*)

1. The regular work week consists of a five-day week of 8 hours per day for a total of 40 hours. Any additional time worked after 5:00 P.M., or on Saturday or Sunday, is considered overtime.
2. Employees who are late arriving for work are penalized as follows:
   - 15 minutes, if they are late by one to 15 minutes;
   - 30 minutes, if they are late by 16 to 30 minutes, and so on.
3. The rate of pay for overtime is one-and-a-half times the regular rate.

Name______________________ Date______________

ANSWERS TO SECTION 16.1 EXERCISES (text p. 708)

Exercise 1, p. 708

Annual Salary	*Payroll Period*	*Gross Pay per Period*
$ 39 000	Weekly	
	Weekly	$ 800
$ 22 750	Biweekly	
	Biweekly	$ 1 250
$ 36 000	Semi-monthly	
	Semi-monthly	$ 1 800
$ 30 000	Monthly	
	Monthly	$ 3 200

Exercise 2, p. 709

Payroll Period	*Gross Pay*
a. Weekly	
b. Biweekly	
c. Semi-monthly	
d. Monthly	

Exercise 3, p. 709

Total Hours	*Regular Rate*	*Regular Hours*	*Overtime Hours*	*Regular Pay*	*Overtime Pay*	*Gross Pay*
46	$11.50					
43	$14.50					
44	$12.00					
54	$21.00					
47	$13.75					

Name____________________ Date_______________

ANSWERS TO SECTION 16.1 EXERCISES (cont.)

Exercise 4, p. 709

Day	*Number of Units Completed*	*Salary*	*Piecework Earnings*	*Gross Pay*
Monday	10			
Tuesday	9			
Wednesday (1/2)	5			
Thursday	11			
Friday	10			
TOTALS				

Exercise 5, p. 710

Time Card
Week Ended July 23 19 – –
Social Ins. No. 642 393 438
Name Frank Windsor

Day	Morning In	Morning Out	Afternoon In	Afternoon Out	Extra In	Extra Out	Total Hours
M	7:58	12:01	12:58	5:01			
T	8:07	12:00	12:57	5:02			
W	7:56	12:03	12:59	5:00			
T	7:59	12:02	1:01	5:03			
F	7:57	12:02	12:59	5:01			
S							
S							

	Hours	Rate	Earnings
Regular Time		14.00	
Overtime			
Gross Pay			

Time Card
Week Ended July 23 19 – –
Social Ins. No. 643 461 217
Name Ray Peterson

Day	Morning In	Morning Out	Afternoon In	Afternoon Out	Extra In	Extra Out	Total Hours
M	7:58	12:01	1:00	5:02			
T	7:59	12:00	12:58	5:01	5:59	8:55	
W	7:57	12:01	12:59	5:02			
T	7:56	12:01	12:58	5:03			
F	7:59	12:01	12:59	5:01			
S	7:58	12:01					
S							

	Hours	Rate	Earnings
Regular Time		12.20	
Overtime			
Gross Pay			

Name____________________ Date______________

ANSWERS TO SECTION 16.1 EXERCISES (cont.)

Exercise 6, p. 711

Salesperson	*Sales for Month*	*Salary*	*Commission*	*Gross Earnings*
Mary Hunt	$ 90 000			
Anna Mocha	$122 000			
Bob Rennie	$ 75 000			
Fay Savard	$316 000			
Paul Thors	$ 50 000			
Gloria Unich	$ 70 000			
Gladys Wilson	$ 26 000			

ANSWERS TO SECTION 16.2 REVIEW QUESTIONS (text p. 732)

Payroll Deductions and Net Pay

1. ______
2. ______
3. ______
4. ______
5. ______
6. ______
7. ______
8. ______
10. ______
11. ______
12. ______
13. ______
14. ______
15. ______

Name______ Date______

ANSWERS TO SECTION 16.2 REVIEW QUESTIONS (cont.)

16. ______________________________

17. ______________________________

18. ______________________________

19. ______________________________
   1. ______________________________
   2. ______________________________
   3. ______________________________

ANSWERS TO SECTION 16.2 EXERCISES (text p. 732)

Exercise 1, p. 732

1.

Employee	*Biweekly Gross Pay*	*CPP Deduction*	*UI Deduction*	*RPP (5%) Deduction*
F. Mazur	$ 965			
C. Koch	$ 990			
P. Parsons	$1 100			
G. Vittelli	$1 050			
Y. Van Del	$1 200			

2. _____ deductions:_____ @ _________ + final deduction of ________

Exercise 2, p. 733

Net Claim Code	Gross Earnings		RPP Deduction 6%		Union Dues		Taxable Earnings		Income Tax Deduction		CPP Deduction		UI Deduction	
10	1 150	—			15	—								
8	1 275	—			15	—								
5	1 325	—			15	—								
1	1 180	—			15	—								
2	1 230	—			15	—								
TOTALS		—												

Name________________________ Date__________________

ANSWERS TO SECTION 16.2 EXERCISES (cont.)

Exercise 3, p. 733

Payroll Journal — For the two weeks ended ______ 19 —

Employee	Net Claim Code	Earnings			Deductions										Net Pay
							Income Tax								
		Regular	Extra	Gross	RPP	Union Dues	Taxable Earnings	Tax Deduction	CPP	UI	Health Ins.	Group Life		Total Ded'ns	
J. Bell	8	1 310 —		1 310 —											

Exercise 4, p. 733

a. An amount kept back from an employee's gross pay is known as a______________.

b. The amount of pay remaining after all deductions have been made is known as______________.

c. Payroll calculations are summarized in a book known as the______________.

d. Keeping back an amount from an employee's pay is called______________.

e. Certain payroll deductions are made on behalf of the federal government. The ______________ ______________system is used to keep track of all of these deductions for all of the citizens of the country.

f. The deductions in question **e.** above are for ______________ and ______________.

g. To assist employers in making the deductions in question **f.** above, the government provides ______________.

h. The CPP deduction and the UI deduction are based on the______________figure.

i. For the CPP, there is a______________figure after which no further deductions will be made for the year.

j. Employers, as well as employees, must______________to the CPP and UI funds.

k. A payroll made every two weeks is known as a______________payroll.

l. The maximum unemployment insurance deduction for a______________payroll period is $42.60.

m. A private pension plan that is approved by the government is known as a______________pension plan.

n. An employee fills out a TD1 form in order to determine the______________.

o. The______________number is based on the figure arrived at in question **n.** above.

p. The deduction for income tax is not based on gross earnings. It is based on______________.

q. The figure in question **p.** above is found by making deductions from the gross pay figure. These deductions are allowed by______________.

r. Most provinces operate a______________.

s. The payroll journal is a______________journal and therefore must be______________.

Name______________ Date______________

ANSWERS TO SECTION 16.2 EXERCISES (cont.)

Exercise 4 (cont.)

List of Words and Phrases

biweekly	income tax	Revenue Canada
Canada Pension Plan	maximum	semi-monthly
columnar	net claim amount	social insurance number
contribute	net claim code	taxable
cross-balanced	net pay	unemployment insurance
deduction tables	payroll deduction	withholding
gross pay	payroll journal	
health insurance plan	registered	

ANSWERS TO SECTION 16.3 REVIEW QUESTIONS (text p. 740)

Recording the Payroll

1. ______
   1. ______
   2. ______
   3. ______
   4. ______
   5. ______
2. ______
3. ______
4. ______
5. ______
6. ______
7. ______
8. ______
9. ______
   1. ______
   2. ______
   3. ______
10. ______
11. ______
12. ______
13. ______
14. ______
15. ______

ANSWERS TO SECTION 16.3 EXERCISES (text p. 741)

Exercise 1, p. 741

GENERAL JOURNAL PAGE ____

DATE		PARTICULARS	P.R.	DEBIT	CREDIT

Name ____________________ Date ____________

ANSWERS TO SECTION 16.3 EXERCISES (cont.)

Exercise 1 (cont.)

Bank

Canada Pension Plan Payable

Unemployment Insurance Payable

Registered Pension Plan Payable

Employees' Income Tax Payable

Extended Health Insurance Payable

Union Dues Payable

Group Life Insurance Payable

Employer Health Tax Payable

Payroll Payable

Salaries Expense

Canada Pension Plan Expense

Unemployment Insurance Expense

Registered Pension Plan Expense

Employer Health Tax Expense

Name______________________ Date______________

ANSWERS TO SECTION 16.3 EXERCISES (cont.)

Exercise 1 (cont.)

6. a.
   b.
   c.

   d.

   e.

Exercise 2, p. 741 (Workbook Exercise)

Examine the following T-accounts and answer the questions below.

CPP Payable

	Debit	Credit
Feb		185.12
		185.12
Mar	370.24	
		190.40
		190.40
Apr	380.80	

UI Payable

	Debit	Credit
Feb		265.35
		371.49
Mar	636.84	
		268.20
		375.48
Apr.	643.68	

Empls' Inc. Tax Payable

	Debit	Credit
Feb		502.36
Mar	502.36	
		525.24
Apr	525.25	

a. How is the $371.49 amount of the UI Payable account calculated? ____________

b. In the CPP Payable account, why does the $185.12 appear twice? ____________
____________.

c. What is the length of the pay period? ____________

d. What amount was remitted to the federal government in March? ____________

Exercise 3, p. 741

1. ____________
   ____
2. ____________
3. a. ____________
   b.
   c. ____________
   d. ____________
4. ____________

Name____________ Date____________

ANSWERS TO SECTION 16.4 REVIEW QUESTIONS (text p. 744)

Payment to Employees

1. ______________________________

    1. ______________________________

       ____

    2. ______________________________

2. ______________________________

    1. ______________________________
    2. ______________________________
    3. ______________________________

3. ______________________________

4. ______________________________

5. ______________________________

   ____

   ____

6. ______________________________

   ____

ANSWERS TO SECTION 16.4 EXERCISES (text p. 744)

Exercise 1, p. 744 (Workbook Exercise)

Shown here is a partial payroll journal for United Wholesale. Prepare the currency requisition form for this payroll.

PAYROLL JOURNAL

Employee		*Net Pay*
Anderson M.		$ 865.56
Chian N.		1 256.12
Gerow J.		1 002.50
Hills A.		852.02
Larocque B.		748.96
McComber J.		1 158.21
Ruf L.		658.87
Spenser M.		876.89
Valela C.		945.17
Zubak P.		1 247.05
Total		***$9 611.35***

Name______________________ Date______________________

ANSWERS TO SECTION 16.4 EXERCISES (cont.)

Exercise 1 (cont.)

PAYROLL CURRENCY REQUISITION — **PERIOD ENDED** March **20,** 19 —

Employee	*Net Pay*	*$20*	*$10*	*$5*	*$1*	*25¢*	*10¢*	*5¢*	*1¢*
Anderson, M.									
Chian, N.									
Gerow, J.									
Hills, A.									
Larocque, B.									
McComber, J.									
Ruf, L.									
Spenser, M.									
Valela, C.									
Zubak, P.									
No. of bills or coins									
Dollar value									

Exercise 2, p. 745

Name____________________ Date______________

ANSWERS TO SECTION 16.4 EXERCISES (cont.)

Exercise 3, p. 746

1. ______
2. ______
3. ______
4. ______
5. ______
6. ______

ANSWERS TO SECTION 16.5 REVIEW QUESTIONS (text p. 749)

Basic Payroll Records

1. ______
   1. ______
   2. ______
   3. ______
2. ______
3. ______
4. ______
5. ______
6. ______
7. ______
8. ______
   1. ______
   2. ______
   3. ______

Name______ Date______

ANSWERS TO SECTION 16.5 EXERCISES (text p. 750)

Exercise 1, p. 750

1. a. Mary's gross pay

   b. Canada Pension Plan

   c. Unemployment Insurance

   d. Registered Pension Plan

   e. Income Tax

2.

Exercise 2, p. 750

1. Box 14 ________
   Box 16 ________
   Box 18 ________
   Box 20 ________
   Box 22 ________

2.

3.

Name ________________ Date ____________

ANSWERS TO SECTION 16.6 COMPUTER REVIEW QUESTIONS (text p. 754)

Using a Computer: The Payroll Module in Simply Accounting™

1. ____
2. ____
3. ____
4. ____
5. ____

ANSWERS TO SECTION 16.6 COMPUTER EXERCISES (text p. 755)

Communicate It (text p. 756)

*(**Note:** Because the remaining computer exercises have no manual applications, in the interest of saving paper, we have deleted pages 514 and 515 from the Workbook.)*

ANSWERS TO CHAPTER 16 EXERCISES (text p. 757)

Exercise 1, p. 757 Using Your Knowledge

PAYROLL JOURNAL

For the two weeks ended ____________

Employee	Earnings				Deductions										Net Pay
	Net Claim Code	Regular	Extra	Gross	RPP	Union Dues	Income Tax		CPP	UI	Ext. Health Ins.	Group Life		Total Ded'ns	
							Taxable Earnings	Tax Deduction							

Name ____________ Date ____________

ANSWERS TO CHAPTER 16 EXERCISES (cont.)

Exercise 1 (cont.)

GENERAL JOURNAL

PAGE ____

DATE		PARTICULARS	P.R.	DEBIT	CREDIT

ANSWERS TO CHAPTER 16 EXERCISES (cont.)

Exercise 2, p. 757

PAYROLL JOURNAL

For the two weeks ended *January 20 19__*

Employee	Net Claim Code	Earnings			Deductions										Net Pay
		Regular	Extra or Commission	Gross	RPP	Union Dues	Income Tax		CPP	UI	Ext. Health Ins.	Group Life		Total Ded'ns	
							Taxable Earnings	Tax Deduction							

Name_______________ Date_______________

ANSWERS TO CHAPTER 16 EXERCISES (cont.)

Exercise 2 (cont.)

2., 3. GENERAL JOURNAL PAGE ____

DATE		PARTICULARS	P.R.	DEBIT	CREDIT

Name ________________ Date ________________

ANSWERS TO CHAPTER 16 EXERCISES (cont.)

Exercise 3, p. 758 **Comprehensive Exercise**

1.

2.

3.

4.

5.

6.

7.

Exercise 4, p. 760 **Comprehensive Exercise**

Part 1

Bank		CPP Payable		UI Payable	

Name ________ Date ________

ANSWERS TO CHAPTER 16 EXERCISES (cont.)

Exercise 4 (cont.)

RPP Payable

Employee's Income Tax Payable

Extended Health Insurance Payable

Employer Health Tax Payable

Union Dues Payable

Payroll Payable

Wages Expense

CPP Expense

UI Expense

RPP Expense

Employer Health Tax Expense

Expenses

Part 2

Cash Paid Out + Amount Owed

Name__________________ Date______________

ANSWERS TO CHAPTER 16 EXERCISES (cont.)

Exercise 5, p. 760 **For Further Thought** *(Use more paper if necessary.)*

1. ____________________
2. a. ____________________
   b. ____________________
   c. ____________________
3. ____________________
4. ____________________
5. ____________________
6. ____________________
7. ____________________
8. ____________________
9. ____________________

Exercise 7, p. 761 **Cases for Further Thought** *(Use more paper if necessary.)*

1. ____________________
2. ____________________

CASE STUDIES (text p. 761)

Case 1 *Wage Increases — What's Fair?*, p. 762 *(Use more paper if necessary.)*

1. ____________________
2. ____________________

Name____________________ Date____________

CASE STUDIES (cont.)

Case 2 *Wage Increases — How Much Can Be Offered?*, p. 762 *(Use more paper if necessary.)*

1. ______

2. ______

3. ______

4. **a.** ______

b. ______

Challenge Case 3 *A Profit-Sharing Proposal*, p. 763 *(Use more paper if necessary.)*

1. ______

2. ______

3. **a.** ______

b. ______

4. ______

Name______ Date______

CASE STUDIES (cont.)

Challenge Case 3 (cont.)

5.

6.

7.

8.

Name Date

CASE STUDIES (cont.)

Challenge Case 3 (cont.)

9.

10.

11.

Name Date